ENTREPRENEURSHIP IN THE THIRD WORLD

ENTREPRENEURSHIP
IN THE
THIRD WORLD

RISK AND UNCERTAINTY
IN INDUSTRY IN PAKISTAN

Zafar Altaf

CROOM HELM
London • New York • Sydney

© 1988 Zafar Altaf
Croom Helm Ltd, Provident House, Burrell Row,
Beckenham, Kent, BR3 1AT
Croom Helm Australia, 44-50 Waterloo Road,
North Ryde, 2113, New South Wales

Published in the USA by
Croom Helm
in association with Methuen, Inc.
29 West 35th Street
New York, NY 10001

British Library Cataloguing in Publication Data

Altaf, Zafar
    Entrepreneurship in the Third World: risk
    and uncertainty in industry in Pakistan.
    1. Businessmen — Pakistan 2. Entrepreneurs
    I. Title
    338.'04'095491   HC440.5
    ISBN 0-7099-0574-2

Library of Congress Cataloging-in-Publication Data

ISBN 0-7099-0574-2

Printed and bound in Great Britain
by Billing & Sons Limited, Worcester.

CONTENTS

Contents

TABLES AND FIGURES

Tables

Tables and Figures

Figures

Tables and Figures

ACKNOWLEDGEMENTS

I owe a debt of gratitude to all those who have
encouraged me in completing this book. It has
been an uphill task. Such are the rigours of
public life. The functions of a bureaucracy in
a developing country are anything but conducive
to academic work. It has its own distinct
culture. One is part of this culture and therefore subject to all its compulsions.

The working schedules had to be so arranged
as to enable me to have two distinct working
plans in the same day. That has meant being
away from my family. Their patience on occasions
was stretched. They have not only encouraged me
but also contributed meaningfully to complete
this work. My brother and sisters and a working
mother and father at 80 have contributed to a
family tradition for hard work.

The present work is in a very difficult
area. The work is open to question. In the
Third World what degree of risk and uncertainty
do these entrepreneurs face? I have tried to
work out a methodology. Unless a true picture
emerges, less developed countries will keep on
chasing an illusion -- the illusion of an
industrialised society and all that goes with
it. The critical factor is entrepreneurship.
It may be difficult to gauge and foresee the
requirements of entrepreneurs but certain things
in society need to be imposed on them, i.e.
intangibles like tenacity, honesty, desirable
motivational levels. All in all it requires
knowledge of human working. The emphasis must
therefore shift to the critical material.

The members of bureaucracy who kept at me
and enabled me to struggle with difficult
concepts is headed by Dr. Tariq Siddiqui, Principal

Acknowledgements

Pakistan Administrative Staff College, Lahore. Arguments with Ahmed Rashid Siddiqui, another stalwart from the Establishment Division, were worthwhile and removed a number of doubts.

There will be errors of omission and commission. The responsibility is entirely mine. If an argument seems too complex and complicated it may be attributed to an inability to put things more logically. To the more generous it may seem to be due to dealing in such complex factors as human personality.

The experience of workshops especially the Entrepreneurship Development Institute at Ahmedabad, India and Leadership for Development at Bethel, Maine, U.S.A., reinforced my views on directing efforts towards the most difficult factor in production -- entrepreneurs. Dr. Patel at Ahmedabad and Dick and Marianne Vittitow at Bethel encouraged me towards this view. The first chapter heavily depends on Entrepreneur Development Institute efforts at bringing logic to the subject under discussion. I am indebted to all the authors who find a place in the listed bibliography. They have sharpened my views one way or the other.

To Abdul Hafeez Kardar -- Sportsman,
Politician - Friend.

It is possible to induce entrepreneurs and to
induct them into an economy. The highly successful programme of the Entrepreneurial Development
Institute of Ahmedabad, India has amply proved
this. By careful construction and reconstruction
of achievement motivation they have been able to
develop entrepreneurs. The possibility has been
successfully demonstrated over a ten year period.
    The evidence in the current work pertains
to analysing uncertainty and risk in an economy.
There are two constraints always mentioned in
any study. Frank Knight was the first one to
indicate this. In the case of developed countries industrialisation was not as urgent a
matter as it is these days. Less developed
countries (Ldcs), with high populations, need a
sector which can mop up surplus labour. The
illusion of industrial society as a desirable one
has been upheld for too long. Policy makers have
taken upon themselves to undertake measures to
accelerate industrialisation. In this the early
entrepreneurs have taken advantage of their
earlier entrance into industries. Their industries are protected not only from competition
but are also provided with all kinds of incentives.
In terms of influence a handful of entrepreneurs
have increased their influence to such an extent
that they can hold a pistol to anyone's head.
Their methodology border's on blackmail. Each
succeeding year's industrialisation problems
add to the incentive schemes of the government
and the benefit of entrepreneurs. The preoccupation, indeed with industrialisation, has led to
a permanent institutional framework to look after
'sick industries'. Experiments conducted within
the economy have rebounded to make matters worse

than before.

The internal world of the entrepreneur therefore assumes significance. Value and attitudes
inculcated in a social framework become important.
In the absence of checks in the economic system,
this value system could be anything but socially
just. Policies borrowed from elsewhere have not
been adapted to local conditions. The result is
in terms of inappropriate policies and a set of
rules without any frame of reference.

Available evidence would have us believe
that risk and uncertainty is very limited in
Pakistan. Risk in the economic system is
virtually negligible. Uncertainty flowing from
Law and Order can lead to, on occasions, loss of
assets. Governments, however, tend to cover such
losses. Such periods are also times of larger
profits. Experience, training and education have
a distinct bearing on entrepreneurial performance.
The relevance of all three has been examined.

The subject is challenging. Within a
dynamic system the entrepreneur will keep on
changing. It is that change that needs to be
directed towards positive action and achievement
orientation. The evidence on static environment
is indicative of rich profits to such as are
aware of them and can avail of them. The ability
of the entrepreneur to play the system rather
than the market assumes significance and
importance. This has further accentuated problems.
A bureaucracy unaware of product requirements
feels that it can marshal the economy in terms
of investment. This has led to various other
anomalies.

Is the market system a better overall
allocative process or is the bureaucratic investment procedure superior? The market has an
inbuilt corrective mechanism. Such a mechanism
is missing in the alternative. The institutions
that serve both systems are different. So, as
and when a change has to come about, the
supporting institutions will have to be suitably
modified.

Chapter One

INDUSTRIALISATION

Pakistan's experience with the process of Industrialisation provides an excellent area for
analysis. At independence in 1947, the country
hardly had any industrial capacity. The emphasis
was mostly on agriculture and that too on peasant
agriculture. Hardly any analytic work was done
in the formative years. The reason for this lack
of effort was the involvement of the majority with
constructing and structuring a new existence.
Other pressing claims, invariably, were of greater
immediate importance and required the attention of
all. Since then a number of studies on various
aspects of industrialisation have emerged (1). A
considerable amount of work remains to be done.
Some difficult questions about the country's
industrialisation have yet to be addressed. One
of the difficult areas and in fact from which most
of the analysis follows has to do with the
collection of creditable statistics. Only the
registered industries' statistics (2) are collected.
Such industry as is not registered is not included
in the statistical profile. A large segment of
the small and medium industry is not covered.
Besides the limitation of physical coverage, the
government functionary collecting such statistics
is normally viewed with concern by the entrepreneur. The nature and transactional experience of
the entrepreneur largely effects his response
towards the information collecting functionary.
Attitudes of the entrepreneurs, therefore, also
effect the quality of statistics. The analysis
that do flow from such statistics are questionable.
Despite reservations to the contrary one has
however to consider the impact of statistics so
collected. That they find marginal utility in
decision making may be correct. They do present,

1

over time, a basis for industrial profile. The structural changes in GDP reflect the growing importance of industry in the country's economy.

Table 1.1 : Structural Changes in GDP (At Constant Factor Cost, 1959-60)

Year	Share in GDP (%)				
	Agricul-ture	Manufac-turing	Total Commo-dity Sector	All Services	GDP
1949-50	53.19	7.75	62.82	37.18	100.00
1954-55	48.02	10.84	61.43	38.57	100.00
1959-60	45.83	12.00	61.29	38.71	100.00
1964-65	39.68	15.04	60.39	39.61	100.00
1969-70	38.88	16.04	61.58	38.42	100.00
1974-75	33.19	15.58	56.09	43.91	100.00
1979-80	31.02	16.32	56.01	43.99	100.00
1980-81	30.19	16.94	55.83	44.17	100.00
1981-82	29.32	18.06	55.87	44.13	100.00
1982-83	28.59	18.58	55.44	44.56	100.00
1983-84	25.94	19.41	54.24	45.76	100.00
1984-85-P	26.28	19.43	54.44	45.56	100.00

P: Provisional

Source: Federal Bureau of Statistics

The share of manufacturing in GDP indicates an interesting feature in the 1970s. There is an actual drop in the share of manufacturing. This was caused by, not an increase in agriculture, but because of nationalisation (3) of industrial units. However, nationalisation did affect different segments of the industrial sector in a variety of ways. A survey of industrial concerns in the small sector (4) indicated that because of the hesitancy of the large sector to invest in industrial projects, there was unprecedented growth in the small sector. Industrial finance had become available to the small scale manufacturing sector. Had this availability of industrial credit continued in the

late 1970s and early 1980s the structure of industrial growth and output may well have been different.
An analysis of the structure of industries and their
proportional increase indicates the trend in current
industrial investment (Table 1.2). The increase in
output indicates that growth in the industrial
sector was a continuous feature. This however does
not indicate either the existence or nonexistence
of spare capacity, nor does it indicate efficiency
in the industrial sector. Table 1.2 also does not
have the production figures in respect of small
scale industry. The output, except for essential
inputs for agriculture, is oriented towards meeting
the demand of the urban sector. The derived demand
of the rural population is seldom catered for in
the allocation process. The allocative process is
such that the demand of the rural areas is either
not known or is deliberately ignored. The nature
of 'product' requirements have been such that
prestige is attached to urban goods. For the urban
consumer prestige and status follow from purchase
of imported products and goods. The market,
because of this kind of structuring for goods, is
extremely thin and limited. Matters are not helped
because of stagnation in agricultural incomes.
    Another feature of the production system is
that if the total industrial sanctions issued
between 1977 to March 1985 were analysed the
emphasis would seem to be towards 'soft' (5)
industries rather than such industries as have a
spin off effect (Table 1.3). These sanctions flow
from an allocative device (6) worked out on the
basis of existing demand in the country. In the
investment schedule which is worked out periodi-
cally for the country the existing capacity, the
likely demand over a fixed period is worked out.
The gap, if there be any gap between existing
capacity and demand, is then the quantum investment that will be allowed. In other words the
bureaucracy determines the derived demand for the
investors. The effectiveness or efficiency of this
allocative process is difficult to state, in the
absence of a 'free choice' in investment. However
such a free choice exists in the small manufacturing sector. In this sub sector investment is
entirely on the basis of entrepreneurial insights
into product supply-demand factors. Feasibility
work is non-existent and the entrepreneur normally
starts his operations not on any 'grandiose' basis
but slowly and proceeds by trial and error. In
the process entrepreneurs build up immense respect

3

Table 1.2: Increase in Production of Selected Industries

	1963-64	1976-77	1984-85	%age increase Col:4 - Col:2 Col:2
(1)	(2)	(3)	(4)	(5)
1- Beverage (000 dozen bottles)	9706	26361	31031	220
2- Cigarettes (Million numbers)	12785	28379	30969	142
3- Cotton Yarm (Million Kg)	198.6	282.6	307.0	54
4- Motor Tyres (000)	59 (1964-65)	148	228	286
5- Cycle Tyres	1795	3461	3074	71
6- Caustic Soda (000 tonnes)	5.4	24.9	29	437
7- Paints & Varnishes (000 litres)	3987	7193	9093	128
8- Polishes & Cream for footwear (Million gms)	369.5	604.1	630.6	71
9- Fertilizers (Urea super phosphate, Ammonium nitrate, Ammonium sulphate) (000tonnes)	158.2	824.2	1765.9	1016
10 Bicycles (000)	97.7 (1964-65)	211.5	361.8	270
11 Electric Bulbs (Million nos.)	6.8 (1964-65)	14.9	33.6	394

Table 1.2: (Continued)

(1)	1963-64 (2)	1976-77 (3)	1984-85 (4)	%age increase Col:4 - Col:2 Col:2 (5)
12 M.S. Products (000 tonnes)	230 (1964-65)	269.6	551.7	140
13 Paper (Printing & Writing) (000 tonnes)	13.5 (1970-71)	18.9	25.5	89
14 Cotton Yarn (000 kg)	437883	282640	343997	-21

Table 1.3: Sanctions Issued by Industry

		1977-83	1983-84	1984-85 (Upto March)	Total
1.	Food , Beverage and Tobacco	5.638	2.076	1.244	8.949
2.	Textiles	7.023	1.868	0.844	9.735
3.	Leather & Leather Products	0.302	0.001	0.027	0.330
4.	Rubber & Rubber Products	2.482	0.132	0.003	2.617
5.	Paper & Pulp Products	1.888	0.873	1.074	3.835
6.	Chemicals, Synthetics, Fertilizers, Chemicals and Petroleum	16.429	6.197	1.718	24.344
7.	Non-Metallic Mineral Products	9.454	3.270	0.391	13.115
8.	Basic Metals	0.684	1.127	0.012	1.823
9.	Metal Products	0.684	1.127	0.012	1.823
10	Machinery other than Electrical	1.126	0.170	0.369	1.673
11	Electrical Machinery, Equipment and Apparatus	1.077	0.469	0.593	2.139
12	Electronics	0.071	0.207	0.218	0.496
13	Transport Equipments	0.619	0.812	0.189	1.620
14	Miscellaneous including Hotels and other services Industries	2.987	0.982	1.029	4.988
	Total	50.003	19.742	8.560	78.305

Source: Ministry of Industries.

for the market place, devising methodology different
from their better endowed and more 'pampered' large
scale entrepreneurs.

Industrial Policy Statement
In a major policy statement (7) the government
identified its major objectives. These were in
the realm of:
  (i)   Emphasis on industry to continue.
  (ii) Shift towards high value added industry.
  (iii) Linkages within the economy to be
        established in such a way that there
        is dispersal of industry in an
        economically viable manner.
  (iv) Market size for Pakistan manufactures
        to be enlarged through aggressively
        supporting manufactured products.
    The policy then states how priority for expan-
sion of industry will be fixed. It states that:
  (i)   Since a steel mill is to go into
        capacity production urgent investment
        is down-stream industry is required.
  (ii) Since there is likely to be high growth
        in agriculture investment opportunities
        for agriculture processing for domestic
        and export markets will be encouraged.
  (iii) Mechanisation would provide linkage
        between agriculture and industry.
  (iv) For the future:
        (a) Defence related industries will
             be given priority.
        (b) Industries based on high sophis-
             ticated technology will be
             provided with special incentives.
        (c) Fiscal incentives for private
             sector so as to set up private
             industrial estates.
    The policy objectives place a premium on
industrialisation. However, the policy statement
does not provide any basis for determining entrepreneurial talent. It assumes that in Pakistan
entrepreneurs are willing to undertake diverse
kinds of industrial activities that exist. This
may be true to a certain extent for areas like
Sialkot, Gujranwala and Gujrat where entrepreneurs
may be available. This is of course for the type
of industry which they want to set up and not for
the kind government wants them to invest in. For
instance specific industry incentives were
provided to the electronic industry for Islamabad
and North West Frontier Province (NWFP) almost two

years ago. Despite this announcement investment is
not forthcoming. In other words industrial policy
assumes that there is (a) no shortage of supply of
entrepreneurs (b) that they would invest in
industry along determined lines.

Sanctioning Procedures
The main hurdle in the investment policies, so far
as the entrepreneur is concerned, is the sanctioning procedures. These are cumbersome and difficult
to play. Human behaviour problems abound.
Although a deregulation commission is working at
simplifying these procedures, it is doubtful if it
can change the relationship between the bureaucracy (or various levels of it) and the entrepreneur. The bureaucracy in Pakistan is interven-
tionist and regulatory. It is in the business of
'overlording' the entrepreneur (unless he has
clout). Even then the chances that an entrepreneur
will sooner or later be taken to task cannot be
ruled out. There are a number of weaknesses from
tax avoidance to evasion, to labour disputes etc
which can attract the attention of the local
functionary.
(i)Projects Exempted: In the industrial policy
statement certain categories of projects are exempt
from sanctions. An entrepreneur may have to go
through the procedures indicated at Figure-I.
(ii)Projects not exempt: Involving fixed investment above Rs.100 million as indicated Figure-II.
      To cover other shortfalls, an Industrial
Facilities Board is in operation in each province
(8). This is chaired by a very high ranking
official (9) and has for its members the representatives from the chambers of commerce, government
departments, financial institutions and utility
organisations. It works as a grievance removal
agency.
      So far as the small industry (10) is concerned
there is in every province a Small Industries Corporation. Industrial Estates have been developed
by these corporations in various locales. Some of
these industrial estates have been developed with
a regional development perspective. The mere
availability of an infrastructure is, however, no
guarantee to its becoming a centre of industrial
activity. Since important inputs in the form of
induced supply of entrepreneurial talent, credit,
technological support, market information are
missing these estates have not been commissioned.
In fact the response has been rather on the weak

Figure I: The Institutional Content of Entrepreneurs

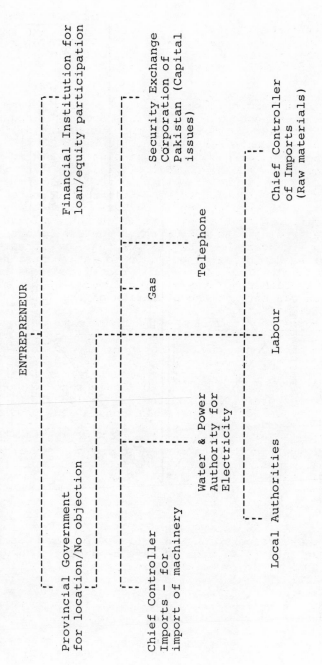

ENTREPRENEUR

Provincial Government for location/No objection

Financial Institution for loan/equity participation

Chief Controller Imports - for import of machinery

Gas

Telephone

Security Exchange Corporation of Pakistan (Capital issues)

Water & Power Authority for Electricity

Labour

Chief Controller of Imports (Raw materials)

Local Authorities

10

Figure II: Entrepreneurial Interactions

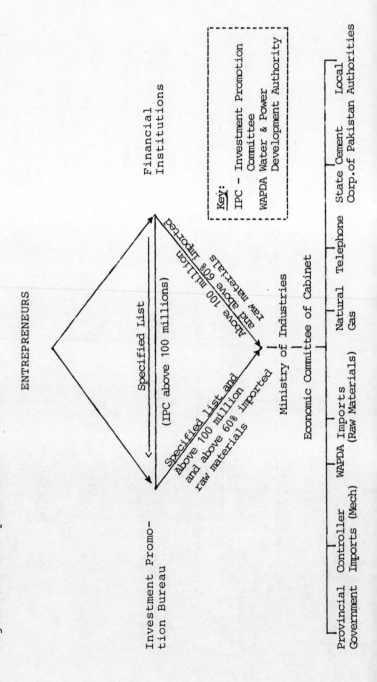

ENTREPRENEURS

Financial
Institutions

Investment Promo-
tion Bureau

Specified List

(IPC above 100 millions)

Above 100 million
and above 60% imported
raw materials

Specified List and
above 100 million
and above 60% imported
raw materials

Ministry of Industries

Economic Committee of Cabinet

Key:
IPC - Investment Promotion
Committee
WAPDA Water & Power
Development Authority

Provincial
Government

Controller
Imports (Mech)

WAPDA Imports
(Raw Materials)

Natural
Gas

Telephone

State Cement
Corp.of Pakistan

Local
Authorities

side.

Deregulation

An important consideration with government policy
of the day is to simplify government procedures.
These procedures have developed over the last three
decades in an effort to control and regulate
industrialisation. These have been in the nature
of piecemeal actions. In other words as a response
to some aspect of industrialisation which was
unacceptable to the policy makers. It would be
impossible to recall the basis for creating such
regulatory actions. In general, though, these
were meant to safeguard the interest of the
consumers. In actual fact this may not have been
the case. It may have only encouraged the propensity towards undesirable control by bureaucracy.

The intention of the present government is
visible in its various policy statements, such as
the sixth plan and the Industrial Policy Statement.

In investment sanctioning it has tried to
liberalise by increasing substantially the limit
on investment requiring sanctions; from Rs.20
million to Rs.300 million in terms of total project
size and from Rs.10 million to Rs.50 million in
terms of foreign exchange requirements.

Similarly the sanctioning procedures have been
considerably streamlined. There are indeterminate
areas which still require consideration at an
appropriate level as a considerable amount of time
and effort is wasted in these areas, i.e. projects
of national importance, industries with excess
capacity and such other industries as included in
the negative list (11). Besides this grey area,
Government has over a period of time centralised
its functioning. The agencies responsible for
ascertaining and determining the pros and cons are
not the final approving agencies for projects.
These projects end up for consideration in the
Economic Committee of the Cabinet (ECC).

Besides this there are a number of industries
whose product is subject to price regulation. The
pricing mechanism is cost plus basis. The basis
seems to be to keep the cost of essentials at a
reasonable level and at the same time to allow a
reasonable rate of return to the investor. This
in actual practice very rarely happens given the
nature and basis of decision making. In fact
policy decisions end up short on both factors.
The normal basis would be to allow free market
forces to take over. This can only happen if
there were no barriers to entry. In fact, despite

liberalisation, barriers to entry are almost
insurmountable. It seems virtually impossible
to counter the methodology of those already in an
industry and enjoying unfettered and unlimited
profits. Needless to say this is the general rule
in all price 'regulated' industries. It is
extremely difficult to work out the exact cost
figures. Both the practised art and the will to
do so may contribute to this weakness.

NOTES

1. These are in the nature of monographs or
ILO/ARTEP studies. Some by Pakistani authors.
2. Registered are such industries as have
been formally approved by the authorities.
3. During the period 1972-77 a spate of
nationalisations affected the working of the
economy. (The industrial Policy provided as an
appendix indicates the details.)
4. See Z. Altaf Pakistani Entrepreneurs,
Croom Helm, London, 1983.
5. 'Soft' -- industries with weak linkages.
6. Industrial investment schedule in which
the demand and supply structure of products is
worked out and the gap determined. This gap is
then the basis for allocation and sanctions.
The schedule is for major industries and completely
ignores the small scale production basis.
7. Industrial Policy Statement, Government
of Pakistan, Ministry of Industries, June 1984.
8. Pakistan has four provinces -- Punjab,
Sind, North West Frontier (NWFP) and Baluchistan.
9. Normally the Chief Secretary (or the
Principal Secretary).
10. Defined as less than Rs.5 million
investment. (1$ = Rs.16/- current rate of
exchange.)
11. A negative list in the Industrial Policy
Statement stipulates areas not available for
investment.

Chapter Two

REAPPRAISAL OF THEORIES OF RISK AND UNCERTAINTY

Developing countries as a rule have taken to
industrialisation in the hope of achieving their
cherished goals. The objectives, hopes and
aspirations are normally based on the current
position that developed countries are in at the
moment. Economic history or the basis which led
to their current position are not known or if known
rarely examined. The visibility and the apparent
strength of these economies are normally related to
their being 'industrialised'. When considering
this 'industrialised' aspect policy makers in the
Third World seek certain obvious and 'easy to
comprehend' options. These are to acquire a
particular technology, capture scale economies,
thereby improving income of the labour force besides
providing fresh employment possibilities. In their
earnestness to achieve these possibilities all
kinds of incentives are provided. The nature of
these incentives are all pervasive. Since political systems are generally unstable in less
developed countries, evidence has it that a newly
installed government has always eulogised and
supported the industrial sector. The support over
a period of time has been seen to decline. Why
so? The reason is that the initial promises and
strengths of industrialisation so strongly advocated are seldom realised. This realisation only
comes with time. For despite all kind of 'support
systems' the industrial sector has generally
failed to deliver its own delineated goals and
objectives, much less fulfil social obligations.
     The entrepreneurial theories (1) advocated,
therefore, need to be reappraised in a different
context. In the context of less developed countries important modifications may well be indicated.
     With the addition of this entrepreneurial

13

factor the entire concept of factors of production becomes unstable. Traditional factors of production, land, labour, capital, once acquired give a stable equation. With the consideration of entrepreneur as prime mover this equation is destabilised, in the sense that a variable factor is now under consideration. The level at which the entrepreneur operates and achieves determines his variability. In developed countries, because of less barriers to entry and exit entrepreneurial performance can be gauged and determined by market forces. Efficiency, competition, production possibilities determine the level at which a particular entrepreneur operates. Not so in the less developed countries. Other factors come into play. The risk of an entrepreneur may be entirely determined by the institutional framework in existence. The uncertainty may be determined by the political system and the prevailing law and order situation. Normally noneconomic factors have not been given due weight in the analysis of risk and uncertainty. Its exclusion would mean partial analysis.

The historical perspective of an entrepreneur in the context of the less developed nations therefore does not hold. Firstly because of environmental reasons. The land-man ratio and other modern pressing claims were not noticeable when most of these early theories were propounded. Secondly the information media was not as 'communicative' nor as quick. Thirdly government intervention in all spheres of life was minimal. There was not the kind of involvement and intervention that is so noticeable these days. Fourthly, the state of the art was not as acute as it was today. Fifthly the nature of markets has changed considerably. Sixthly, the lobby groups of the entrepreneurs vis-a-vis the counter force of the existing industrialists make for a continuous tussle in government industrial policy. These and a number of other issues and competing claims make analysis that much more complex. The concept of free market is a far fetched concept. The more relevant would be a 'fixed' market. Forces in play defy established rules. The reasons may or may not be in the field of economic policy making.

It would be unfair to consider all entrepreneurs as operating on the same plane. Within the entrepreneurs great diversity is noticed. This diversity may be due to scale, specific industry or geographical reasons, so that even here the nature of risk and uncertainty will differ. The

more relevant question seems to be -- Does the
entrepreneur bear any risk or uncertainty? The
evidence that is available in the Pakistani context
has been analysed in the remaining chapters. The
uncertainty element seems to be dependent on the
political system. Even here and according to the
appreciation of the problem by the entrepreneur,
enough safeguards have been brought in.

The arguments given above are not meant to
indicate that the entrepreneur receives everything
without any effort. His effort is diverted
towards, in the case of the large entrepreneur --
(i) the credit markets; (ii) the project sanctioning authorities; (iii) institutional contact.

The credit markets in Pakistan are extremely
limited. The headquarters are located at the major
port city Karachi (former capital). Policies are
not decentralised. In any case even if these
policies were decentralised, given the constraints
in the system, checks come in sooner or later. The
bureaucracy, in order to make a system foolproof,
tends towards over structuring regulatory policies.
The project sanction procedure had become so
perverse in Pakistan, that it would take years
before formal approval is accorded. The caveats
that are added by the bureaucracy require further
effort by the entrepreneur. However, once these
formalities are covered and he is on his way his
risk and uncertainty are considerably reduced if
not removed altogether.

The question that one must address oneself to,
then, is he an innovator in the Schumpeterian
sense? The underlying basis in this thesis was
again one of risk. The entrepreneur in organising
something new was taking on a new 'risky' arrangement. This presumably also meant a reconsideration
of raw materials, production systems, marketing of
goods etc. Such a necessity arises where the
competition in a system overtakes the earlier
efforts of the entrepreneurs. In other words, the
entrepreneur is all 'eyes and ears' to competitors
and in order to stay ahead of the pack he innovates.
The need for this kind of innovation may not be
there in less developed countries, with demand
for goods always in excess of supply (even of
consumer goods). The excessive population trends
also increase the demand for a product. The only
safeguard is to have a product which is of acceptable quality. In the case of the entrepreneur
who seeks substantial rewards and knows how to
'play the game', the lion's share is available from

the credit market.

For the medium and small entrepreneur, policies generally are not as helpful. Some of the more persistant do manage credit facilities but these are after considerable effort and time. The entrepreneur who thinks small is the one who may bear the maximum risk because of his inability to play the capital markets. There is no loan facility, no banker's equity, in other words hardly any institutional support. His capital is his own, earned over a period of time.

The project sanctioning authorities and those involved in the project formulation work in complex and complicated structures. Most of these organisations work to the disadvantage of the many. Under the garb of allocative efficiency an investment schedule determines whether an industrial project can be sanctioned or not. It is not necessary to differentiate between products and their special importance. The very concept that the bureaucracy can develop such an investment schedule is ill conceived. It would be virtually impossible to determine the demand, firstly for an existing product and secondly about a future product. The result in both cases could mean misallocation of investment.

The documentation and feasibility studies pose another area of difficulty. The documentation is peculiar to each organisation. The relevance of information sought in each document is questionable. Some information is only sought because it could be relevant at some future date. Some of the information is hypothetical. Its validity and reliability can always be questioned. The feasibility studies on the other hand determine the cost of a number of factors which ultimately reflect on the profitability of the enterprise. These costs are so balanced as to fulfil a routine. Playing these capital markets successfully is more than half the battle. Where the entrepreneur is so totally dependent on a centralised capital market, a basis other than market success is generally the criterion for obtaining scarce financial resources.

The overriding consideration then is the level and kind of institutional contact that is maintained by the entrepreneur. Obviously the new entrant hardly has any knowledge of either the rules of the game or how they are played. The institutional contact may be indirect. The political or the influential entrepreneur has the

wherewithal for this kind of contact. It is
the production based entrepreneur who suffers
from lack of contact. It is therefore obvious
that risk and uncertainty are manifested
differently for different categories of entrepreneurs.

Entrepreneur may, therefore, be added to the
original list of factors of production. The reasons
for this being so are different than in the more
developed countries where capital markets follow
their own criteria and nuances. The large industry
entrepreneur must, as already stated, know how to
operate capital markets, institutions where projects
are sanctioned. Chances are that all financial
risks will be covered. It is the production based
medium or small level entrepreneur who really has
to push himself in all directions to make a success
of it. The Schumpeterian concept, I am afraid, is
less obvious. The reason is that the entrepreneur
has generally managed to transplant an existing
system. The effort is more in the nature of an
all encompassing borrowing. Turnkey arrangements
are implanted without due regard to either their
appropriateness or their utility. The net result
is a consumer trend forced upon the urbanites and
held up to the rural population as the ultimate in
obtaining quality of life. In other words status
illusions are brought into a nation state when
priority may lie elsewhere.

In a different sense the Schumpeterian concept
is achieved. The new product brings with it a new
arrangement organisationally. In the context of
a less developed country such a situation would
occur every time there is a new firm coming up.
Its uniqueness, in the context in which it was
probably used in the first instance, would be very
rare. It would, for instance, mean that the
entrepreneur was and is capable of modifying a
process so as to be in tune with the existing
market requirements.

Knight (2) considered the entrepreneur as the
carrier of risk. Evidence available indicates
that financial risk in Pakistan for an industrialist seemed to be non-existent. This is not to say
that there were no failures. To be sure these
failures were there. These were due to reasons
other than market risk. Normally entrepreneurial
delinquency was the reason. Even as of today,
government's of the day tend to prop up such
delinquent behaviour (3). In other words entrepreneurs have played truant either by misutilising

17

funds or by obtaining incomplete or ineffective technology or by not having the appropriate man-power. Normally whenever a sick unit is reported or a demand set up by the respective chamber of commerce, everyone in that particular industry (or group) sets up a similar demand. A committee in the Ministry of Finance considers these risks and provides appropriate response.

Recent Economic Thought

In recent economic thought (4) the entrepreneurial concept has come to mean getting to terms with all kinds of coordinative activities. If Kilby's (5) activities were critically revisited a different scenario would emerge.

Perception of market opportunities may not be so important as the desire to enter a specific indus-try where administrative fiat has made it impossible for others to enter. The barriers to entry are administered to ensure the continuing profitability of those in the industry. So primacy for the entrepreneur may be to break through such rigid structures.

Obtaining control of scarce resources is again a matter of how the 'entrepreneurial influence' operates. The resources are so scarce as to be available to the 'big sharks' only. Now policies such as balancing, modernisation and replacement (BMR) have been developed to ensure the continuing and growing requirements of those in lucrative industries. This is ostensibly for improving the competitiveness of the firm. Such an outcome would be an exception. For despite all efforts at increasing competitiveness in national and international markets, the products of such firms have to be protected behind high tariff walls. The myth of comparative cost advantage in inter-national markets remains illusive. This is one of the basic reasons why the export oriented policies for value added goods are subsidised. Similar arguments can be furthered for purchase of inputs, as well as for marketing of products and responding to competition.

Kilby, of course, was considering the corporate sector entrepreneur who plays by well intentioned and successful institutions. Such is not the case in Pakistan, either for the corporate sector entrepreneurs (except a few) or for the medium and small level entrepreneur.

If current literature is weak in determining the economic basis of entrepreneurs, how must this phenomenon be explained? In India (Gujrat State) an indigenous model has been developed. Although the Centre for Entrepreneurship Development is involved in trying to develop and create entrepreneurs, their basic abilities can be determined from the various methods and programmes that have been devised (Figure III).

The approach is an all encompassing one but it basically considers human traits. The human traits assessed (Figure IV), according to Patel (6), include (i) the need to achieve, (ii) risk taking, an intelligent calculated risk, (iii) positive self confidence, (iv) initiative and independence, (v) problem solving, (vi) hopeful about future and increasing level of aspiration, (viii) need for power, (ix) time boundness -- tend to do things in a time span, and (x) need for power.

The basic and critical trait strengthened is the need for achievement. Risk taking is covered by a supervised feasibility study of the market which the entrepreneur carries out himself (Figure V). As a result of this study a familiarity with the subject is developed which leads to increased self confidence and initiative. It is much too early to state as to whether dependency on the Centre for Entrepreneurial Development is increased. Because of the study of the market, doubts and fears tend to be removed. Since this is also supervised the demonstration of this ability indicates the success or failure of the enterprise (Figure VI). Entrepreneurs have an acute desire to search the environment. This search is furthered in the Centre when they are asked to study and identify the industry of their choice in a real situation. The basis for choice of industry has to be explained and the economics essential to success collected and interpreted (Figure VIII). The programme has achieved a high success rate.

Once a project plan is discussed and approved, a one window operation for credit is carried out. The credit requirements and disbursements are not at the headquarters of the financial institutions but at the industrial location. The advantage of such a transparent occasion ensures besides publicity a building up of confidence in the would-be entrepreneurs (Figure VIII).

The location, generally, determined for the entrepreneurs is such as to take into consideration all possible requirements. In other words industry location is based in the most desireable location

(Figure IX). There are, however, some limitations to the programme:
(i) The target group is the small entrepreneur. Those that would not otherwise be able to push themselves to the level required. So a new potential methodology for supply of entrepreneurs has been developed.
(ii) The markets those would-be entrepreneurs study are localised, regional markets. The overall national market analysis is not there.
(iii) The production base is at a low technological level.

Entrepreneurial Development, as determined in Gujrat, is a function of:

Figure III: Affecting Entrepreneurial Development

$ED = f\ (Et,\ Op,\ Sk,\ Pr,\ F,\ If,\ En.)$

ED = Entrepreneurship Development.

Et = Entrepreneurial Traits.

Op = Opportunity.

Sk = Skills.

Pr = Project Report (Plan).

F = Finance.

If = Infrastructure.

En = Environment.

Source: International Workshop for Entrepreneurial Development - Gujrat, 1983.

To explain entrepreneurial development the theorist must therefore delve into not only economics but also psychology of the entrepreneur as well as social environments obtaining in the area. The three must work together. The psyche of an individual will vary with the experiences and cultural norms of the individual and the country. Every country must therefore determine its own basis for increasing the supply of entrepreneurs (Figure X).

Figure IV: Entrepreneurial Traits

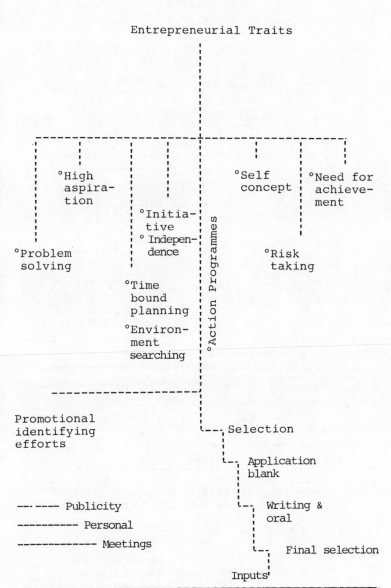

Source: International Workshop for Entrepreneurial Development – Gujrat, 1983.

Figure V: Entrepreneurial Opportunities

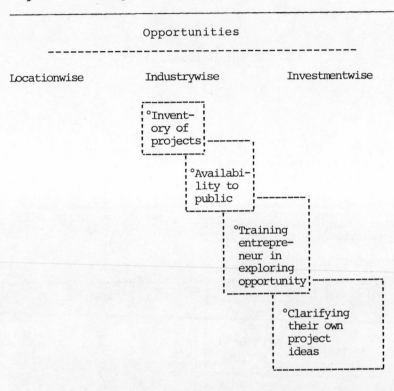

Source: International Workshop for Entrepreneurial Development - Gujrat, 1983. (Same source for Figure 6)

Figure VI: Entrepreneurial Skills

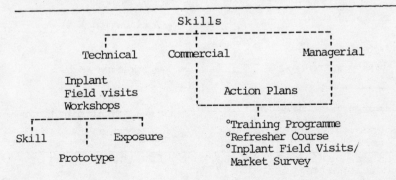

Figure VII: Project Plan

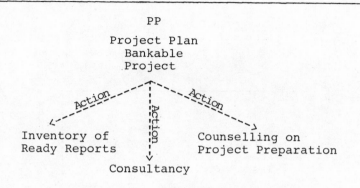

Source: International Workshop for Entrepreneurial Development - Gujrat, 1983

Figure VIII: Finances Requirements

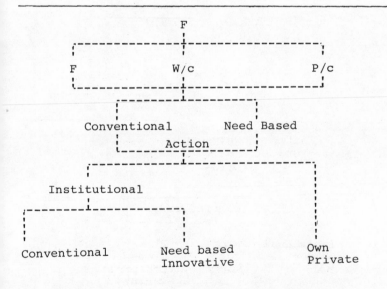

Source: International Workshop for Entrepreneurial Development - Gujrat, 1983.

Figure IX: Infrastructural Requirements

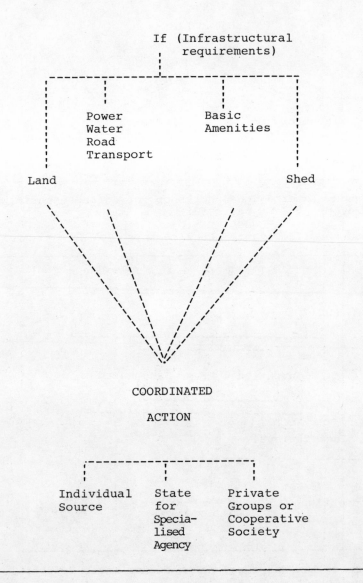

Source: International Workshop for Entrepreneurial Development - Gujrat, 1983.

Figure X: Entrepreneurial Linkages

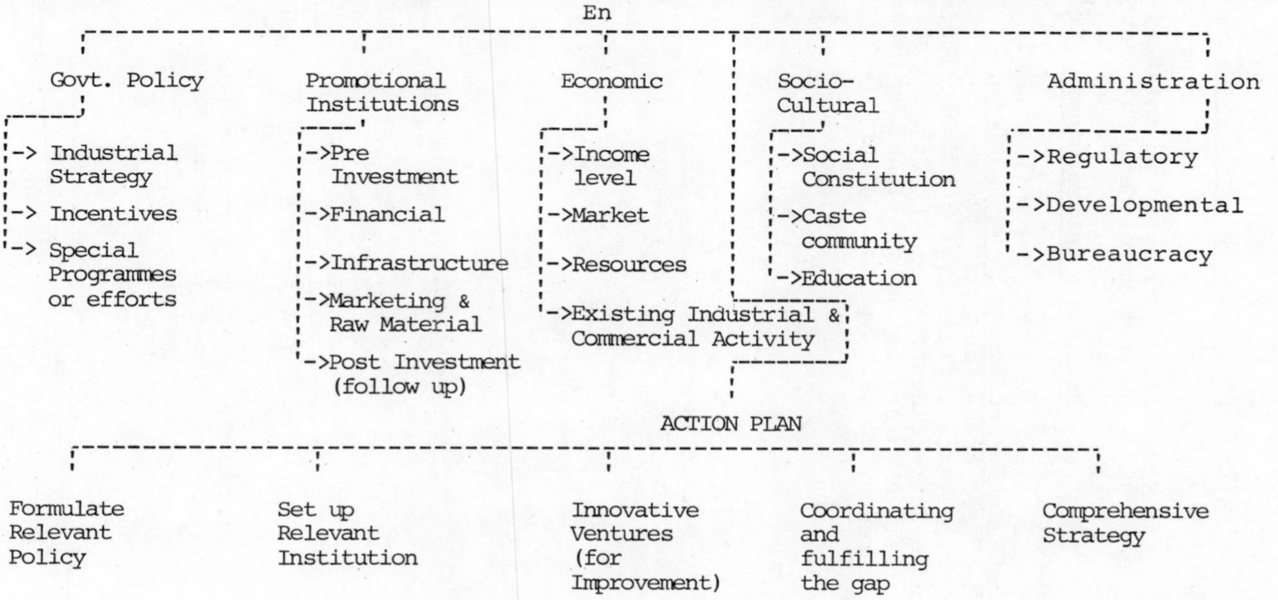

En

Govt. Policy	Promotional Institutions	Economic	Socio-Cultural	Administration
-> Industrial Strategy	->Pre Investment	->Income level	->Social Constitution	->Regulatory
-> Incentives	->Financial	->Market	->Caste community	->Developmental
-> Special Programmes or efforts	->Infrastructure	->Resources	->Education	->Bureaucracy
	->Marketing & Raw Material	->Existing Industrial & Commercial Activity		
	->Post Investment (follow up)			

ACTION PLAN

Formulate Relevant Policy	Set up Relevant Institution	Innovative Ventures (for Improvement)	Coordinating and fulfilling the gap	Comprehensive Strategy

Source: International Workshop for Entrepreneurial Development - Gujrat, 1983

NOTES

1. Z. Altaf, <u>Pakistani Entrepreneurs</u>, Croom Helm, London, 1983.
2. Ibid.
3. 438 Sick Industries approved for Revival till August 1985 - Dr. Mahbub-ul-Haq, Business Recorder, December 6, 1985.
4. Z. Altaf, <u>Pakistani Entrepreneurs</u>, Croom Helm, London, 1983.
5. P. Kilby, 'Hunting the Heffalump' in <u>Entrepreneurship and Economic Development</u>, P. Kilby (ed), The Free Press, New York 1971.
6. V.G. Patel, 'Identifying and Developing Indigenous Entrepreneurship -- The Gujrat Model', lecture delivered at the International Workshop on Entrepreneurial Development, Gujrat, 1983.

Chapter Three

STIMULATING ECONOMIC ENVIRONMENT

It is proposed to examine, in this chapter, the
manner in which entrepreneurs were induced towards
industrial activity. Almost the first act in 1947
was a call to 'faithfuls' (1) to come back to
Pakistan, to help the country through the initial
period of difficulty. During the first three years
these personal calls abounded. Industrial policy
was so widely interpreted that, irrespective of
the project, anyone who came forward was allowed to
invest. Policy making started in the early fifties
and has since continued.

Evidence indicates that environment plays a
crucial part in not only inducing entrepreneurs but
also in specific industry investment of these
entrepreneurs. The entrepreneurial response is
dependent on how lucid and widely circulated and
perceived an incentive policy is. The effort of
the government is therefore to evoke a 'sympathetic resonance' to its policies.

In the case of Pakistan, government did play
a very crucial role. Policies, were devised and
implemented but it is impossible to state the
validity and reliability of these policies. There
can never be any absolute measure. A relative
measure, however, is available. The responses can
be ascertained by time periods and these can be
compared. Such relative measures have their limitations as there can be multiple reasons for
investment. Data gathering has hazards for the
entrepreneur. For instance production statistics
can be utilised by the revenue system for realising
its own objectives. If the data is used for
repressive purposes, it will hardly be reliable or
valid. Under such circumstances a credibility norm
has to be developed between the statistician and
the entrepreneur. The basis for such trust

creation is dependent on personal contact. Trust
in such societies, once developed, is rewarding and
information sought can come through (2). In the
absence of a bare minimum of trust distorted
figures are likely to be provided. For instance
if capacity utilisation is the basis for taxation,
then there is no way that reliable figures for
production would be available. That is asking for
the heavy hand of the administration to eventually
land on the enterprise that supplies the necessary
information. The administration will accept everything which increases government revenues. Once a
tax base is established, it keeps on increasing, in
a given proportion, no matter what the state of
profits or finances of the enterprise are. So the
first protective device of the entrepreneur is not
to provide the required data.

Assumptions on data are also interestingly
made. For instance despite the 1975-76 survey of
small industries the growth of small industry is
assumed to be at the rate of population increase
i.e. 3 per cent. In the Punjab where an industrial
survey was undertaken, the growth indications were
much in excess of this and varied in industrial
classification terms between 30 per cent to
130 per cent (3).

It is obvious that given these limitations
some alternative methodology was required. At a
very basic level therefore entrepreneurs were
asked questions to determine the impact of government incentive policy. Answers were solicited to
such questions as awareness of incentives, whether
these were applied for, as also whether the entrepreneur's firm was a beneficiary of these incentives.
In case they were not, reasons for not being
beneficiaries were obtained. Yet another indication of relativeness would be whether any help was
obtained on first investment or second or whether
any of government's much announced advisory centres
played any part in inducing the final step.
Advisory centre information was sought on choice of
technology, choice of industry or any other
industrial requirement. A normative question was
put to them to elicit whether government agencies
are a requirement of our time.

Before we start analysing these responses let
us first examine the nature of incentives that the
government offered. That the economic environment
is not independent of the other environments i.e.
political, social and administrative, is all too
obvious. Occasional reference to political, social

and administrative factors will be made, where
these factors have overriding importance and have
dwarfed economic thinking and economic rationality.

Fiscal Incentives

Fiscal incentives have followed a pattern consist-
tent with the stop-go policies of the government
of the day. Pakistan's taxation system is
dominated by indirect taxation to the extent of
about 85%. The balancing of the budget is not by
fine tuning but by tinkering e.g. an investors
demand for reduction in interest on fixed investments was accepted and reduced from 14% to 11% but
the special depreciation allowed at the rate of
15% was withdrawn. Similarly the Corporate Tax
was increased to 55% from 50% but this was offset
by withdrawal of tax of 10% to 15% on bonus shares
of public and private companies. Such offsetting
practices and complicated procedures have understandably upset the industrialists and the entrepreneurs. The internal revenue representative is
a fact of life in all capitalist countries whether
developed or not. Such complex conditions, which
are continuously modified mean one of two things:
(i) either the industrialist/entrepreneur comes to
terms with the system and accepts everything that
comes his way, or (ii) seeks to mould the tax
system in such a way that it helps him to the
maximum.

When the second of the two categories is taken
up as a response the entrepreneur creates an
atmosphere through the media and through the
Chambers of Commerce such as to influence the
policy making decisions. As a last resort he may
try and influence the outcome of a decision
through monetary considerations.

Influence of Taxation. For analytical convenience
the tax structure may be divided into (i) direct,
and (ii) indirect. Income tax and super tax form
the first category and import duties (sales tax on
imports and excise tax etc) come under the second
category. The direct system formed the major
instrument for increasing investment and for
inducing entrepreneurs into the system, generally
via tax holidays and various exemptions from
income tax. The indirect tax system was and is
utilised primarily for placating existing demands
of the various Chambers of Commerce and other
bodies for rebates on existing sales and excise
taxes, or on imports of essential items. The tax

holiday has varied from 8 to 6 to 4 to 2 years. At
the moment it is utilised for removing regional
disparities or for inducement to specific industries. The two specific provisions for location
by geographical and industrial positioning do
conflict but generally the industrialising effect
of the former could not be denied and is referred
to in Table 3.9 (page 52).

The inducement by industry meant that such
industrial direction had to be identified as was
a pioneering start requiring specialist skills, a
highly trained labour force, a raw material source
etc. In short, an industry which raised the level
of all kinds of production and knowledge frontiers.

Exemption from income tax and other taxes
followed on certain conditions:
(1) Industries based on indigenous raw materials.
(2) Industries providing incentive, for industrialisation (appropriate and far reaching backward
and forward linkages) and capital formation.
(3) Industries willing to invest 60 per cent of
their profits in the same industry or any other.

In addition, exemptions were also allowed for
capital gains tax and wealth tax. The domestic
industries were also entitled to depreciation and
in some cases (non-tax holiday areas) to accelerated depreciation.

Rebates. Besides exemption from direct taxes the
export industries were allowed rebates on imported
raw materials directly utilised in the production
process. These export industries were also exempt
from excise duty.

Import Duty. The nature of import substitution
industrialisation policies followed meant the
utilisation of this source (also known as custom
duty) from mere revenue raising to a protective
form. The underlying philosophy for a protective
cover was to provide, over a period of time,
sufficient time for the industry to improve its
efficiency. The protective tariff cover was to
be removed once the industry had been placed on
a sound basis. It was thought that such policies
would help develop nascent industry to a stage
where it would be competitive and able to with-
stand market pressures.

The protective duties were further utilised
on a sliding scale, low duties on capital goods,
comparatively high on imported raw materials and

highest on consumer goods. There were further
variations within each group depending on how
reliable and essential a product was considered
to be.

Export Duties. In addition to custom duties, there
were export duties on a number of traditional
primary commodities, primarily for the purpose of
inducing some form of value added processing before
export. In later years, two of the most important
traditional export commodities i.e. rice and cotton,
were brought under State Trading Corporation.

Commercial Policy. Aspects pertaining to exchange
control, import licensing, and export promotion
will be examined.

Foreign Exchange Control Policy. The exchange
control policy was designed to regulate the inflow
and outflow of foreign exchange. It became an
important policy instrument for industrialisation,
as it was not only a scarce resource but it also
provided to the industrialist an over valued
currency (4) which could be utilised for windfall
gains. The allocations were made by a high
powered committee.

Import Licence (5). The foreign exchange control
policy saw its outlet through the allocation of
various categories of users. It thus became an
instrument for resource allocation involving three
dimensions: (i) what to import, (ii) how much to
import, and (iii) who should import.
    We will not go into details as to how this
policy operated except to state that further sub-
divisions came in e.g. commercial, industrial,
regular, irregular, once-off etc complicating its
administration. The administrative discretions
thus created served as a powerful basis for streng-
thening a few and strangling many of the aspirants.
    This control mechanism's application to
commercial imports meant that no foreign exchange
was available for goods to compete with locally
manufactured goods. So since 1952, when it first
came into operation and thereafter, this operated
as a very strong protective device for the
industrialist/entrepreneur.

The Export Bonus Scheme. Pakistan's first devaluation in 1955 did not help the subsequent valuation
of the currency. For a variety of reasons, the

overvalued currency was 'propped' up by administrative price control and rationing. This administrative price control led to the creation of the
Export Bonus Scheme. Under this scheme exporters
were allowed to retain a fixed percentage of their
foreign exchange earnings. These were tradeable in
the open market and the premium rates varied
between 150 to 180 per cent, in practice nearer the
upper limit. This meant that multiple exchange
rates were in operation for those requiring foreign
exchange and unable to do so under the Import
Licence schemes.

The method and the procedure was extremely
complicated. Administrative machinery besides
being inadequate could not be expected to come to
the rescue of the entrepreneurs, simply because the
two spoke two different languages. Communication
between the two could only be possible through
means other than normal appreciation. Administrative discretion gave way to jockeying, to graft
and to host of other discouraging factors.

Tables 3.1 and 3.2 indicate the impact of
Bonus Imports as recorded between 1959-60 to 1967-
68. The bonus scheme was discontinued thereafter.

Table 3.1: Bonus Imports and Total Imports
(Rs Million)

Year	Total Imports	Bonus Imports	Bonus as % of Total Imports
1959-60	2461	131	5.3
1960-61	3188	146	4.6
1961-62	3109	165	5.3
1962-63	3819	201	5.3
1963-64	4430	237	5.4
1964-65	5374	270	5.0
1965-66	4208	328	7.8
1966-67	5192	442	8.5
1967-68	4655	513	11.0

Source: Dr. S. Haq - Currency, Devaluation,
Balance of Payments and Economic Development:
Research Report No.3. United Bank Limited,
Karachi 1968.

Table 3.2: Comparison of Bonus Imports
(Rs Million)

Years	Consumer Goods		Raw Materials		Capital Goods	
	Value	%	Value	%	Value	%
1959-60	40	30.5	37	28.2	54	41.3
1960-61	45	30.8	14	9.6	87	59.6
1961-62	66	40.0	43	26.1	56	33.9
1962-63	77	38.3	55	27.4	69	34.3
1963-64	85	35.9	91	38.4	61	25.7
1964-65	140	51.8	81	30.0	49	18.1
1965-66	141	43.0	139	42.2	48	14.6
1966-67	215	48.6	168	38.0	59	13.3
1967-68	280	54.6	184	35.9	49	9.5

Source: Dr. S. Haq - Currency, Devaluation,
Balance of Payments and Economic Development:
Research Report No.3. United Bank Limited,
Karachi, 1968.

Effects of Export Bonus Scheme. In many ways the
Bonus Voucher Scheme proved a blessing to the
entrepreneurs. It assured first and foremost, the
continuous development of markets via consumer
goods import and therefore the non limitation of
import substitution possibilities (Table 3.2)
so that the momentum of this kind of industrialisation could go into the 1970s and the 1980s.
Secondly it made available scarce foreign
exchange, albeit at high costs, but certainly
better than 'starving' the entrepreneur of this
highly priced requirement.
Thirdly it did discriminate against export of
raw materials and provided incentives to manufacture of processed commodities.
Fourthly it raised the protective effects of
tariff by raising the domestic cost of imports and
thereby encouraged, indirectly, more effort in
import substitution policies.
Fifthly, and this is a contentious point, some
economists felt that this encouraged corporate
savings trends (7) as the marginal propensity to
save in this sector is higher than the average
propensity to save. Other economists (8) do not
necessarily agree with this point of view.
There were other economists, namely, Mallon,
Soligo, and Stan and Thomas who doubted 'price
subsidies' and questioned the validity of and

economic rationale of policies by stating that
'..... producers could export at a loss to the
country but at a profit to themselves' (9) or that
the '.....present structure of the bonus rate is
such that those industries which have the highest
import content are receiving the largest export
subsidy through the bonus scheme (10), or that
'the failure of the scheme to work more smoothly
over the years may be attributed to the inflexi-
bility and unresponsiveness of the economy .....
additional policies to exploit changing conditions
are believed to be necessary conditions for
achieving better results' (11).

The controversial views aside, the fact that
import substitution and industrialisation did take
place cannot be denied. The answer as to 'who'
carried out this industrialisation would be more
pertinent to our present work but no such effort
was made to relate the beneficiaries and to have
a particularly hard and good look at them.

Subsequent Export Incentives. A host of fiscal
incentives like the rebate on custom duties, rebate
of excise duties, refund of sales tax, and income
tax concessions on export earnings have been
introduced and continue in force.

The only point in their administration worth
mentioning is that the involvement of the administrative machinery with the entrepreneur/industria-
list becomes ever more complicated (12).

(a) Monetary Concessions. Monetary measures are
mainly export credit guarantees both at the
preshipment and postshipment stages. Export
finance is available at an interest rate of 2
per cent per annum. The Banks in turn are eligible
for refinance from the State Bank at zero rate
of interest.

Separate schemes for export of machinery and
non traditional exports are in operation with one
major difference. In the Export Finance Scheme
meant for non-traditional other than industrial
machinery, the exporter is allowed credit on the
basis of previous years' performance. Similarly
schemes involving insurance, idemnity schemes of
the State Bank of Pakistan are in operation.

(b) Special Concessions. Special licensing facilities are allowed to industries exporting goods,
usually as a percentage of their exports and

preferential treatment is provided to any entrepreneur wanting to manufacture goods for exports by
allowing imports of banned importable items.

But by far, in this category, the most
important facility to entrepreneurs is to import
plant and machinery for the establishment of
industrial units on credit and to pay for it out
of export earnings. Such units must guarantee to
export at least 50% of their production. In some
cases this has been reduced to 25% or 33% depending
on nature of goods produced and the kind of
competition encountered in world markets.

(c)Other Measures. Concessional inland freight
rates, facility for travel abroad, and establishment of trade offices abroad are some of the other
measures provided as incentives.

Tariff Protection and its Effects.
Pakistan followed the classical mould for using initially,
the infant industry argument for its tariff protection
policies. It was argued, and justifiably, that as
a result of obtaining factors in the economy no
industry in an Ldc would have comparative cost
advantage unless protection was provided; and that
over a period of time, as the learning process
developed the industry requirements, the cost of
factor inputs would ensure a reduction in cost,
ultimately leading to removal of protective tariffs.
That such protective industrialisation also
created external economies was also held to be an
important basis for diversification and industrial
development. Thus the industry created specifically under such protection needs to be viewed in
a larger social context. In the context of a
social criterion allowing for other economic
sectors to interact with it, in terms of subcon-
tractual activities developing in the locale, one
can find a positive reason for imposition of such
tariffs. Viewed in the larger context of import
substitution, where initial but dormant, comparative cost is said to be available, initial
industrial threat meant a higher cost to the
consumer. Over a period of time this cost was to
fall and the product become competitive in the
national as well as the world economic order. But
tariff protection by itself does not help; other
reinforcing policies i.e. exchange controls and
quantitative restriction on imports need also to
be imposed. All these factors add of course to

the rapid industrialisation and ignore efficiency of production, quality and price of domestic goods. Above all once established they forget consumer welfare. No government agency has systematically and continuously analysed and removed or reduced high tariff values on the basis of improved factors of production.

The second argument, briefly referred to, is the external economies argument. This is socially profitable in as much as it creates rather than relying on pre-existing service sector as in a developed country i.e. transport, insurance, banking, skilled labour market, training facilities and is an impetus towards entrepreneurial activities. These sectors are effectively under the 'umbrella' of a giant/large corporate entity created in an industrial wilderness. Either the state or state induced entrepreneurs will have to do the pioneering job. The infant industry 'argument stretches beyond the external economies case' (13).

Other reasons have also been attributed to the need for tariff protection. For our limited purposes, the basic reason is what started the issue. In the case of Pakistan foreign direct investment never came despite very high tariffs, or if it did, it was hesitant for a variety of non-economic reasons.

Over the years, the Tariff Commission was responsible for ascertaining the reasons for the imposition and degree of imposition of tariff protection. Arguments raised varied from sheer moral' or national argument to quality and industrial infancy. Thus paint and varnish argue that the industry is vital to defence need (period of tension with India being a motivating force in this reason), and so forth (14). It seems that when it came to seeking a 'monopoly' position in the market no holds were barred.

The other side of the coin, of course, was for requests on banning restrictions on imports, full rebate of import duties on raw materials and purchase of products by nationalised industries (irrespective of price and quality aspects). The minimum protection requested for instance by the paints, varnish industry was 75 per cent, while in the case of paper it was 65 per cent.

Tax Holidays
Tax holiday is a major incentive offered by Ldc. Pakistan was no exception to the rule. The

system was implemented with growing discretion and
systematic elimination of high growth areas. This
made the dispersal of industry by geographic
location an important corner stone of its social
criteria. The social benefits of such actions are
impossible to compute but reference has already
been made to such vertical and horizontal social
benefits at Lawrencepur (Table 3.9).

(a) Geographic or Backward Areas Incentives. The
current geographic/backward area incentive includes,
besides a tax holiday for five years, exemption
from payment of customs duty on imported machinery
and equipment plus a similar exemption for indigenously fabricated capital goods. For semi-
developed areas there is 50 per cent relief on
standard customs duty on the import of plant and
equipment for projects to be located in industrial
estates throughout the country. For the Pakistan
Industrial Credit and Investment Corporation
(PICIC), one of the two main credit agencies, the
impact of such incentives was as follows:

Table 3.3: Investment - New and Expansion Projects
(Rs Million)

Regions	No. of projects in Plan Period 1978-83	Amount	Per cent
1. Tax Holiday[a]	9	151	29
2. Industrial Estates[b]	9	101.82	19
3. Specified Semi-developed[b]	19	141.60	27
4. Non-Concession Areas[c]	19	129.94	25
		524.36	100

Source: Pakistan Industrial Credit and Investment
Corporation Limited, Karachi.

a = 100% tax holidays plus 100% concessions on
    import of machinery etc.
b = 50% tax holidays plus 50% concessions on
    import of machinery.
c = No tax holiday area. Fully developed

Table 3.3 shows the growing dispersal to less developed areas (29%), specified semi-developed areas (27%), non-concession areas (25%) and industrial estates (19%). The poor response in industrial estates is rather surprising but the pattern in Pakistan is one of either complete saturation or no industries. In Sialkot, Gujranwala, Gujrat, the demand has not been fulfilled whereas in other industrial estates there has been virtually no responses. Problems in both categories do exist. These will be referred to when the response of entrepreneurs is under consideration.

b) Specific Industry Incentives. The Specific industry incentives are in three manufacturing industries i.e. Textiles, Agricultural implements and Garments industry.

Textiles industry finds its place due to a number of sick mills that are there in the sector. The result has been that others have utilised the internal weakness of the units to their advantage. In fact the feeling in both IDBP and PICIC is summarised as ... 'as regards profits, the efficient and honest entrepreneurs seem to be doing much better than before and have consistently declared higher dividends (15).

The second industry is the Agricultural implements industry. This industry provides links to the green revolution and its prominence was officially recognised in 1976, resulting in positive response from entrepreneurs not only in the industrial areas but also in the rural areas. Such a recognition never came in the other ancillary industries in the mid sixties (16).

The third industry similarly is relatively new and is export led - i.e. the Garments industry, where the export performance indicates the effect of exemption. The increase in exports for two years between July 1976 and June 1978 is of the order of 16 per cent by value and 118 per cent by quantity.

Effect of Tax Holiday. As a crude measure, Azhar and Sharif carried out a sensitivity analysis to determine the profits that were earned by tax holiday companies between 1959-60 and 1970-71. The assumptions which were utilised for computation of results were different proportions of equity and borrowed capital and using different rates of net profit on total fixed capital. Accordingly their results show a windfall gain for the 40 firms in this sample to the extent of Rs 864 million (40:60 equity/debt, net profit 10%), Rs 1149.9 million (30:70 equity/debt, and 10% net profit), Rs 1293 million (40:60 equity/debt and net profit 15%). The conclusions that Azhar and Sharif arrive at are as follows:

'For the tax holiday to have an appreciable effect on industrial dispersion it has to be incorporated within a regional development plan ... There is little point in granting tax holiday in areas without amenities.'

It seems that in the 1970s a different view altogether was being taken. The decisive impact of tax holiday was highlighted by PICIC in the following manner:

Table 3.4: Tax Holiday Regions (PICIC Sanctions only)   (Rs Million)

Province	Period	No	Amount
Baluchistan	July 1970 - June 76	3	26.6
	July 1976 - June 80	9	138.28
Azad Kashmir	July 1970 - June 76	-	-
	July 1976 - June 80	4	49.72
N.W.F.P.	July 1970 - June 76	-	-
	July 1976 - June 80	3	62.00

Source: Pakistan Industrial Credit & Investment Corporation Limited.

The impact of tax holiday in 1970s is apparent. The two have different approaches. It is difficult to relate the Azhar and Sharif findings to their ultimate deductions (17). The loss to government revenue seemed to be uppermost in their empirical research. When entrepreneurs are required to take on new ventures in far flung areas inducements of the kind provided are required.

In the preceding section a broad overview of government incentives has been provided. It is of course important to determine how the entrepreneurs perceive these incentives, or to be even basic, whether they are aware of these incentives. To determine this specific questions were put to the entrepreneurs.

Awareness of Incentives
To the generic question, whether they were aware of

incentives, 87 per cent replied in the affirmative and only 13 per cent said they were not aware. The awareness level was considered for all kinds of incentives, so even if the entrepreneur was aware of one incentive it was accepted as a positive indication that the government had managed to communicate with the entrepreneur or would-be entrepreneur.

The second basis was to determine whether the awareness of incentives was put to any use and therefore entrepreneurs were asked to indicate whether they had applied and if they had, the field was further narrowed to determine which specific incentives had been applied for. Understandably some were easily availed while others required lobbying and considerable effort. These will be dealt with later. The effort will be to try and determine the means by which governments of the day are influenced by entrepreneurs.

Table 3.5: Awareness of Incentives

	Incentive	Aware/ Utilised	Not aware/ Not utilised
		(Percent)	
1.	Knowledge	87	13
2.	Applied for	78	22
3.	Tax holiday	26	73
4.	Accelerated depreciation	63	37
5.	Reinvestment allowance	41	59
6.	Import duty relief	32	68
7.	Import licence	70	30
8.	Any other	26	74

From the responses above a fair degree of popularity of the various government measures can be ascertained. When it came to applying for any benefit 9 per cent of those aware did not apply. The explanation provided by the entrepreneurs was generally along the lines of government incompetence and red tape. In fact status has now permeated along industry lines. An entrepreneur in a beverage industry (18) is in a lower status order than a textile owner and therefore can be taken liberty with. The surprising fact was that only 26 per cent were aware of tax holidays.

Similarly awareness of import duty relief at 32 per cent was on the lower side. Generally the import duty relief is the most difficult to obtain because of the nature of administrative procedures. The relief is provided by an agency which probably is one of the most difficult agencies to deal with i.e. the custom (19) authorities. Not only is the only port of Karachi cluttered and haphazardly managed but slow and cumbersome procedures, followed by corrupt practices make life almost impossible for those unable to influence decisions.

The best course open is to pay the duty and set up the industry as soon as possible. In fact matters have gone to such an extent that some of the machinery (20) never leaves the premises and after 3 years (the time allowed for 'ripening') the machinery is auctioned. Such auctions are now awaited by the middle level and smaller industrialists. The cost, though, is exhorbitant in as much as idle machinery stays at the port warehouses without being utilised for a substantial period of its life. Import licence facilities and accelerated depreciation are in the higher awareness category at 70 per cent and 63 per cent. Import licence as already indicated is the lifeline of the industrialist/entrepreneur. Without raw materials he has one of two options, either to shut down or to produce quality goods at exhorbitant cost. The entrepreneur generally has to obtain the raw materials at a premium from the grey/black markets. For the remaining 30 per cent raw material is unimportant and these include the Ceramics industry, the textile units (small) and even the Agricultural implements (21) industry where 306 agricultural manufacturing units in the Punjab are listed, of which 128 listed units do not have any access to imported raw materials. This is a case of extreme limitation as entrepreneurs may exist in the economy, as have purchased raw materials from other entrepreneurs or from the open market. Those without import licences may well be greater than those not using imported raw materials but who manage to obtain import licences.

The only other tax significantly and specifically indicated was the reinvestment allowance allowed by the government (41 per cent). These allowances both at the actual operational level and at the export level have assumed significant proportions. Those who exported in the 1960s have seen the importance and impact of the export Bonus

Scheme (EBS). Since a market for export Bonus Vouncers existed bringing in premium to the extent of 180 per cent, the entrepreneurs saw this as a means of getting rick quick. Because of accelerated industrialisation, balance of payments strain could only be reduced either by curtailing imports or increased export earnings. These earnings led to EBS and every time exports stagnated resulting in strain on balance of payments, the slab of EBS incentive was increased from 10% to 20% to 30% till eventually, in some cases it rested at 40%. Forty per cent of foreign exchange could be transacted at 180% premium. No wonder, it led one entrepreneur to remark that the net profit per spindle per day was Rs 1. So that for the smallest unit it was Rs 12,500 per day (22). These are mammoth incentives, much beyond 'generous tax concessions' (23). Add to this Papaneks incisive statement, 'tax evasion widely and effectively practised' (24). Papanek was merely touching the tip of an economic windfall.

Impact of Education, Experience and Training

The increase in experience is directly related to awareness of incentives. In the higher experience category i.e. above 16 years, there was a 100 per cent response indicating awareness of what was happening between the industry and other areas i.e. Government and its policies. The lowest awareness of incentives was shown by the experience group which was in the 1-5 years category. The ones with no experience conformed with the total average i.e. 87 per cent and determined what the industrial requirements were and what benefits from government policies could be obtained. So with the passage of time and as the supply of entrepreneurs increased, government policies managed to filter down to the new and emerging entrepreneurs. To what degree (25) was this information available and the form in which it was available are difficult to state. Assumptions could however be made. In the case of the inexperienced and uneducated the information system most probably was informal, by word of mouth. Entrepreneurs during the course of the interview did mention how sometimes there was grave danger of misallocation of resources because of sometimes the seeming rush of entrepreneurs in a particular field. Where profits were exhorbitant such a rush would be visible.

When considering education, the more the number of years spent in education the more the

likelihood of the entrepreneur being aware of
incentives. Although there is a progressive
improvement in the information levels with
increased education, the knowledge even at the
highest level is not 10 per cent indicating what
has already been stated i.e. that universal
knowledge of all incentives is not commonly known
or even easily available.

Probably the worst informed are the trained
categories, with the self trained i.e. ironically
those who have worked hardest and usually unsocial
hours, unaware of the benefits that could accrue to
them. This is not in the least surprising
considering that these entrepreneurs are from the
very lowest social milieu and their efforts are
really to get away from the clutches of a terribly
powerful and vicious poverty trap. Afraid as they
are of losing their hard fought emergence, they are
thankful for little mercies. Three-fifths in this
category were not informed of any incentives. The
apprentice category again suffered, as they
operate at a minimal organisational level, much as
the self trained do.

Impact of Awareness of Incentives (26)
The awareness of incentives and their impact on
entrepreneurs may be gauged from Table 3.6. In
the small sector maximum benefits having been
obtained from Import licence (30%) and Accelerated
depreciation (28%). The importance of import
licence has already been highlighted and accelerated depreciation benefits accrue at the time of
assessment of corporate/income tax. Such benefits
are calculated either by the internal Revenue
Officer or the legal intermediary placing the
accounts before the tax department. The least
known is Tax holiday (9%) and Import duty relief
(10%) despite the fact that these two incentives
provide the maximum financial reward. In the
medium size category again the popularity of Import
licence (19%) and Accelerated depreciation (16%) is
obvious while again Tax holiday (5%) and Import
duty relief (7%) confirm the earlier pattern. In
the large sector Import licence (21%) and Accelerated depreciation (19%) hold primate positions but
again in the large sector the main point of
differentiation is that the overall differential
between benefits from incentives is less. Thus no
incentive has a response less than 13%. Tax
holiday and Reinvestment allowance are weakest at
13% and 14% respectively.

A point that is worth making however, is that roughly 20% of the entrepreneurs did not respond to the word economic incentive despite a detailed explanation of the mechanism and the instruments of policy. Clearly then, the government was missing out on its extension work. The majority of these were in the small sector and had moved up from very humble beginnings. In order to streamline functioning, it would be desirable to reach these entrepreneurs. But in the real world of the Ldcs this is more easily said than done. The offices

Table 3.6: Awareness of Incentives - Quantification of the Impact   (Per cent)

Size	Aware-ness		Tax Holi-day		Acc. Dep.		Rein. Allow.		Import Duty Relief		Tariff Pro-tect.		Imp. Lic-ence		Other	
	Yes	No	Yes	No	Yes	No	Yes	No	Yes	No	Yes	No	Yes	No	Yes	No
Small (0-50)	36	9	9	39	28	20	15	33	10	38	15	33	30	18	8	40
Medium (51-200)	22	2	5	21	16	10	12	14	7	18	12	14	19	6	2	20
Large (201±)	24	2	13	15	19	8	14	13	15	12	15	12	21	6	13	15

are normally located in large towns and even when the offices are located in relatively smaller towns, demotivated individuals find themselves filling such jobs. Occasionally these jobs are not filled. Dual responsibilities were also common, as also Industrial Development Officer, Gujrat, was residing in Sialkot, a distance of 40 miles (usually a hazardous journey), the Industrial Development Officer, Gujranwala, living in Gujrat - again a distance of 40 miles of hazardous commuting and the Industrial Development Officer, Jhelum, non-existent. The job was covered by the Gujrat officer, who as stated earlier lives in Sialkot. The Industrial Development Officer, Sialkot, is a war veteran still in command position, unable to communicate with the entrepreneurs. In fact the organisation and division of responsibility leaves much to be desired. PICIC/IDBP have offices in main towns of Pakistan/provincial capitals. With

the authority passing into the hands of the large
entrepreneurs, by virtue of their being the
Chairman of the Board of Directors, the field for
economic benefits has considerably narrowed. The
board does not function to the exclusion of benefits
to the members of the committees. Rather they have
to be satisfied on a priority basis. It is, therefore, not surprising that despite thirty seven
years of experience, some of these institutions
have never gone beyond their own front door to
carry the message.

Ranking of Incentives
Entrepreneurs were also asked to respond to these
incentives by ranking them in order of significance,
vis-a-vis their own industry. Each one was able to
respond according to his knowledge of the kind and
nature of incentives. Out of a possible 196
responses, the maximum response in having applied
and received an incentive and considered important
the maximum indication was for Import Licence (107),
followed by Accelerated Depreciation (98), Tariff
Protection (69), Reinvestment Allowance (64), Import
Duty Relief (46) and Tax Holiday (44). The
variability in response is significant and is
dependent on their appreciation and knowledge of
the incentives offered.
        Table 3.7 places the responses in perspec-
tive. Since the responses are multiple, a row
indicates multiple responses within say Tax
holidays and columns will be for comparison between
incentives in terms of most acceptable.
        Of those who applied and received benefit,
67 per cent considered import licence as the life
line to existence. Its requirement to the modern
industrial structure is exceedingly important and
relevant not only for continuous import of raw
material but also for import of spares and
machinery. Another 19 per cent gave it secondary
importance but placed it high. The indigenous
industrial sector performs adequately on indigenous
raw materials or on 'crumbs' thrown by the large
modern sector. The indigenous sector's ingenuity
is remarkable. Its ingenuity has led to a remarkable policy, known as the Destruction Certificate.
The 'Destruction Certificate' is operable for
all those who import machinery on licence to
replace an outdated, obsolete machinery. At the
time of the installation the entrepreneur has to
inform the Industries department, who then send a
representative to see that the old machinery is

45

destroyed in their presence and before the new one
can be installed and commissioned. This rather
surprising policy is followed with exceptional
conscientiousness. It does not strike the department's mind that the obsolete machinery could be

Table 3.7: Ranking of Incentives
(Multiple responses)

Incentives	Ranking (per cent)						No. of Responses
	1	2	3	4	5	6	
1. Tax Holiday	52	20	14	11	2	–	44
2. Accelerated Depreciation	14	23	29	9	16	9	98
3. Reinvestment Allowance	6	30	28	13	19	5	64
4. Import Duty Relief	22	35	22	15	4	2	69
5. Tariff Protection	23	35	13	22	6	2	69
6. Import Licence	67	19	7	5	1	2	107

utilised elsewhere. As a result an important
source of machinery at minimal price has been
unnecessarily strangulated. The reason provided
for this repressive measure is that a number of
unregistered companies/firms are unnecessarily
cropping up. That is indeed a unique reason. The
bureaucracy is thus provided a whip hand in the
matter.

The second largest primary response was in the
area of Tax holidays, although the number of persons
responding were the least (only 44 out of 196). All
these were in the large sector. Of those, 52 per
cent considered Tax holiday as essential and 20 per
cent placed these in 2nd response. But the fact
remains that the administration of this benefit
is so detailed and time consuming that anyone
thinking of doing so at this stage of the industrialisation will either need to have direct access
to the most powerful authority or go through
procedural delays which could easily run into four
or five years, by which time all projections, costs
and benefits become meaningless.

Even where the government has tried to stream-

line procedures in order to make matters easier,
the industrialist still has to obtain 'No Objection
Certificates' which are extremely time consuming.
In any case when with rules, provisos are added,
the bureaucracy positions itself for a repressive
interpretation of discretion. The matter is
challenged first at the lowest level and can only
be put right at the highest level - nearly a 1000
miles away. During this process the industrialist
wastes precious time. The response of the large
sector industrialist is to employ a 'retiring
official' (27) so that administrative problems
are ironed out. A medium or a small entrepreneur
cannot afford this or his management is at such a
stage that he views outsiders with suspicion.

The next two incentives in order of preference
are Tariff Protection and Import duty relief.
Tariff Protection determines the competitiveness
and hence the efficiency of an industry. Given the
objective of monopolists to maximise profits in the
short and long term, one important way was to
ensure that competition from more efficient
producers was limited (28). This could be done by
a continuous effort at high effective tariff
protection. Operationally this could be translation of objectives into maximising share of assets.
This would also restrict new entrants. Thus
where government was to sanction, monopolists
applied for larger sanctions, and once created,
pointed to excess capacity not being utilised
because of competitive factors and tried to have
imposed a higher slab on tariff protection.
Similarly import duty relief is normally available
for imported machinery in less developed areas and
also for balancing, modernising and replacement.
It thus acts partly as a reinforcement to the tax
holiday already discussed. All these policies
were mutually reinforcing and led to excess
capacity creation, rather than fuller/extensive
utilisation of capacity. Azhar and Sharif on the
basis of their report have concluded that this led
to 20 per cent excess capacity creation (29).

Accelerated depreciation and Reinvestment
allowance similarly played a reinforcing role.
The rates for these two vary significantly. It is
virtually impossible to determine the cost
increases to the consumer as a result of implementation of these policies. Till such time as there
were supply constraints in the economy these may
have been necessary but in their absence, continuation of these policies could only mean further

47

distortions in price. How far this distortion has
gone is difficult to analyse but a comparison
between ex-factory price with the CIF price of the
competing import products would yield the extent
of the problem.

If the analysis of ranking was limited to size,
then the preponderance of the large sector in terms
of obtaining benefits is inexhaustible. The
smallest sector (30) (0-10 category) is bereft of
any benefits because of the level at which they
operate and the organisational nature and level of
work required to be done. Although slightly better
off, the medium level suffers from the same problems,
while those in the small, modern 11-50 category
seem to derive some benefits from these incentives.
The basic reason for this of course is that at
this level the production units are probably the
most capital intensive and therefore although the
size by employment is small, size by sale outstrips
the other categories.

Location

The incentives policies followed were for dispersal
of industry and to reduce inequality in the country.
The measurement of such policies can be possibly
by techniques for market economies but such a
treatise is dependent on a considerable number of
assumptions. Such a measurement is not proposed
for a variety of reasons. For one, the single
most important consideration simply is that if the
production process can be geared into action, the
goods so produced can be sold no matter what the
'level of inefficiency and quality is, both being
reflected in the ultimate price of the goods'.
This may sound a very extreme view but one has only
to follow the strands. Initial inefficiencies have
not led to subsequent efficiencies and neither
have these been reflected in the price structures.
In fact, policies are then structured to ensure
the continuance of a project once started. The
reality really is that if a unit is set up and it
does not 'continue production' it becomes an eye-
sore. It stands out and the government invites
criticism for misallocation. If the next government decides its misallocation, it still cannot do
anything because of the capital that will be made
out of it by political opponents. The realities
of jobs in a limited economy do have an overriding
consideration. The writer does not envisage any
change in these policies. It is for these reasons
that threat of closure is a signal for hard times

not only for the unit but also for the government
of the day; since equity participation by semi-
government agencies is helpful in another manner
i.e. they are carriers not only of government
policies on the Board of Directors, but carry back
firm, industry requirements. Usually two or three
people are on 30-40 Boards of Directors. The
continuous projection of difficulties means that
these representatives are required to have these
policies modified. That is also to their benefit
otherwise they may well be questioned as to their
performance on the Board of Directors. So, in
essence, once a unit comes into production, and
continues to be so, its success is more or less
predictable. This is in the context of large
corporate sector industries and not in the case of
the self propelled, hard working, self developed
entrepreneur.

For the smaller sector, government suggests
that these industries be located as far as possible
in the Integrated Rural Development Programme (32)
(IRDP) Centres and Cooperative Farming Centres (33).
This is, of course, subject to availability of
specialised skills. So far as the small sector is
concerned one can safely state that there was and
is no apparent government influence.

The entrepreneurs were questioned on their
attitude to location policy. Over three-quarters
stated that they had set up industry in their home
town and 22 per cent stated that they had taken
industry away from the home town. These were
mostly in the large corporate sector with a well
developed management structure. Thus industries
which found movement away were in the Textile
sector. If export was taken as a criterion for
determining success, then some of the units
located in remote areas have been and are amongst
the most successful. The advantage, of course,
is the absence of industrial relations problems,
which as explained before have been dealt with in
a manner other than under the stipulated, statutory rules. Some of the industries, of course,
are not footloose because of raw material
availability i.e. glass and ceramics and those
dependent on the markets i.e. marble industry,
cutting and polishing, auto equipment.

It is not surprising to see that the small
industry is home town oriented. Berna (34) found
a similar overwhelming majority where choice of
location was determined merely because of the fact
that the entrepreneur was living there.

Considerations like availability of labour, availability of supervisory skills and infrastructure facilities seemed to have played no part in the majority of the decisions.

The larger sector industrialists, especially of the post 1972 era, wanted to get away from existing industrial areas. These areas had become hot beds for industrial and political strife. Wherever there was a conglomerate of firms the likelihood of extra holidays and consequent disruption of production was a real one. Conditions like a speech of the President meant that crowds had to be brought in to hear the speech, political rallies meant absence from work, and worst of all industrial demands usually took on a personal vendetta quality. Entrepreneurs therefore tended to move away from existing industrial complexes. The disadvantages like skilled labour etc were easily countered by bringing in skilled personnel from other areas. Since accommodation is provided there is no difficulty in obtaining such personnel either from an own unit or 'poaching on another unit'. These village giants have cropped up in the most unlikely places, and one industrial family in particular built up a 'cross advisory service'(35). This is called 'progressive environment change'. This family, along with another Memon family, systematically developed far flung areas. The labour turnover in their concerns is minimal but ever since the middle east rush, they have experienced labour shortage. Probably the most astonishing fact is the speed with which village labour was trained and utilised. Between 1972 and 76, this Chinniotti Sheikh family set up seven composite (36) textile mills, apparently without a hitch of any kind. Table 3.8 gives the indication by size of firms located in home town.

Table 3.8: Industries by Location (Per cent)

Size	Home town	Away
Small	45	5
Medium	19	5
Large	11	15

Since Tax Holiday and Import Duty Relief were the major incentives for location, the entrepreneurs knowledge was checked by industrial classification. Approximately 26 per cent were aware of the tax

holiday and 32 per cent were aware of import duty
relief; so that there was a positive indication
between the industrial location policy of the
government and the response by the entrepreneurs.
Which industrial sectors responded to these incentives? The Textile sector was the front runner
followed by Footwear and leather, Agricultural
implements, and more recently Metal machinery
and Electric fan industry.

Industrialising Effect
As a means of discerning the effect of industrialising, we look at two units set up by the same
entrepreneur (37) in two districts (38) of the
Punjab.

Attock District (39). The Lawrencepur Woollen and
Textile Mills came into existence in 1954. The
population of the district in 1972 was 982,000
and the area 4148 sq.miles with a population
density of 237 persons per square mile. The crafts
known in the area were manufacturing manual spice
grinder (made of stone) and indigenous shoes,
inlaid with gold and silver thread embroidery.
These were the only skills known. Infrastructural
facilities were limited and barely adequate yet
the first modern production unit changed the
history of this district.
    Before 1954, there were only two indigenous
brick kilns in the area and two ice and cold
storage units. At the moment there are fifty-one
large modern industrial units in an area which
could almost be considered completely barren and
devoid of any productive activity. The skills in
the population were non-existent. The industrialisation effect goes beyond Hirschman's forward
and backward linkage as well as Nurkse's
horizontal effect. What is clear in the pattern
(Table 3.9) is the wide range of industry that has
developed in the area. The brick manufacturing
industry indicates the momentum and the growing
strength of industry.
    The pioneer effects of the Lawrencepur Textile
Mills at Attock are indicative of a surprising
amount of spread of industries. It is difficult to
attribute primacy to any specific action but
despite poor infrastructural facilities there is
an array of industrial establishments. The area
is practically free from any industrial strife.
This area has been for many years, a conflict zone
between landlords and peasants and .....'although

Table 3.9: Industrialising Effect - Attock and Vehari

Industry	Years when established		No. of units established	
	Attock	Vehari	Attock	Vehari
1. Commodity Processing	1970s		3	10
2. Ice & Cold Storage	1970	1956/71/ &2	1	4
3. Electric Furnace	1970		1	-
4. Turbine Pump[a]	1959		1	-
5. Engineering Works	1957		1	-
6. Textiles (Woollen and Cotton)[b]	1975/77		4	-
7. Petroleum Refinery[a]	1973		2	-
8. Industrial Gases	1974		2	-
9. Marble & Tiles/ Building	1965/74		2	-
10 Sheet Glass	1969/78		2	-
11 RCC Pipes	1954/60/64		4	-
12 Brick Manufacture	1956/1979		30	-
13 Cast Iron & Foundry	-	1972/75	-	4
14 Cotton Ginning	-	-	-	5
Total:			53	23

Source: Directory of Industrial Establishments in Punjab Government of Punjab, Lahore. January 1980

a = Joint Ventures
b = Excludes Lawrencepur and Burewala Textile Mills.

for the moment the landlords may seem to have won
the day (40)' leading to upheaval in agricultural occupation. Ejection from a normal occupation may well be reason for the work ethic,
industriousness and orderly industrial relations.
This may well be the reason for entrepreneurs to
leave developed areas and make up skill shortfalls
though ethical strengths.

Vehari District. The same entrepreneurs set up a
similar unit in Burewala in 1954. The population
in 1972, was 1,027,000 and an area of 1685 square
miles with a density of 609 persons per square mile.
The area is agriculturally one of the best in
Pakistan. The infrastructural facilities are
better than those in Attock.The main industry in
the area despite this early pioneering effort is
indigenous cotton ginning and commodity processing
(edible oil and oil extraction). The area has
remained an agricultural area. Better agricultural
endowments meant the relative less importance given
to industrial development. How would the entrepreneurs know the difference between the two districts?
In the absence of any formal studies and analysis
the'gut feeling' or informal knowledge provided by
the same entrepreneur probably acted as a catalyst
for one district. Neither was there any depth in
industrial activity, nor was there the spread that
one saw in Attock district.
     The pioneering effect of the enterprise in
Attock relative to Vehari, although not measured,
is definitely of greater significance than the
one at Vehari.

Government Influence on Investment
Entrepreneurs were questioned as to the role of the
government in influencing their investment
decisions. The responses sought are in Table 3.10.
56 per cent stated that influence was on second
investment. But when specifically questioned on
the nature of influence and whether it affected
choice of technology or industry or other industrial
requirements the response indicated 7% positively
for technology, 6% for choice of industry and 13%
for other requirements i.e. site location,
infrastructure etc.
     The apparent disparity between government
influence in a general sense and then in a specific
sense needs to be explained. Most of the entrepreneurs considered government a non-entity, a face-
less unit in the distance churning out what should

be done but not explaining how or the manner of
going about solving problems. When response
followed, the entrepreneurs would return disappoin-
ted because the enthusiastic responder would find
himself handed from one official to another, till
he ended up at a ridiculously low level (41),
status and information wise.

Of the 28% aware in first investment, 11% are
in the Textile industry and 4% in the Chemical and
glass industries. The predominance of textiles
goes back to the influence of the large modern
influential sector. The textile sector was tightly
controlled by the early entrants. Any subsequent
entrants therefore had to use political or
bureaucratic influence. The Chemical and glass
industries are machine paced industries, capital
intensive in nature. The Glass industry was part
of tied aid, so that any entrepreneur wishing to go
into this industry had predetermined technology
choice (from East European countries).

Once the ropes were known and once initial
hesitation was removed there were indications
that government influence had doubled i.e. from
28 to 56 per cent. Realisation that government
was a source of information was therefore becoming

Table 3.10: Government Influence on Investment
(Per cent)

S.No.	Influence	Yes	No
1.	1st investment	28	72
2.	2nd investment	56	44
3.	Choice of technology	7	93
4.	Choice of industry	6	94
5.	Other industrial requirements	13	87
6.	Government necessary to advise	80	20
7.	Consider other industries	54	46

relatively common among second investors.

In the matter of choice of technology and
choice of industry the sample of entrepreneurs
response was 7 and 6 per cent respectively. There
may be a degree of sample bias but probably once
an entrepreneur had decided the nature of his
investment, he found the government policy could
be moulded to his desire. Some of the sample
entrepreneurs never went to the government in the

first place. They sought no recognition, no benefits. In a matter of fact way, they set about
their task. Only where the choice was between
second best entrepreneurs i.e. not the influential
large sector, but the persistent aspiring, predis-
posed entrepreneur, they received tied aid projects,
in which there was no flexibility. Obviously it is
advantageous to have foreign exchange at one's
disposal and choice of technology from a range of
countries (as well as choice of brand names) rather
than tied project aid from East European countries,
with no reliability as to availability of spares or
future modernising or balancing prospects.

In terms of other industrial requirements, 13
per cent of the entrepreneurs replied in the
affirmative. Again, given the nature of an entrepreneur's experience with bureaucracy, would there
be chances of his returning to the same agency?
For the large sectors land prices are dispropor-
tionately distorted in favour of the industrialists.
Land is procured by the government for industrial
usage at a much lower than market price. This
unnecessarily raises the demand of the large modern
entrepreneur (42). Land is acquired under the Land
Acquisition Act, in which the agricultural land
prices are fixed on the average of the last three
years' sales price. If the transaction in that
area is, say, 1950 then the last transaction along
with the previous three determines the average
price. Agricultural transactions do vary with the
quality of land but in recent times, market price
differentials are inflationary and there is a steep
rise in land prices. So anyone acquiring land
along with industry is hedging strongly against any
losses.

In industrial estates the advantage of a
developed site with electricity connections and
other amenities (43) is a boon. In less developed
countries everything is in short supply. Electricity connections should not be thought to be
routine matters. They take time (as much as 6
months to a year) and even other inputs i.e.
influence, graft etc.

If the response was so poor in a technology
and industry direction, can the government play any
positive role? It seems that an overwhelming
majority (80 per cent thought that government was a
necessary requirement and should be involved in the
industrial process. That is true. Take one
specific aspect i.e. Law and Order. In case of any
conflict violent Law and Order disputes take place.

Arbitration is rarely resorted to as the problems
are not purely industrial relations oriented.
Rather a political tinge is often visible. On
such occasions government has to intervene and
delay can lead to further difficulties. There are
a number of similar examples where instructions
have been issued to District Offcers, for both
industrial and political reasons, to maintain
harmony.

If government is necessary to the extent of
80% and influence on first investment only 28%,
did the entrepreneurs consider other possible
industries? Over half of the sample said they did,
indicating that when risky situations are visible,
decisions narrow down to a single choice after much
deliberation and discussion.

A further probe was made into the aspect of
choice of industry i.e. the direction taken for
industrialisation. Table 3.11 indicates how the
choices were made by the entrepreneurs.

Table 3.11: Origination of Idea for Industry

	Idea	Per cent
1.	Friends' Advice	7
2.	Relatives	17
3.	Own Decision	73
4.	Financial Success	3

The preponderance of own desire is really an
indication of the strength of the family inputs
(via the extended family). Relatives are once
removed from the extended family and usually are
individuals considered successful. Their advice
is almost invariably binding and that is indicated
by the 17 per cent response. Friends, surprisingly,
are next in prominence and over the economist's
favourite rationale, financial success.

Implications. Government's continued assertion of
good intentions can be ill served by an ill trained
and ill conceived bureaucracy. Such a bureaucracy
would be weak in implementing policy. This weakness would continue in the future as it is seldom
self-corrective. To increase government's credibility and to market itself effectively government
and the bureaucracy need to have more extension
feelers into the economy, not policy making

institutions located in high and mighty places.
Industry and entrepreneurs at the first and second
stage are not comparable to the large scale industries' brief-case toting executives. To the
former these institutions, by there very stature,
are awe inspiring.

How does the bureaucracy guide and control?
Since all control is bureaucratic, immense
discretion is with them. While 'guidance' takes
a back seat, contradictory rules and procedures
are to be implemented in order to control the
entrepreneur. The knowledge gap between theore-
tical and practical reality is ever increasing.
As industry passes on to an ever increasing
technological stage, this divergence will keep on
increasing. Any obstacle being time consuming and
an additive cost factor, the bureaucracy will keep
on adding to the cost of a project by (a) its lack
of knowledge of requirements both technical and
others and (b) by its own peculiar inertia and
lack of decision making.

The lack of technical information could be
rectified either by leaving the matters to the
entrepreneurs themselves or by inducting a
horizontal level of experts and consultants.
Unfortunately these technical consultants were in
short supply, although they are now available.
The difficulty now is in terms of determining and
assessing a new technological basis for setting
up an industry.

There are a variety of other adverse conditions
which do not permit the entrepreneur to use the
government as a prop for covering all those weaknesses which he has. In this, the worst sufferer
is probably the craftsman entrepreneur, to whom
everything seems like a maze. It is therefore
open to question, whether under such restrictive
and adverse conditions government serves as an
obstacle or as an accelerator to industrial
development. The explanation lies, probably, in
the resilience of the entrepreneurs who with no
alternative meaningful occupations, decided to
surmount and overcome all obstacles.

Market
The mechanics of import demand will not be under
consideration but rather the peculiarities of
markets in less developed countries. For a product
there are a number of demands not necessarily
dependent upon 'product differentiation' but
dependent on the level of disposable income.

Although product differentiation is visible in the
developing economies as well, the range of this
product differentiation by quality and price is
minimal or very narrow. In the less developed
countries the quality range could be very substantial. Accordingly price would vary with
quality, the variation between minimum and maximum
varying between 15-20 times depending on the products, with the low quality emerging from
indigenous and the better quality from modern
industry.

     This follows of course from the inequalities
inherent in the system. As real disposable income
varies significantly, tiers automatically develop
between the various segments of the community.
These come to be reflected ultimately in the
purchasing power of the inhabitants of the country.
If disposable income is less, purchasing power
being limited, these consumers (poor) will purchase
inexpensive, low quality products in preference
to higher quality, more durable goods. In the
recent past incomes in this sector have risen
because of repatriation of earnings from abroad.
The preference for durable luxury goods has
increased while the expenditure on essentials
still is at the basic minimum (44).

     The practical consequences for the craftsman
entrepreneur are extremely beneficial. His low
quality goods have a market. Their entry to
industrialisation is inexpensive, the continuation
of production much cheaper. This is due to very
low overheads and (most important) reliance on
indigenous raw materials assures them a share of
the market. As already indicated the majority
of the skills are learnt in this indigenous sector
through informal training.

     The second consequence of market segmentation
is its implication for the size of the market.
Imports are generally considered as a measure for
size of market and therefore determine the size
of manufacturing plant to be installed. The size
of a market by imports underestimates the size
of market because it does not take into consideration sub markets, and other shifts in demand. This
import measure is also in part responsible for
administrative barriers to entry (45) and also for
creating monopoly profits. Despite economies of
scales, and despite infant industry arguments,
these large units have not considered consumer
welfare at all. Instead every time they have had a
problem they have convinced the government that the

58

problems are exogenous in nature and not endogenous
to the firm. Subsidies and benefits were/are
sought and obtained. Unconnected markets are
therefore possible and indeed exist, making it
possible for marginal industries to become viable.
These in turn could lead to other industries
becoming viable. A chain effect is thus created.

The entrepreneurs in the sample were asked to
respond to reasons for choice of industry, as well
as reasons for elimination of other industries as
and when considered. Table 3.12 indicates the
responses. For those with a positive attitude,
market and experience were major reasons. The
favourable market was a gut choice rather than any
formal market study. The entrepreneur in Ldcs does
not consider sale products as much as he analyses
the transformation seen in the owners of units and
firms. The modern sector industrialist is earmarked
as doing well by the manner of his living. The
more conspicuous the consumption the better the
living and therefore the higher the profits. At the
indigenous level i.e. the craftsmen entrepreneur
level, any indication of improvement via modern
gadgetry (cars, TV etc) is an indication of profitability and growing prosperity. In Pakistan and in
other societies in less developed countries
interaction between families is a source of information. This information acts as an indicator to
other possible entrepreneurs.

Craftsmen entrepreneurs simply emulate the
example of another craftsman. In bazaar economies
knowledge of performance is common, and there are
no barriers to entry: others simply make their way
into the industry at the lowest level; still others
initiate by taking on a job subcontracting a part
for a composite unit. Traders with 7 per cent are
really bazaar merchants who realise supply and
demand factors for the goods, realise that supply
will be erratic for a number of reasons common to
Ldcs, i.e. high transportation cost, natural
disasters etc. and therefore know that their goods
no matter of what quality will always sell. Simple
technology with 5% and high profitability with
4% are the other reasons for choice.

On the negative side 13% considered that the
industry they eliminated from their choice was for
reasons of market saturation, 38% thought they had
no experience and that it was better to go into an
industry one is familiar with. Poor profits was
a high at 19% indicating that even if the entrepreneurs were not opting for maximising profits, they

at least did try to balance profits in some meaningful way. Technological complexity affected another
3%, while in the 'others' category, lack of adequate
resources was the main bottleneck.

Table 3.12: Reason for Choice/Elimination of
Industry

S. No	Reason	Entrepreneur's reason for choice (%)	Entrepreneur's reason for elimination (%)
1.	Market	39 (Large)[a]	13 (Poor)[a]
2.	Experience	38[b]	38 (No)[b]
3.	Profitability	4 (High)[c]	19 (Less)[c]
4.	Incentives	1	-
5.	Technology	5 (Simple)[d]	3 (Complex)[d]
6.	Traders	7	-
7.	Any other	6	22 (Credit etc)
8.	Govt. interference	-	5
		100	100

N.B. a,b,c,d: parentheses give the value attitude
used by the entrepreneurs in their responses.

Chambers of Commerce and Industry
In the country there are two main, influential
Chambers of Commerce and Industry (46) one each at
Karachi and Lahore. These two houses provide the
collective voice to the government on the various
issues. They not only influence but they also
modify government policies which are regressive
and repressive for the member entrepreneur.
        For the executives (47) of these Chambers
it is always a cose of tightrope walking but by
now they are versatile and flexible in their
approach to the bureaucracy, to the Chief Executive
and to foreign trade missions. The Chambers
continue to analyse government policies and are in
constant contact through their specialised sub-
committees with the government on matters of
concern to their member entrepreneurs. Their
objective may indicate welfare of the entrepreneurs
but their action is limited to their members'

problems.

The Chambers therefore provides an important intermediary and probably, in the absence of academics and media, constitutes the only body which evaluates government action. The Lahore Branch of the Chamber is significantly different in one way. It has constantly advocated the cause of the small industrialist and pointed out to the government the role of the small entrepreneur in any economy.

In the Punjab this role is played by the smaller Trade Associations. Their performance however is weak compared to these Chambers of Commerce and Industry.

The members, a President and a Vice President of the Chamber of Commerce as well as one Trade Association President were interviewed. The nature of the problems were different. Whereas the Chamber was demanding incentives, to increase its existing profitability, the trade association was dealing with very basic issues of getting decisions early, of getting financial institutions to open branches/offices in small towns. Particularly interesting was the confirmation that large industrialists manage to get things done. They can get finances, then move to the Federal Government and have tariffs and taxes manipulated to their benefits. On the other hand, no matter how genuine a request was, the small entrepreneur was unable to convince the relevant authority. Even the financial institutions, despite government instructions, do not hold meetings as statutorily required. Credit obtainable, by those who can, from Industrial Development Bank (IDBP) can take anything between 1-2 years. There are procedural problems. One of the most difficult to fulfil to the entire satisfaction of the processing agency is their credit forms. In the absence of surveyors, any kind of valuation on immobile assets can be questioned. This can always be used as a basis for explaining delays and bureaucratic inefficiencies.

Bureaucratic Regulation
We have described the important policy instruments formulated for accelerated industrialisation. Whether these are used in a progressive manner or implemented in a restrictive manner is to a large extent dependent on the quality of bureaucracy. Policies devised at the highest level are to be implemented by a small time government functionary, the custom inspector and the lower tiers. These

are low paid men, wielding considerable authority and power. These men have to interpret a growing number of government rules and regulations and apply these regulations to a growing complexity of products entering a country. The statutory regulation orders (48) can hardly be all encompassing. Since laws of construction would of necessity have to be applied to a majority of the cases, the natural consequence is that the exercise of executive discretion is dependent on the ability of the field functionary. Is then the cure in delegation of and decentralisation of authority?

For the entrepreneur, decentralisation of authority is essential. If this decentralisation is not there, he makes it available by his own methods. He may use influence, graft or a mixture of the two or cultivate and strike a friendship. A deal has to be struck. The petty official, knowing his strength, could either allow a benefit immediately or create untold misery and difficulty for the entrepreneur. Since Pakistan follows the American administrative system of quasi-executive courts, an appeal to the vertically integrated officer may occasionally being relief, but would never bring an improvement to the system because he would not like to pass harsh criticism on his own subordinates. Besides the subordinates losing grace, the department itself would be in disgrace. Further, any pointing of misdemeanour would mean his own inability at some later date to help a friend in release of goods from the customs. All these acts are mutually reinforcing and it is sufficient to point out that there is an imbalance between power, authority, responsibility and living standards. What could you expect from a petty official who is allowing entry of restricted or banned or altered goods amounting to millions of Rupees, when he himself is living hand to mouth. Try reason with a person of such authority (49). All this leads to red tape, delay of an extraordinary kind.

Aware, as the various governments were of this problem, it could not be tackled for the following reasons:

Firstly the entrepreneur himself was and is guilty of misconduct. In order to circumvent rules and regulations or whatever shortfalls they start wooing petty officials. In time the official realises that this could be a source of earnings.

Secondly reform in the system starting right from 1948 (50) was aimed at improving the administrative system. What these commissions did was to

look at the administrative system, not in terms of
improving channels and removing bottlenecks in
public dealings but in terms of various streams of
recruitment which comprised the administrative
services. Thus besides there being about 20
superior services recruited via an examination
system and an unnumbered subordinate and petty
services, the questions addressed by these
commissions and UN Advisors was how to balance the
promotional and recruitment aspects between the
various recruited streams. The lower ranks, more
in number, clamoured for upward mobility. The
other superior ranks i.e. the Postal Services,
irrespective of the nature of their experience
sought jobs in other disciplines. The net result
was (a) conflict between the services (b) public
dealing relegated to secondary position (c) wastage
of time and effort.

The policy was further complicated by the
concept of 'lateral entry' (51) in 1973. Lateral
entry was to be on the basis of 'meritorious'
individuals/Pakistanis recruited from all over. In
fact it led to party loyalists' recruitment. The
lesson was well learnt by the next government, who
started an en masse recruitment of their own
loyalists. This led to a continuous dimnuition
in morale. Escape from reality could be by moving
to international institutions and that is what
the better ones did.

Thirdly in any developing country all kinds of
channels are either 'clogged' or blocked. A
specially designed effort is called for to clear
these channels. Entrepreneurs realised that
special inbuilt relationships were called for. The
nature of these relationships varied and depended
on the nature of the work, to say the least.

Fourthly in other countries expatriates (52)
held a whip hand in industry, in Pakistan these
were replaced by the early entrepreneurs, who had
virtually every agency at their beck and call.

Change and Instability
Pakistan of 1947 is difficult to envisage, even for
those who lived (53) through that period. Human
beings were in abundance, all else was in short
supply. Pakistan was an economic wreck and an
economic monstrosity, a moth eaten state. Besides
economic weaknesses, political and social unrest
has bedevilled the state since 1947. Rising social
expectations, with sloganeering by politicians or
those in power, meant that sooner or later

63

disillusionment was to catch up as the gap between
the promised and the actual grew. Impressive
arrays of figures indicating growth meant nothing
to the silent masses, who got up each day to find
sloth, slums and misery around them. Realisation
in time also came that the rich were obtaining
economic benefits without putting in any work.
The result of all such realities is reinforcing.
The system suffered disruptions, uncertainty at
regular periodic spans. Law and Order was to be
maintained at all costs and if factory labour was
out of step, the Law and Order agencies i.e.
magistracy and police were to bring the culprits
to book. Various rules broke down because of the
refusal of authorites to understand the nature of
changing conditions, of inflation and growing
disenchantment.

       To the entrepreneurs it meant an increase in
risk and uncertainty. New ventures were required
to pay back the earlier investment. It also meant
disruption in production and trade. The trade
disruption meant that hoarding practices became
important and consumer welfare invariably took a
nastly blow. The entire period of the fifties was
one of political lobbying, or strikes and counter
strikes, followed by a relatively stable period in
the 1960s under President Ayub. But two wars in
1965 and in 1971-72 and Civil Strife in 1968-70
meant a set back for the investor.

       In early 1972 came the threat of nationalisa-
tion. This threat stayed till 1977. During the
period the entrepreneurs who suffered received no
compensation (54) or received bonds (55) redeemable
in the distant future. The main effect of nationalisation (56) was that the large, modern capitalist
sector became wary of the economic climate. To
guard against any further nationalisation, the
emphasis was on short term credit, reduced self
monetary involvement. Even bonus payments to
labour were made from short term borrowings from
banks. The rush was on to take away whatever one
could from the unit/firm. Only a handful in the
large corporate sector decided to go into industry
under changed circumstances. The debt-equity
structure was drastically changed to include the
extra added risk, from 60:40 to 70:30, then to
80:20 and finally ended up at 90:10. In some
cases the financial institutions have provided
100 per cent capital, leaving the entire control
to the private sector i.e. a state enterprise in
private hands.

The public sector, since 1977, is operating differently. Private sector representatives have been provided key positions on the Board of Directors. It is too early to state the effect of this on the economic environment except that the private sector has been very buoyant since 1977. The period 1972-77 was the time of the small industrialist (57). In fact there have been significant effects of nationalisation.

For one, the big houses have decided to divide assets and to be independent, if not in fact, at least in theory. No joint financial statements are published. Legally these are independent and separate entities.

For another the large houses have since taken to small capital intensive industry, with innovative products i.e. chipboard from rice waste.

Entrepreneurs stated the effects of instability and changing conditions. These unstable conditions were divided by most of them into political and economic and their considered view was that 'economic stability' depends on political stability. We now have politically stability in the country. Therefore economic stability should now have precedence over political stability. All our policies should now be geared to make the country economically stable (58).

Interplay of Incentives and Disincentives

We have seen how incentives are provided through policies and we have highlighted some of the impediments in the environment. How did the individuals respond to the incentives and to the impediments? Basically the entrepreneur believed in himself. If an incentive helped it was accepted as a gift; if it did not or if there were difficulties it was projected as 'the will of God'. This fatalist concept, far from being an impediment has enabled entrepreneurs not only to explain their own difficulties but also explain individual performance differences. As it happens the good times and bad times, in terms of contacts and connections, alternate. If 1950-60 and 1960-70 was the era of the modern sector, and the small sector stayed in the background, the era 1970-77 was one of the small entrepreneur, not in terms of financial institutions as such but in terms of influential connections. Political representatives at ward level became important and minor difficulties i.e. electricity connections, recognition by authorities (thus enabling them to become

contenders for import licence) and host of petty
pin pricks unnecessarily causing discontent were
removed. Why did they not go in for higher and
better incentives? The problem really existed in
the perception of the individual. To the small
sector industrialist this perception simply meant
the removal of existing difficulties and contra-
dictions. To a small sector machine paced industrialists it meant obtaining a plot/site in an
industrial estate. To another it simply meant
obtaining freehold rights so that he became
owner of the area and therefore 'master' of his
place of work. That limited the instability as
the entrepreneur perceived and the importance of
such requirements are real and not to be down-
played.

The disincentives or adverse circumstances
under which the entrepreneurs operate need to be
considered in greater detail. The entrepreneurs
were asked to explain their difficulties.

(a) Human Resources Shortage. In the 1950s and early
1960s Pakistan lost a majority of its skilled and
unskilled labour to the United Kingdom. In search
of cheap labour, the former Commonwealth countries
i.e. India, Pakistan and the West Indies provided
draft labour. This labour operated at the lowest
level, underwent a period of supervised in-job
training and more or less permanently emigrated.
The decision was government to government.

The present emigration to Middle East and
other African countries i.e. Libya, Nigeria, Uganda
and Zambia is of a different kind and nature. This
mass movement of human beings is (a) temporary
(b) for specific skills (c) via management consultants and not government to government.

Although it is difficult to foresee the
pattern of current or subsequent expenditure of
their earnings preliminary studies indicate that
62.6% is in consumption and 37.4% in investment,
of which Real Estate at 23% is the front runner,
followed by Own Business at 8%. Agricultural
machinery, Savings Scheme, Industrial Schemes and
Transport together constitute 6.2% of the investment (59).

The immediate impact is of course the loss of
skilled personnel. That this has affected production and productivity is not in doubt, although
the magnitude of the problem is difficult to
comprehend. The salary differentials are such a
great inducement that it is difficult to check the

outward flow of skilled personnel. When administrative measures were brought in, evasive action was taken by those desiring to leave the country.

Entrepreneurs reported theft of letter heads so that the intending emigrant could write his own testimonials. Malpractices and exploitation of labour by management consultants caused such strains that the Federal Government was forced to set up its own Emigration Bureau and statutorily control these malpractices.

The net result in terms of costs, when skilled labour is replaced by relatively less skilled or less efficient labour, can lead to --
(1)   Modification of labour intensive technology and subsequent purchase of ever increasing capital intensive projects.
(2)   The relative scarcity of labour means that demand for skills is at a premium and a scarcity value needs to be paid.
(3)   For every inefficient replacement pushes up costs as there is inevitably an increase in break downs of machinery and an all round increase in waste.   This means either an excess inventory of spares of haphazard local fabrication, which could damage the entire back up system.

The entrepreneurs have sought to hold these limitations by providing salary differentials and excellent supervisory status positions.   There is greater assertion of non-economic factors and ever increasing respect, which is lacking in Mideast emigrant situations.   Some have even helped their best workers to jobs abroad hoping that the loss would be temporary and these individuals would return ultimately to the fold.

(b) Upper Strata Social Milieu. In Pakistan there are hardly any expatriate firms as in Nigeria and other African countries.   But the large modern sector has taken their place.   The small entrepreneur, and the large modern sector entrepreneur live in two distinct worlds.   While the smaller is unaware of such things as public relations, social contract, the large entrepreneur believes in such extra working relationships.   He does understand the advantage of being on the right side and manipulates the environment to his advantage.   All correspondence and all activity is in English, to which only the large sector entrepreneur responds; the smaller is ill at ease with such communications.   As a result the small level entrepreneur suffers from personality situations which leave

him in a not altogether beneficial position
vis-a-vis the economy
In any interaction between diverse economic
sectors, in which blatant differences are visible,
the lower economic sector generally misses out on
the benefits and receives all the negative factors.
The net result is that the small sector continues
to live in the shadow of the large sector. Even
the medium scale efficiently run units tend to
miss out. Basically the nature of organisation
and the kind of firm determine how far one can
travel in the incentive line.

Thus in the case of a foreign entrepreneur,
who was hedging against insecurity and instability
in his area, he decided to preempt these factors
in trying to enter the large corporate sector in
Pakistan. In fact he preempted bureaucratic
delays and this is what he said: 'one of the
discouraging factors is of course delays. With a
confounding number of agencies and the stages
involved in the sanctioning of a project it often
turns into an exasperating experience for the
private investor, foreign as well as domestic' (60).
This was the subject of a Presidential Directive
with orders that all the projects of this entrepreneur should be sanctioned within 7 days under
orders. This was done:
'In respect of incentives ..... there are
discontinuities and anomalies inhibiting a truly
massive inflow of capital for the optimum realisation of the economy's potential ..... acknowledged
the potentially beneficial effect of these
measures but he maintained ... the incentives
left not enough to stimulate the ambition of the
foreign private investor .... (61) .... and
then went on to blackmail concerned departments by
saying he had very useful discussions with
President and the Finance Minister and he was
confident that his projects would be useful for
Pakistan' (62).

The marvel of creative vision as he was called
had effectively warned all the departments involved
in sanctioning of investment projects. Firstly he
made it clear that he could reach the very top and
therefore would brook no nonsense. Secondly he
warned the bureaucracy and thirdly he made it clear
he was looking for special treatment where incentives were concerned.

Discrimination of this kind has always worked
for the modern sector and against the smaller
sector. Ironically this may also prove the point

of discrimination between the Islamic foreign
private investor and the Islamic domestic private
investor, both in the very large scale of operations. That has to be seen.

(c)Acquisition of Capital Goods and Supplies. Frequently enterprises operating in Pakistan do not
order the appropriate design equipment for local
conditions. This difficulty over a period of time
has been removed but there still is considerable
wastage due to inappropriate equipment, delays
caused in shipping and transportation to site.
Pakistan is served by one port (the other is not
yet ready) and first priority is to imported food
stuff and agricultural inputs. In the order of
priority capital goods have a low base resulting
in either ships charging for excessive waiting
time or simply going away and unloading the cargo
elsewhere in one of the Middle East ports from
where it comes by barges.

(d)Infrastructural Problems. The country geographi-
cally has more length and less width and this
length gets narrower when the area where industry
is located is identified. As a result all roads
and railway connections tend to be in a distinct
pattern following the rivers. There is very little
lateral railway connections or road connections
and in fact barring Punjab the road and rail
network does not serve the other provinces even
adequately.
     The transportation system affects the size of
the market. Firstly availability of transport
fixed the geographic size or width of the market.
Secondly the cost of transport will influence the
volume of exchange or the depth of the market.
Thus if transport costs fall the producer receives
a greater income for his commodity and the price
of manufactured goods offered is equally reduced.
After 1973, transport costs have increased
enormously. With just one overburdened highway
(63), the chances of either improving the 'width'
or the 'depth' of the market are virtually
non-existent.

NOTES

     1. Faithful - followers of Islam. Pakistan
was created on the basis of religion.
     2. As the writer found during the course of
his interviews with entrepreneurs. This held for

all categories.

3. Z. Altaf, <u>Pakistani Entrepreneurs</u>, Croom Helm, London, 1983, pages 163-164.

4. Pakistan has now moved to a floating exchange rate.

5. Under the existing arrangements the import policy has been considerably liberalised. There is now a negative list and a restrictive list.

6. This is heavily based on various government publications and reports.

7. M. Baqai,'Corporate Savings in Pakistan', <u>P.D.R.</u>(Pakistan Development Review), Spring 1965.

8. Thomas Mallon and others.

9. Richard Mallon. 'Export Policy in Pakistan', <u>P.D.R.</u>(Pakistan Development Review), Vol. VI, No.1, Spring 1966 - page 74.

10. R. Soligo and J.J. Stern, 'Export Promotion and Investment Criteria', <u>P.D.R.</u>(Pakistan Development Review), Vol. VI, No.1, Spring 1966 - page 56.

11. A. Khaliquzzaman Ahmed, 'Export Bonus Scheme', P.D.R.(Pakistan Development Review), Vol. VI, No.1, Spring 1966, page 36.

12. Deregulation committees have been set up and the first set of policies was implemented in 1984. The second phase of deregulation is under consideration.

13. P. Bardhan, 'External Economies, Economic Development and the Theory of Protection', <u>Oxford Economic Papers</u>, 1964.

14. Tariff Commission Industry Report 1952.

15. Pakistan Industrial Credit and Investment Corporation Ltd - Internal Report - page 8. Also in Z. Altaf, <u>Pakistani Entrepreneurs</u>, page 26.

16. E.H. Smith & T. Durrani 'The Diesel Engine Industry of Daska op cit and Keneda & Child - 'Links to the Green Revolution' op cit.

17. B.A. Azhar and Sharouf M. Sharif, 'The Effects of Tax Holiday on Investment Decisions: An Empirical Analysis', <u>Pakistan Development Review</u>, Vol. XIII, No.4, Winter 1974.

18. This particular industrialist, at an appropriate time, went into the textile industry.

19. Dry ports are now being established in the country. This will ease the congestion at Karachi.

20. Circulars issued by the Central Board of Revenue to determine the status of the incoming machinery. It is almost impossible to define the exact nature and kind of machinery, given the vast range and the changes in the capital goods market.

The net result is that the entrepreneur is at the mercy of the custom functionary at the port of entry.

21. The agricultural implements industry despite a 10 year tax holiday has been a disappointment in another sense - it has been extremely conservative in improving implement design or in introducing new implements. It has also been a disappointment in terms of using improvements in metallurgy.

22. Interview with an entrepreneur who from peddling his wares on a cycle went on to become a leading industrialist.

23. G.F. Papanek, Pakistan's Development - Social Goals and Private Incentives, Harvard U.P., Cambridge, 1967, page 34.

24. Ibid., page 34.

25. This was limited by the quality of information available as well as the entrepreneur's own receptiveness.

26. Size definition is by labour employed - small - 0-50; medium 51-200; large 201±.

27. Retirement age varies from 58-60 years.

28. The Investment schedule restricts entry. Demand projections made by government functionaries, under the impression of proper allocation of resources, ensures these entry restrictions. The more influential manage to circumvent this. A case in point is the beverage industry.

29. B.A. Azhar and S.M. Sharif - The Effect of Tax Holiday - op cit.

30. The small sector has been further subdivided for the purposes of analyses.

31. The location policy announced by the government has also taken into consideration ecological and environmental requirements. Punjab Province has also given this prominence.

32. Integrated Rural Development Programme was a fad of the 1970s in the agricultural field. It was for providing 'inputs' to farmers from one scope. Not a single project has ever been sanctioned for IRDP.

33. The same is true for Cooperative Farming Centres.

34. James J. Berna, Industrial Entrepreneurship in Madras State, Asia Pub. Ho., Bombay, 1970.

35. A total of 15 large sector industries have been set up by this family.

36. A composite mill is both a weaving and a spinning mill - 25000 spindles and looms in ratio of 1:400 spindles.

37.   The entrepreneur is from a Memon family. The two units are cotton textile and woollen cotton and textile, both based on local raw materials.

38.   The two districts are Vehari and Attock. The former in the affluent, agriculturally irrigated grainery and the latter in an arid, semi-mountainous, rain fed agricultural area.

39.   Directory of Industrial Establishments in Punjab - Government of Punjab, Lahore is the data source.

40.   Nigar Ahmed - Peasant struggle in a Feudal Setting, Rural Employment Policy Research Programme, Geneva, International Labour Office, 1980.

41.   At the policy making level there are 5 tiers besides the tiers in the attached departments. All of them are bereft of economic or engineering knowledge and are from 'generalist' services.

42.   The Sugar Mill demand is now 40 squares i.e. 1000 acres, the justification being requirement for a research farm.   In fact what happens is that after a couple of years the agricultural land (barring factory area) is sold at a further low price to the owners by the Board of Directors (themselves).   So in the process of becoming industrialists they also become agriculturists/ landowners.

43.   A Facilities Board now functions in each province and is headed by the Chief Secretary (Administrative head).   The Board facilitates installation of utilities and considers delay cases.

44.   Z. Altaf, Pakistani Entrepreneurs, p. 25.

45.   Through creation of and adherence to Investment schedules.

46.   A number of them have now been established dependent on industrial development.

47.   Not so, they are now politically active and very influential.

48.   Talking in terms of incoming goods at port of entry.

49.   A much more restrictive power is the power to arrest for suspicion.   This, under the Criminal Law could be wielded by a Foot Constable - drawing a salary of Rs.800/- p.m. ($50/-).   The Foot Constable is usually illiterate or has up to 5 years of education.

50.   There have been innumerable reform commissions, the last one in 1978.

51. The Administrative Reforms 1973 were based on the Fulton Committee Report.

52. Mary P. Rowe - 'Indigenous Industrial Entrepreneurship in Lagos' Nigeria, Ph.D. thesis, Michigan State University, 1972, pp. 77-78.

53. The writer went through that period as a young boy.

54. Market value of shares of 3 companies Ravi Rayon, Metropolitan Steel, and Synthetic Chemical was Rs 10.00, Rs 6.92 and Rs 5.13, their break up value for bonds were given as Rs 2.57, Rs 2.08, and nil respectively.

55. At a very low rate of interest i.e. 7%.

56. Z. Altaf, Pakistani Entrepreneurs, page 18.

57. Ibid., pp. 163, 164.

58. Lahore Chamber of Commerce and Industry, Annual Report 1972 - Memorandum submitted to the President of Pakistan, Lahore May 20, 1972.

59. The State of Pakistan's Economy 1970-71 to 1979-80, Islamabad, Institute of Development Economics, 1980, page 46.

60. Galadari on New Horizons for Pakistan - Interview. The Pakistan Economist - April19-25, 1980, pp. 8-9.

61. Ibid., page 9.

63. This is now being improved. A systematic road network in the rural areas is receiving high priority. In the Punjab Province, the construction of roads is almost at the rate of 1000 miles per year.

Chapter Four

UNCERTAINTY AND RISK

In any economy opportunities exist, and although
dependent on various factors, these opportunities
may vary considerably. The appreciation or rather
the perception of these opportunities impels the
would-be entrepreneurs towards translating their
ideas into action. Each entrepreneur, as a result,
views these opportunities and the consequences
thereof in their own individualistic way, and in
that sense each perception is unique to the
entrepreneur.

Two consequences emerge as a result. Frank
Kinight, considered these two aspects as uncertainty
and risk (1). The entrepreneurs as a result of
converting their ideas into action bear the responsibility and consequences of such decisions. This
identification enabled the entrepreneurs to differentiate between uncertainty and risk. When
conditions were uncertain the situation was such as
to defy quantification. A 'gut' feeling in such a
situation was not possible as in this part of the
real world probability determination has no
meaning. Uncertainty brings with it violent and
volatile situations. The intensity of the
uncertain conditions in Pakistan during the period
1968-72 (2) could not have been perceived under
any kind of probabalistic determinism (3). There is
no way to foresee the future and therefore no way
to cover up these eventualities. In the Third
World, despite government involvement, institutions
cannot be created to cover such kinds of uncertainty.

The associative aspect of uncertainty i.e.
risk can be computed. Under such circumstances
risk computation can mean reduction of uncertainty.
Even here accurate powers of prediction are
required, which are more or less non existent.

74

Institutións normally operating in the less
developed world do not cover even risk. Whatever
risk coverage exists is dependent on the government
of the day and to the insurance companies (to a
very limited extent).

Entrepreneur's Variability

Frank Knight's entrepreneur seem to emerge with a
minimal homogeneous knowledge, judgement and foresight, confidence and organisational ability (4).
It may be safe to assume that although the ceiling
in these conditions may differ and may be reflected
in their profits, the flooring or the base from
which they start is the same. An entrepreneur, in
the developed countries endowed with knowledge, in
an imperfect market, under conditions of disequili-
brium, makes profits. In an Ldc, where the degree
of market imperfection is greater, where equilibrium
theory does not hold, where governments through
incentives further distort the imperfect situation,
profits far exceed logical expectations. Equally
when the system is under duress the loss can equal,
if not exceed the earlier profit. The entrepreneur
and the enterprise may thus swing between two
extreme points.
     The variability in the entrepreneur's skill
has so far not been highlighted. Each entrepreneur,
if one were to go by Knight's contentions, varies
in terms of knowledge, judgement, foresight,
confidence and organisational ability. Differ
they well might because of the inherent difference
in the nature of human beings and their uniqueness.
At the entrepreneurial level what makes this
difference significant is the difference between the
indigenous and the modern corporate entrepreneurs.
The difference is highly significant. Because of
qualitatively improved inputs into entrepreneurial
development in the large modern corporate sector
one can only see the 'political entrepreneur rather
than the economic entrepreneur' (5). An improved
input therefore was responsible for this shift.
According to Hannah (6) this also formed an
entrepreneurial effort and with increasing government involvement, even in the developed economies,
is a living reality. In the Ldc the ever increasing
government involvement has taken the form of a
mixed economy i.e. the government not committed to
either a capitalist or a socialist economy but to a
blend of the two systems. In such an economy an
intricate number of sub-systems are in operation.
The capitalist system, in its pure form is visible

at the level of the craftsman entrepreneurs; the
mixed economy entrepreneur visible at the level of
the craftsman entrepreneur turned progressive
entrepreneur - not entirely corporate and not
entirely dependent on the government. Having
started as a craftsman entrepreneur a relentless
effort and identification of opportunities may
have led them to reaching the progressive level.
The last category is the political entrepreneur,
who by virtue of his contacts started as a coordi-
nator, hiring factors of production from the
market in which this category of entrepreneur was
supported and subsidised by the political system.
This difference stands reflected in their attitude
to uncertainty and risk. The economic entrepreneur
believes in a reward system based on market forces
while the political entrepreneur believes in a
protected system. It would not be an exaggeration
to say that the incentives are predominantly for
the political entrepreneur and any benefit that
accrues to the economic entrepreneur is by virtue
of a positive default - an unwitting and unforeseen
blessing and help. The mixed economy entrepreneur
shifts and alternates between the two, consciously
seeking the rewards of hard work but also seeking
the political benefits as and when he can.
Although unable to influence policy at the level of
government, this category is nevertheless able to
cover significant grounds behind the scenes.

Uncertainty

How does uncertainty affect these categories? To
the political entrepreneur uncertainty emanating
from the political system has effects in the
following ways:

Firstly since these entrepreneurs are held up
as the unacceptable face of capitalism, politicians looking for popular decisions use them as
scapegoats and in the process enhance their own
reputations as upholders of the public good. As
a result a spate of nationalisations took place
from 1972-77 (7).

Secondly in Ldcs national integration is
generally weak and secessionist tendencies exist.
This is the only sector which is utilised for
national integration and for removing or reducing
regional disparities i.e. the House of Adamjees
invested in former East Pakistan, and Sind. The
loss of assets in East Pakistan when the state of
Bangladesh was created meant the loss of 70 per
cent of their assets, for which no compensation

was paid. Similarly Memon entrepreneurs lost their assets.

Thirdly when powerful individuals see a profitable concern and set their mind on acquiring it. The deal is generally behind doors and in case the entrepreneurs resist such a change, the powerful individual, by virtue of his whip hand in government can either increase competition by inducing policies detrimental to the well being of the enterprise i.e. removal of tariffs etc or by asking the Inland Revenue department to reopen the tax returns and reassess not only the tax for the enterprise but also the personal tax of the entrepreneur. Such methods are powerful means to subjugate the entrepreneur and the enterprise. There are various corollaries to such strong arm tactics.

Some of the non economic factors creating uncertainty have been stated and conditions under which they might appear indicated. Economic uncertaintly can also emerge when, as for instance, for a number of years, the strain on the balance of payments was such that raw material and spare parts could not be imported; also under conditions when the geopolitical situation forced Pakistan to divert its budget towards defence purposes leaving the industrial sector high and dry. In other words economic means are diverted towards an emerging crises.

For the economic entrepreneur uncertainties are of a different nature. Unable to hire expertise and skill and living under and working under twillight conditions these entrepreneurs, on occasions, barely exist. What are these occasions? Usually these occasions are wars and Law and Order situations. It is on such occasions that they may even have to exist by borrowing from institutions. Since their markets are extremely narrow and their customers at the lower end of the living heap, they have less disposable income or only marginal disposable income. Any factor that creates instability or uncertainty causes considerable consternation. The mixed economy entrepreneur survives, probably better than any other. To him the perfect hedge for uncertainty was to maximise real estate holdings. These entrepreneurs normally utilise any excess amount for purchasing/building not only extra residential accommodation but also commercial shopping centres thereby gaining in two ways. The property was normally against the names of some members of the house thus lowering the

Inland Revenue's tax slab on their profits/earnings.
Secondly the rental benefits can be shown as insignificant by either first taking an excess of goodwill amount usually unaccounted for in the books
or secondly showing rental less than actually paid.
There were therefore considerable possibilities for
avoision, i.e. avoidance and evasion, in the real
estate business. Given that such countries are
given galloping inflation significant returns are
obtainable in the real estate.

Risk

Although it may be difficult to separate uncertainty
and risk, an effort in this direction will focus on
the non-quantifiable, non-manageable aspects and on
the other hand the quantifiable, reducible area in
which an enterprise would of necessity operate.
The entrepreneur bears the uncertainty as well as
the risk (8). Corporate level ownership and control
continue with the entrepreneur. There is not the
kind of divorce and the shareholding base is not
as wide as in the developed countries. There is no
question of a separate mangement. Owners provide
the management and all or majority of the critical
functions, the remaining management positions
going to the members of the extended family and
thereafter to members of the community. Only in
very rare cases are executive positions provided
to qualified professionals. Therefore the risk is
firmly with the entrepreneur. The capitalist or
financier bearing the risk, in the Schumpeterian
sense, is non-existent. The role of the financier
is ever increasingly going to the financial intermediaries. The debt-equity ratio, in the case of
the political entrepreneur, has moved from the
original 60:40 to 80:20 or 90:10, and in a minority
of cases the entire finances are provided for,
though this extreme situation is very limited.
Even in the equity of say 40 per cent the political
entrepreneur is provided another 20 per cent by the various
equity supporting intermediaries. Of the balance
20%, 10% of the funds, approx., is from commissions
which accrue to the purchaser for buying machinery
(9) etc. That leaves the entrepreneur providing
the balance of finances of 10 per cent. In the process,
on the board of Directors the entrepreneur picks up
two or three representatives of the financial and
equity intermediatires. The risk shift has therefore moved from the political entrepreneurs to the
financial institutions. The economic entrepreneur

and the progressive entrepreneur bear their own
risk (10) entirely. Probably only the working
capital, on occasions, is their only short term
borrowing. They do not have any differentials in
interest rates from the capital markets and in
fact when taking a short term overdraft pay as much
as 20-25 per cent interest. Survival becomes that
much more difficult. In this category the role of
perception is different than that in the case of
the political entrepreneur. Unable to hire factors
of production the entrepreneur has a beginning
usually in a 'twilight building' under sweat
conditions. At this stage entrepreneurs risk is
maximum. The ability to survive is dependent on
continued production. The profit margin in such
cases is marginal and is considered sufficient if
it provides for survival. The leisure hours of
this class of entrepreneur are non existent.
Theirs is a toil and a slog. Believing in their
expertise and skill their ladder climb is
difficult and over a span of time. Their movement
out is limited. In a sense they make machines do
much more diverse jobs than originally meant for.
Vintage lathe machines, die casting machines are
invariably improved to provide better service and
product. There are no drawing boards when a
technical problem emerges; it is more trial and
error. The problem is perceived and then corrected.
There are no barriers to entry at this level
or minimal barriers to entry. Success is noticed
and followed. The risk may be minimised in the
macro sense but in the micro sense the entrepreneur
still needs to produce the goods that will fetch
him a share of the market.
The knowledge that capital markets are
insufficient exerts another kind of risk and
pressure, though the beneficial aspects of the
extended family are already stated. Although
financial requirements are minimised by the size
of the enterprise, the entrepreneur, if not
initially, then subsequently required capital.
This capital is provided by the extended family and
is more or less in the form of an interest free
loan. So Vinson's condition to a certain extent is
fulfilled (11) with a comparable, indirect responsibility, much larger and greater in nature, having
been created. Two conditions operate for recall of
this loan i.e. firstly when the loaner himself is
in need or secondly when the enterprise is doing
well enough to pay back. If the loanee is unable
to pay back, the moral shame becomes oppressive,

and social ostracism follows. The stakes are high
and the options not to succeed almost completely
absent. Other forms of help may also come about
but these are in the nature of supplementary
supports. Basically the entrepreneur himself needs
to prove his worth and achieve glory or shame.
High accolades are available for the successful.

Do capital markets or scarcity of capital
limit the entry of entrepreneurs? It is difficult
to provide an omnibus answer to such questions.
Suffice it to say that Alexander's (12) contention
'that such conditions limit the pool from which
entrepreneurial talent can be recruited' or
Schatz's (13) contention that 'scarcity is only an
illusion' in the case of Nigeria only supply part
of the answer so far as Pakistan is concerned. For
those in the 'talent pool' without the necessary
credit to hire factors of production the requirement is a political and bureaucratic clout. That
comes in a time span, as and when the right 'friendship fits' are available in the environment. So
in that sense these only delay entrepreneurial
entry. For the economic and progressive the
situation is different. The economic entrepreneur
enters at a level and based on his own expertise
and skill or on the arrogance of his knowledge
of the production process. It is the progressive
who suffers not so much from credit shortages as
from entry barriers. His response is therefore
different. He looks for units not doing well -
those wanting to opt out. These he acquires.
This allows him the ability to then challenge
and contest the political entrepreneur.

Are there other limits to entrepreneurial
recruitment? Do other jobs limit recruitment?
The majority of the entrepreneurs when checked for
motivation expressed a desire for self employment.
To put it strongly this desire is augmented by 'to
be free of other people's power' (14).

Rewards of Uncertainty and Risk

Perception of uncertainty and risk determines the
response of the entrepreneur. We have indicated
the flexibility in response for the three categories of entrepreneurs normally found. This
categorisation, needless to say is not watertight
but it does enable us to look at the various
entrepreneurs in an analytical perspective. Some
may question the mixed economy entrepreneur
(normally in middle category) being referred to
as progressive. The reason for such a reference

is merely to indicate that the firm is in a progressive flux i.e. increasing in size, and always
on the look out for technological improvement. It
is in these firms that technologies are adapted,
that appropriate technology becomes operative. The
political entrepreneur is a borrower, and hires
factors on the basis of established institutional
credit lines. Their worth lies in providing a basis
for others to invest in unattractive locations. The
industrialisation effect is noticeable.

The last word goes to Frank Knight (15) -
Uncertainty exerts a fourfold tendency to select
men and specialise functions:
(i) An adaptation of men to occupations on the
basis of kind of knowledge and judgement (ii) similar selection on the basis of foresight for some
lines of activity call for this endowment in a very
different degree from others (iii) a specialisation
within productive groups (iv) those with confidence
in the judgement and disposition to back it up in
action specialised in risk taking.

The human response to uncertainty, risk and
limitation was based primarily on human ingenuity.
Where uncertainty was maximum the entrepreneurs
came in collectively. The two Chambers of Commerce
at Karachi and Lahore went around the corridors
of power in 1972-73 inviting those in authority to
speak at the Chambers, to somehow establish
communication links. The entrepreneurs were well
aware that the new government was not only based
on a socialist ideology but also with slogans for
the poor. The political contest was a complete
upset of official predictions (16) and the
entrepreneurs were caught unaware. Matters were
not helped when after the break up of the country,
at his first major appearance the President stated
'I know when you are paying genuine compliments
to me. Some of the people in the second and third
rows exchanged sarcastic glances when you uttered
compliment words. I watch everyone' (17). The
effort had miscued. The realisation came
immediately but till the very last days the
Chambers kept on talking of 'political sagacity'.
Not for a moment were they reactive. Entrepreneurs
suffered continuously, they were imprisoned. Fear
set in and some left for the Middle East. Others
simply allowed the enterprise to go to seed. They
knew that long knives were out, that the labourers
were going to be the informers on any malpractices
and evasions of tax. In fact 'midnight raids' were
common in an effort to obtain information indicating

transactions not shown in the account books.

The uncertainty and fear permeated to all sectors of industrial activity. Entrepreneurs tended to look over their shoulders rather than put themselves to the inevitable grind that was a requirement, particularly in those turbulent times. Suddenly the established industrial relations code was modified. Since industrial labour provided the 'political muscle' as and when needed they were to be placated, whatever their demands.

Uncertainty also came from the immediate loss of a market. The loss of East Pakistan was a severe blow to the inefficient producers. For far too long they had dumped their goods in that market. While the political entrepreneur suffered, the economic entrepreneur and progressive entrepreneur continued to expand and increase. The political system never felt threatened from these entrepreneurs as they were never identified. Neither were they visible. So for these categories of entrepreneurs uncertainty and risk perception was different.

The other reaction was to take the economy to a position where the political leaders had no option but to seek the help of the entrepreneurs. This happened in the textile sector and despite the buoyancy of 1973, textile exports stagnated, industries closed down and suddenly the political government was looking for ways and means to prop up the industry. So successful was the effort that although ideological and political demands were made for nationalisation, the government retreated. So a threat was removed. The effect on the economic and progressive entrepreneur was also visible. They started dividing their units so that the size looked smaller than it actually was. 'Safety' money was being paid to local political representatives. While all this was happening, a credit squeeze was applied. Capital intensive basic industries with long gestation periods in the public sector were being favoured in the investment schedule. Government policy had shifted from import substitution of consumer items to heavy basic industries a replica of the Mahanlobhis plan implemented in India in the fifties. An ever thicker slice of the capital market cake was therefore to go to these industries being set up in the public sector. This of course, led to a spin off, which accelerated the development of an indigenous intermediate and capital goods industry.

The political entrepreneur utilised the 'escape' process as a defence mechanism as well.

82

Some of them went as Third World multinationals to
Tanzania, Saudi Arabia, to the Middle East, some
even to Ireland and to Canada. Others realised
that manufacture was a 'thankless' task and
reverted to trading. One of the most successful
steel entrepreneurs of Lahore started trading in
carpets. There is now no desire to go into
manufacturing, his export profits are of such a
nature. There is no need to deal with problems
like industrial relations, shortage of raw
materials and overbearing officials.

If uncertainty was not computable, how did
they hedge against it? For one, the system of
incentives was utilised to push up profits
artificially. The protection of infant industry
started the system of tariffs. Tax holidays and
the other incentives had a similar role. Every
time a manufacturer's problems cropped up, it was
somehow related to the policies of the government.
Either incentives were not enough or anomalies
were existing. So the government kept on relenting.
When an existing government did not, the next
government relented in an even bigger way, in an
effort to find support. Its lack of experience
further benefited the political entrepreneurs.

When policies were to be devised to increase
efficiency and competitiveness, out came the
Businessmen's Seminar, the media utilisation to
explain what the industry problems are, how
difficult it really is. The arguments for high
tariffs were justified and additional reasons
like market conditions etc were provided. Artificial shortages were created at will. The inevitable
result of all these policies and tactics/strategies
was windfall profits. The pay back period was
reduced considerably but where the financial statements were mandatory, the enterprises continued to
show losses.

For the political entrepreneur this uncertainty and risk could also be reduced simply by
increasing the debt in the debt-equity ratio, and
bringing in more institutional equity participation.
This has been happening in Pakistan, so that the
debt-equity mix within industries and between
industries is very variable. Needless to say there
are important implications for, not only the high
cost of the product, but also for the government.
Not only do the financial institutions have
extraordinary commitment in the project but there
are immense welfare implications. In order to

then make the industry viable, suitable government policies have to be devised. The stranglehold of the large modern entrepreneurs, as well as their influence, is ever increasing.

In any Ldc where induced capitalism based on import substitution was brought about, the question of ultimately controlling and directing modern corporate sector entrepreneurs becomes an essential task. Since governments tend towards instability, and the bureaucracy by its very nature no longer provides the iron frame, effective sanctions for policing and maintaining the political entrepreneurs within bounds is a daunting task. Pakistan is no exception to the general rule. It is impossible to maintain an even handed policy for all categories of entrepreneurs. Some of the political entrepreneurs not only get away with 'murder' but also take their vendatta to personal levels and ensure the removal of any bureaucrat who does not work in harmony with them. Policies in such situations are limited to placating the powerful.

The economic and progressive entrepreneurs did not play any role of this kind. Their strength was in their own expertise and skill. This seems to be a universal phenomenon (19). The financial intermediaries and the government, in developed and Ldcs, seem to ignore the small sector, though the degree and nature is different. And what of Knight's (20) uncertainty which exerts certain tendencies? In mixed economies, unless conditions are taken as close to free market or capitalist system the adaptation of men to occupations on the basis of kind of knowledge and judgement embodied in management is enough to coordinate factors of production. This would certainly be so if management was the critical factor. It seems, though, that Frank Knight and Nigel Vinson (21) both talk of a knowledge and judgement based on production and technical skill. Moreover the adaptation was to be voluntary and that is why Vinson makes the further point that survival and success follows to those, in the capitalist, free market system, who not only know 'what' to do but 'how' to do it (22). It seems that the political entrepreneurs 'what' in the Ldc needs to be suitably augmented by the 'how' factor. This could only come about with competition and removal of barriers to entry. As long as walls are kept around the enterprises, for whatever reasons, these protective walls will keep on rising. This

adaptation developed in Nigel Vinson when he moved
from the work bench to the sales office in the
plastics industry. So at a very young age he was
able not only to see the production possibilities
but a gap in the market. Himself a product of
encouragement by his former boss, he has developed
six entrepreneurs from within his concern (23).
We find that in Pakistan this spin off is noticeable
in the economic and progressive entrepreneurs and
that for the period 1972-77 when the modern sector
entrepreneur was under 'political fire' these
categories of entrepreneurs were supplied to the
economy.

What has been stated for one of Knight's
conditions also holds for the remaining i.e.
selection on basis of foresight, though in Pakistan
it may be argued that this foresight could be found
in traders. It seems that given certain conditions
the trader is certainly well equipped. Empirical
studies (24) on entrepreneurship have borne this
out, though in recent years because of occupational
and social mobility, others are entering the arena.

A similar argument for the third condition
of Knights i.e. a specialisation within productive
groups, seems now to be overtaken by the ability
to have influence with the supervisory authority
(government), availability of credit lines (from
financial intermediaries). The third ability in a
modern information, patent technology based world
is not difficult to obtain, provided the cost can
be borne. The objective conditions of the
progressive and economic entrepreneur though are
based on such specialisation. The stronger the
specialisation and the better the ability the
quicker and easier is the transition from the
economic to the progressive category.

Finally those with confidence in their
judgement and disposition to back their inner
strengths by action seemed to specialise in risk
taking. For those operating in the home market
and those in the export market the basis of risk
is different. The home market protection, as it
is, requires a different category of consumer
perferences to cater for, while in the export
market the competitiveness and efficiency required
are different.

Methodology of Risk Measurement
Invariably the mantle of industrialisation whether
in a centralised planned economy or in the

capitalist or in a mixed economy depends on the
level of risk and uncertainty that entrepreneur or
individual is willing to bear. It may be argued
that in a centralised planned economy and in a
public sector mixed economy the entrepreneurial
classification and the basis are changed to a
considerable degree. That may be and probably is
the case but other kinds of risk on these
managerial entrepreneurs (25) cannot be denied.
In projects where the prestige and stake is linked
with the prestige and stake of the nation, the
risk may indeed be very high. In strictly economic
terms the uncertainty and risk mentioned earlier
though is not relevant. Samples of questionnaires
provided to entrepreneurs manning state enterprises
in Pakistan have adequately borne out this point
(26). Some of them were even not aware of simple
facts about the enterprise. Some pleaded recency
of posting as an excuse for lack of basic information. Even less was known about the production
process. Everything was referred down the line.
In any case the turnover of the Managing Directors
was so frequent that it was not surprising that
the impression that some were marking time was
irresistible.

Questions were devised to elicit response to
the factors which were responsible for entrepreneurs' movement towards uncertain and high risk
ventures. To say that a protected market, a
highly sympathetic environment and unlimited and
untapped demand cushioned this risk would be to
deny them the credit of their courage and ability
in the face of such overwhelming odds as were
faced by Pakistan in the late 1940s, and early
1950s. There were overbearing uncertainties and
risks encouraged by economic, social, political and
policy variables. If everything was for the
picking as is generally assumed, Pakistan should
have been a haven for foreign direct investment.
Despite its special incentives Pakistan has been
considered a poor area for foreign investment.
It is classified as a highly unattractive and risky
area for industrial ventures. This meant that all
the benefits which do accrue from private foreign
investment i.e. flow of technology, management
ability development etc were not available to the
country. In such circumstances, the response came
from within the country. Since advisory and
extension services were and are practically non
existent the entrepreneurs were left to operate in
an industrial jungle. That the entrepreneurs

preserved and prospered and are today where they
are, does not mean that credit should not be given
to them. Those were turbulent times. An aspect
normally overlooked when considering political
entrepreneurs is the effect they have on the
economic entrepreneur. The economic entrepreneur
survived in a manner indigenously devised and
executed. The progressive entrepreneur, the
midway house, is in many ways a creation of the
'indigenous system'. We shall in what is forthcoming see how these entrepreneurs rationalised
uncertainty and risk.

To obtain a quantifiable measure of risk
entrepreneurs were asked to state the finances
with them at the time that they ventured into
industry. They are then asked to state the
requirement for that particular industry at that
particular time. Answers were then solicited as
to how the shortfall in finances was met –
whether established financial intermediaries
provided the credit, whether equity participation
was sought and available. So far as profitability
was concerned, entrepreneurs were asked to state
how their earnings compared with the target that
they had when they considered investing in the
project. These were considered on a five level
scale starting from very good to very poor. Then
the actual position was ascertained, whether the
profits after tax were much larger than they
thought and once they had committed themselves,
they were asked to give rough percentage figures.

In Pakistan, financial statements do not have
the credibility that prevails in other countries.
In any case these statements are utilised more for
tax purposes and not to show the state of affairs
to the shareholders. There is no concept of
interim six monthly statements. Neither is the
Association of Chartered Accountants in Pakistan in
a position to lay down standards and accounting
principles. The economic and progressive
entrepreneurs invariably do not have any such
accounting requirement. The tax computation is
done by the Inland Revenue authorities on the basis
of scrutiny of original books. There were some
very frank admissions and much depended on the
rapport established with the entrepreneurs.
Profit figures were sought as percentage of sales
and since sales figures were already obtained, it
was possible to arrive at absolute profit figures.
The pattern of rapport generally dictated the
sequence of questions concerning such sensitive

issues.

Motivation

Before we go into the realm of determining
uncertainty and risk it may be appropriate to
look at the inner propelling forces. The profit
motive occupies a predominant place in the models
of economic theory and the early work by Papanek
(27) emphasised the primacy of and the uncompli-
cated nature of entrepreneurs' motives in Pakistan.
Other case studies and empirical work indicated
complexity (28). The unwinding of this complexity
was undertaken by Rowe for Nigeria. In the case
of Pakistan more or less the same basis was
developed with one difference. The questions
pertaining to motives were explained in great
detail and individuals were asked to go back in
time span to the earlier years of the firm. A
great emphasis was placed on a friendly cross
examination if only to counter Papanek's opinion.
'The kind of ex post facto explanation is not very
reliable, because a brief interview question cannot
generally elicit motives for past actions. However
since the natural inclination would be to give
patriotic and other altruistic motives rather than
strictly economic ones, any bias in the answers
is likely to be in favour of patriotism or
altruism' (29). In as much as routinely structured
questions could lead to distortions in response,
Papanek was making a very worthwhile criticism.
Such a criticism may even be more valid for mailed
questionnaires where supplementary questions are
not possible and there is no communication with
the responder. Keeping this in mind considerable
effort was spent in trying to unravel the mysteri-
ous world of motives. So a continuous probing did
improve the chances of obtaining precise answers.

The other important point to remember is that
Pakistanis' bias for patriotism and altruism is
natural. Such a mass migration for the sake of a
country is unheard. Pakistan, one of the two
ideological states created in the twentieth century,
received as many as 6 million people who left their
permanent abodes for the love of this country. So
a fair amount of responses towards altruism and
patriotism should not be a surprise.

Table 4.1 gives the first four responses from
a possible thirteen reasons. The strongest
responses, not only as a first response but as a
second, third and fourth response came from

Table 4.1: Motivational Responses: Pakistan and Nigeria
(Per cent)

Reason	1st Response		2nd Response	3rd Response	4th Response
	Pak	Nig.[a]			
1. Inheritance	23	(-)	4	N	N
2. Profit	19	(48)	15	7	13
3. Security	N	(20)	6	6	9
4. Fatalistic (Born to do it)	N	(4)	N	N	N
5. Accidental	N	(4)	N	N	N
6. Status	3	(6)	N	8	18
7. Satisfaction	7	(5)	8	15	-
8. Away from family work	N	(-)	3	N	N
9. Provide jobs to extended family including friends	N	(5)	5	9	14
10 To help country	27	(1)	12	14	14
11 Self independence	11	(6)	24	19	14
12 Experience	3	(-)	15	19	12
13 Any other	N	(-)	3	3	3

N.B. (i) Nigerian responses considered are only first responses.
   (ii) Percentage figures do not add up to 100 because of elimination of weak responses.
  (iii) N - No response.

(a) Source M.P. Rowe, 'Indigenous Industrial Entrepreneurs in Lagos, Nigeria', p. 153

patriotism. Most of them who gave this response spoke of the immense sacrifices that were made by them to reach their own homeland. Credit for the experiences and the manner in which they picked up the loose threads is indicative of their tenacity and resilience. Nineteen per cent of the entrepreneurs stated profits as a motivational basis for

the first response and 15% as a second, 7% as third
and 13% as fourth. The strength of profit was
explained by the entrepreneurs as not an end in
itself, but as a means to achieve further ends.
When it is seen as an end in itself, and there
were a few examples of this nature, stagnation
and no growth was visible in the enterprise. It
might be difficult to evaluate the power of this
motive given that it may and does militate against
Islamic values. As against this 48% of the Nigerian
entrepreneurs gave profit as the reason for going
into industry. The response of the Nigerians was
overwhelmingly for pecuniary reasons.

In the case of Pakistan, inheritance was
powerfully placed in second place with 23%,
indicating the existence and strength of the
extended family system. Sons stepped into the
shoes of their elders. Did not this indicate
a weakening in entrepreneurial attitude? It would
if the inheritor were to allow the enterprise to
go to 'seed'. Such was very rarely the case. The
entrepreneurs, invariably a product of the industrial milieu, seemed to perform better than their
forefathers, an improvement over what their
elders had left.

Self independence and satisfaction, both
conditions of non economic nature and internal
to the entrepreneur, seemed to hold sequential
importance in first response and powerful secondary
sources of motivation. Experience by itself did
not indicate a primary motive and was weak at 3%
as the first response, although as a source of
supporting secondary motive it showed a 15%, 19%
and 14% for a second, third and fourth response
respectively.

Five initial responses were negligible. These
were security, fatalistic i.e. born to do it,
accidental, away from family work, provide jobs
to members of the extended family. Secondary
response in the last named i.e. providing jobs to
extended family and friends, evolved a 5, 9, and
14 per cent response. In the case of Nigeria, the
motivations were completely different (so far as
primary responses were concerned). Security
formed a very high basis for going into industry
(20%), after profit motive at 48% and a joint
poor third response of 6% for status and self
independence.

Effects of Education on Motivation. How did independent variables like education, experience and

training affect motivation? To analyse this the
twelve specific variables and one general variable
indicated in Table 4.2 were cross tabulated against
education.
     Table 4.2 gives the tabulation of multiple
responses and how education affected each subset
of motivation considered and constructed. We will
be considering row and columns as per analysis
requirement. Where the enterprise was inherited
even there the level of education was considered
as vital and important. Educationally two periods
are important for dropouts i.e. just after 5 years
of education or 10 years of education. Although
the occupation was more or less given, the
entrepreneurs who stepped into the enterprise were,
irrespective of other motives, given a level of
education which in some cases exceeded that of the
father's. The pattern in Table 4.2 when viewed
in totality indicates that the level of education
raises the level of response so far as other
motives are concerned. For instance, and since
multiple responses (4 for each entrepreneur are
under consideration here) the highest educated
i.e. 13± show a response of a higher category
in economic and non economic motivational practice.
     In economic terms 43 responses for profit out
of a total of 102 responses does indicate the
growing awareness and importance attached to this
aspect by the more educated. The other responses
which were significantly higher and non economic
in nature in the educated category (13± years)
were self independence at 62 out of 131 and
patriotic motivation helped the country at 57 out
of 128 responses. Status, satisfaction were the
non economic factors considered essential. In
other words economic factors, welfare (job
providing) and experience held reasonable strength.
At the lower end of the educational attainment
i.e. less than 5 years, only independence and
patriotism at 11 and 10 responses respectively
seemed to have any degree of strength with a strong
showing for profit, patriotism, and altruism in
the 6 to 10 years of education category, though the
responses difference varied between the highest and
this category to the extent of 15-20%. The irresistible conclusion is that with increased education, the general level of motivation and the
degree of intensity of the inner driving force
take on not only a sharper but also a more compel-
ling aspect. Independence as a motivational
factor and patriotism are two non economic factors

Table 4.2: Education and Motivation

Motivation	0	1-5	6-10	11-12	13+	No. of Responses
Interitance	3	2	16	11	26	58
Profit	2	8	30	19	43	102
Security	1	4	10	9	17	41
Fatalistic	1	–	2	1	3	7
Accidental	–	1	2	1	5	9
Status	–	3	14	11	30	51
Satisfaction	4	2	17	9	29	61
Away from family	1	–	7	2	4	14
Provide jobs for friends	3	5	15	6	21	50
Help country	3	10	38	20	57	128
Self independence	1	11	38	19	62	131
Experience	4	8	28	21	33	94
Any other	1	1	5	2	5	14

(Years of Education)

which are common to all categories. Even in
developed countries (30) the urge to be independent
of the consequences of others' decisions seems to be
a powerful basis for entrepreneurship. The idea of
not being a subordinate to another's decision
making process, therefore, runs common to Ldcs and
to developed countries.

Experience and Motivation. When the second input
variable, experience, was tabulated, results
indicated (Table 4.3) that the three strongest
incentives for the experienced were work independently, help the country and experience. The
profit motive, though, seemed to be an underlying
response in roughly 19% of the entrepreneurs in
the experience category, 1-5, 6-11 and 11+ years.
The strength of non economic factors is again
visible. Experience, as a motivating factor is
of equal strength throughout, though why 24 per cent
of the inexperienced feel this way needs to be
explained. A current attitude amongst the entrepreneurs was that knowledge and expertise which
developed through production skills was an essential
requirement, for (a) it reduced input costs,
attributed to information and location for production of goods and (b) there was less chance of loss
through purchases where the throughput in one
production process did not balance the throughput
in another process. Every time a decision on technical matters was required, these two basic defi-
ciencies came up and the entrepreneur had to depend
on outside sources.
It would be difficult on the basis of education
and experience to point to the primary strength
of an inner driving force. All that can be said is
that besides the profit motive, there were other
non economic forces which played an important part.
In fact the identification of pure inner driving
forces would be hazardous and would be simplifying
the decision making process of the entrepreneur to
a very basic and simple level.
In order to ensure strength and success of
their inner desires certain steps, needless to say,
must have been taken by these entrepreneurs.
Almost the first logical idea to come to any
entrepreneur's mind is a place to start and to
establish lines for finance (31). In the Third
World, premises are easily available and the
extended family system does provide the finance.
It is certainly not important to have palatial
premises but 'twilight buildings' are almost surely

Table 4.3: Experience and Motivation

S. No.	Motivation	Years of Experience				Total No. of Responses
		0	1-5	6-10	11±	
1.	Inheritance	19	16	6	17	58
2.	Profit	46	17	21	18	102
3.	Security	18	6	8	9	41
4.	Fatalistic (Born to do it)	2	1	2	2	7
5.	Accidental	5	1	-	3	9
6.	Status	23	12	7	9	51
7.	Satisfaction	29	9	9	14	61
8.	Away from family work	8	1	3	2	14
9.	Provide jobs to friends and family	20	10	7	13	50
10	Help country	55	22	22	29	128
11	Work independently	51	29	24	27	131
12	Experience	24	21	19	30	94
13	Any other	6	2	4	2	14

the first requirement, so that initially when
everything is in short supply the credit requirement is minimised. In Third World countries,
where extension services are not as well developed,
where local resources are not so easily manageable,
an effort was made to gauge what kind of help or
consultancy was sought by the entrepreneurs.
Forty-one per cent of the entrepreneurs sought
consultancy services with the maximum response
coming from those that wanted to help the country,
those who thought profit was a motivating force,
and those who wanted independence. These 41% were
further required to state whether the consultancy
sought was local, foreign or both local and
foreign. The responses for local and foreign
consultants were evenly matched (local 51 per cent,
foreign 43% and 6% both local and foreign). The
categories which were again prominent in obtaining
consultancy, whether local or foreign, were those
indicating a pecuniary and patriotic desire of
helping the country. The inner driving forces
consistently unimportant and least indicated were
the non economic forces i.e. fatalistic, accidental, away from family work. As a further check
as to what kind of consultancy was sought, the
entrepreneurs were asked to state whether it was
merely advice or on a turnkey basis. The maximum
response came from, firstly those who wanted to
work independently, secondly from those who wanted
to develop the country and thirdly from those
seeking pecuniary benefits. The point of significance so far as the determination of and fulfilment of inner desires was concerned was that all
those indicating profit as a motive, patriotism,
or status, or independence of action were either
from the large sector or from the capital
intensive medium scale machine paced technology
which conforms in our scheme of things with the
political and the progressive entrepreneur. The
entrepreneur, obviously, did take all the steps
that were considered necessary and important to
hedge against risk and in furtherance of his
motivations.

Profits and Motives. The details of empirical
evidence by twelve specific and one general motive
need to be elaborated if only to determine to what
extent objective desires were matched by performance. Since multiple response (up to a maximum
of four) had been obtained the total responses do
have a bias to that extent although this should

not affect either the performance of the enterprises
or the direction of that performance i.e. whether
reasonably good/bad/or indifferent. Table 4.4
provides the details.

The first three so far as failure were
concerned were those who had opted for desire for
independent work, profit/pecuniary benefit and
those who wanted to help the country. Although
others like those trying to provide jobs for
friends and relatives also had failures, these
were not significant. At this point in time one
can only indicate the basis for this performance as
being due to insufficient knowledge, skill or whatever. But the fact remains that in an economy
where profits were for the asking the poor performance indication connotes a high risk/uncertainty
existence. In fact those in the second slab
(i.e. 1-12,000) cannot be said to be successful
either, because in comparison to other avocations
this would be poor performance and not adequate
returns on one's investment. The 3rd and 4th
categories, i.e. 12,001 to 50,000 and 50,001 to
100,000 are the entrepreneurs who have done
reasonably well. The entrepreneurs with the
motives pertaining to experience, independent work,
and help the country are in the non economic area,
where pecuniary benefits have a fairly good
representation, while those doing not so well are
the ones with motives bordering on security,
fatalism, accidental, and away from family work, as
their motivating force. Any figure above
Rs 100,000 shows the entrepreneurs doing exceedingly
well, and the entrepreneurs sample shows that
practically all categories are represented i.e.
the representation of these motives is as follows:
Inheritance (32) 43/58, Profit 68/102, Security
28/41, Fatalistic 3/7, Accidental 7/9, Status 41/51,
Jobs for relatives and firends 26/50, Others 7/14.
The high scoring in the profitability of the
entrepreneurs especially where such diverse motives
are concerned points to the complexity of motives
in entrepreneurs. Entrepreneurs, it will be
recalled, were given the option to rank motives.

Table 4.4: Motives and Profits

			Profit	Slabs					
	0-0	1-12,000	12,001-50,000	50,001-100,000	100,000-500,000	500,000-1000,000	1,000,000-3,000,000	3,000,000+	Total
1. Profit	12	5	10	7	25	11	17	15	102
2. Security	5	1	5	2	10	4	8	6	41
3. Fatalistic born to do it.	–	1	2	1	2	–	–	1	7
4. Accidental	–	–	2	–	3	1	2	1	9
5. Status	5	–	3	2	16	6	11	8	51
6. Satisfaction	1	3	9	4	18	6	9	11	61
7. Away from family work	5	–	2	2	2	1	1	1	14
8. Jobs for relatives and friends	8	1	9	6	12	2	7	5	50
9. Helps country	11	4	14	13	37	8	22	19	128
10. Independent work	18	4	16	10	33	9	25	16	131
11. Experience	6	2	11	11	26	8	15	15	94
12. Any other	3	1	3	–	3	1	3	1	14
13. Inheritance	1	2	7	5	21	6	8	8	58

NOTES

1.   Frank Knight, Risk, Uncertainty and Profit.
Boston, Houghton Miflin Co. 1921, pp. 231-32.
2.   In fact some of the economists publishing
books on Pakistan's economic miracle hastily
entered footnotes. Events had not only caught up
but had thrown some of the contents out.
3.   One lending house lost as much as 70% of
its total assets.
4.   Frank Knight, Risk, Uncertainty and Profit,
pp. 268-70.
5.   Dr. L. Hannah - 'The Prime Mover of
Progress - Papers on the Role of the Entrepreneur,
London, Institute of Economic Affairs, 1980,
pp. 53-54.
6.   Ibid., p. 54.
7.   (i) Economic Reforms Order, 1972.
(i) Industrial & Corporate Reforms 1972
(iii) Exchange Reforms Order 1972 (iv) Insurance
Reforms 1972 (v) Nationalisation of Banks 1974
(vi) Nationalisation of Flour Mills, Oil Expellers
and Rice Husking Units 1974.
8.   Frank Knight, Risk, Uncertainty and Profit,
p. 296-300.
9.   Interview with a political entrepreneur.
Occupational mobility was from feudal to industrial
aristocracy.
10.   N. Vinson, 'Successful Entrepreneurship
based on Inquiry and Invention' in - The Prime
Mover of Progress, p. 64.
11.   Nigel Vinson, 'Successful Entrepreneurship,
p. 64.
12.   Alec P. Alexander, Greek Industrialists,
Athens Centre of Planning and Economic Research,
Greece, 1964, p. 34.
13.   Sayre P. Schatz - The Capital Shortage
Illusion.
14.   Nigel Vinson, 'Successful Entrepreneurship
based on Inquiry and Invention', p. 63. Vinson
makes a similar point, expressing his own motivation towards entrepreneurship.
15.   Nigel Vinson, 'Successful Entrepreneurship
based on Inquiry and Invention', p. 63. Vinson
makes a similar point, expressing his own motivation
towards entrepreneurship.
16.   The elections of 1970 held by the Army
when Pakistan was united. The Awami League in E.
Pakistan had an overall majority. For the first
time political control was likely to pass to the
East Pakistanis.

17.   President's address to the Chambers of Commerce at Karachi in 1972.
18.   Z. Altaf, Pakistani Entrepreneurs, Croom Helm, London, 1983.
19.   Nigel Vinson, 'Successful Entrepreneurship based on Inquiry and Invention', pp. 63-67 passim.
20.   Frank Knight, Risk, Uncertainty and Profit.
21.   Nigel Vinson, 'Successful Entrepreneurship based on Inquiry and Invention.
22.   Ibid.
23.   Ibid.
24.   G.F. Papanek in the case of Pakistan, Sayigh for Lebanon, J.J. Carroll for Phillippines, and Owens and Nandy for India.
25.   Signifying entrepreneurs who have not taken the entrepreneurial decision to invest and who are paid by the enterprise (State).
26.   Five Managing Directors were given these questionnaires.
27.   G.F. Papanek, Pakistan's Development. Social Goals and Private Incentives, Harvard U.P. Cambridge, 1967, pp. 46-55 passim.
28.   M. P. Rowe, 'Indigenous Industrial Entrepreneurship in Lagos, Nigeria', Ph.D. Thesis, Michigan State University, 1972, p. 154 and Y.A. Sayigh, Entrepreneurs of Lebanon, Harvard U.P., 1962, p. 105 are amongst those who did suggest the complexity of motives.
29.   G. F. Papanek, Pakistan's Development. Social Goals and Private Incentives, p. 53.
30.   Nigel Vinson, 'Successful Entrepreneurship based on Inquiry and Invention', pp. 63-67 passim.
31.   Nigel Vinson, 'Successful Entrepreneurship based on Inquiry and Invention', p. 63 makes the same points and emphasises minimising cost and expense in the early ventures even in developed countries.
32.   Denominator denotes total responses in that area.

Chapter Five

RISK MEASUREMENT AND COVERAGE

Basis for Evaluation
A value judgement as to superiority of the method
employed needs to be looked at in terms of obtaining effectively correct data. The normal
accounting methodology suffers from certain drawbacks, namely:
(1) The accounting practices are not well developed. Barring the corporate sector, financial
statements are not compiled regularly or assidu-
ously. In fact there being no such situation in
which management/ownership are divorced, the need
for keeping shareholders regularly informed does not
arise. This follows from the fact that ownership
stands secure at having 51 per cent of the shares.
Ownership, even if the management holds minority
shares, is not threatened because of interlocking
share purchases and noticeable interlocking
directorates, in which community feelings and
mutual support work to the exclusion of other
things.
(2) The financial statements downplay the profit
figures as all sales are not recorded. Normally
entrepreneurs keep two sets of books, one for the
tax man and the other for their own use. Sales
transactions do not usually figure in the final
statements and normally the tax authorities work
out the basis for revenue by rules of thumb which
they have developed over a time period.
(3) The assets of a firm are difficult to assess
because of the variability in costs. How should
vintage machinery be assessed? Should it be at
actual cost or, should it be at replacement value?
If it is at actual cost a lathe machine would value
about Rs 1000/-, and if at replacement cost,
Rs 25,000/-. So the majority of the entrepreneurs
tend to take things as 'they come'. In less

developed countries, similar differences exist.
Machine essentially performing the same functions
are priced differently in the United States, Italy,
Spain and Sweden (1). Besides variability in these
costs there is a fair degree of over invoicing
involved and artificial upward pushing of machinery
costs mostly in the nature of corrupt practices
(2). Similarly, differences on infrastructure
exist as well.
(3) Cost benefit analysis as practised in theory
does not have even the remotest application with
the majority of the entrepreneurs. The analysis is
normally carried out by government owned industrial
credit institutions at the behest of the entrepreneur. The analysis essentially is utilised as a
discretionary basis to allow access to some for
monopoly profits and to others denial of these
profits. Thus it is the 'political clout' which
determines the figures which are utilised in these
cost - benefit analyses.

These are then some of the shortcomings in the
system. Most of them are basically human behaviour
oriented problems and do not in any way indicate
the uselessness or otherwise of the methodology.

The procedure followed for this research was
much more basic and much more rudimentary but it
was more appropriate in as much as it provided
probably a more reliable basis on which to proceed.
The reliability of responses was dependent to a
very large extent on the contacts utilised for this
purpose. If the contacts were persons with
established credibility and known to be members
of the industrial ingroup, the writers credentials
were soon established. If these were dubious,
rapport and credibility establishment was very
doubtful. Generally the acid test was whether I
got them to sign the questionnaire. This, I did
not. In Pakistan and possibly in other Ldcs trust
establishment is not dependent on the written word.
In fact when one 'gives one's word' the defence of
that word develops one's reputation. No degree of
broken words can be repaired, in such a cultural
milieu. The normal impersonal basis noticeable
in a capitalistic economy is not visible, so that
normal acceptable yardsticks in western capitalist
economies break down. So despite the apparent
verbal basis for determining an entrepreneur's
personal assets, requirement for industry, sales
figures, and profits as a percentage of sales,
there were apparent merits in the methodology
employed. In fact the only criticism leviable is

that possibly the entrepreneurs did not entirely indicate their personal assets. This may be accepted firstly because of the informal basis of valuation of property and secondly it is anathema in the extended family system to point out one's share of inheritance in family property. To that extent the personal assets may be undervalued.

By virtue of their assets the entrepreneurs were divided into six groups. The basis for risk calculation was to divide the requirement for industry by the personal assets, both figures being provided by the entrepreneur. Similarly the performance ratio was determined by dividing the profit (determined as a percentage of sales) by the personal assets with which the entrepreneur ventured forth. This provided a basis to the entrepreneur for determining the time period in which he would recoup his investment, a more gut feeling and not the acceptable rate of return or pay back method for assessing the basis for investment. The capital asset pricing model in which capital markets play a decisive role is inapplicable in Pakistan and in Ldcs in general. The sources of risk and return are not that easily influenced. These risk, uncertainty and return factors bear their own momentum.

To come to any analytic basis, besides the identification of sources of risk, these risky and uncertain conditions need to be broken down into simple constituent parts by specialised agencies. These agencies in fact should be accessible to entrepreneurs. These agencies in turn must have their 'feelers' in the market for all kinds of diverse information. Even such a simplified basic model is unavailable to the entrepreneurs who more or less rely on their own information, knowledge and financial requirement. Given all these constraints it becomes exceedingly difficult for an entrepreneur to decide between projects or to think in terms of alternatives. These alternatives, already limited by the entrepreneur's socio-economic history, are further constricted by the lack of sympathetic resonance from such sources as are available in the government and the market. Of necessity then the entrepreneurs rely on indigenous methodology and arrive at industry investment decisions by such methodology.

A few of the entrepreneurs interviewed who had resorted to cost-benefit analysis spoke of the methodology as only necessary to pass through the

administrative barriers created by the government
and its agencies. This analysis, to the entrepreneur, is both time consuming and expensive and
permits the administrative agencies to utilise
their discretionary power (3) and act as a basis
for entry barriers to any industry. All that is
required is to quiz figures and return them for
reverification and this can take place as often
as one likes.

It is for these reasons that a different
basis was considered for determining risk and
uncertainty. To the extent that bias can never
be excluded, the figures may be slightly underestimated, especially personal assets and profit.
Even with this caveat the only basis for arriving
at realistically correct figures of profit,
returns etc is dependent on a personal equation.
A personalised system is in operation.

The entrepreneur's assets at the time of entry
into industry indicate that in the sample 6 entrepreneurs started with less than Rs 1000, 24 with
between 1000 and 50,000, 16 with between 50,000
and 100,000, 91 between 100,000 and 1,000,000, 34 between 1,000,000 and 5,000,000 and 19 above 5,000,000 (Table 5.1).

The definition of assets includes movable
and immovable assets. The attachment of valuation to assets of an immovable nature is very
variable and dependent on the influence of the
entrepreneur. Worthless assets, since there is
normally no concept of valuation surveying, could
be used as collateral assets or valuable assets
down graded if so considered by the financial
intermediaries. Discretion in this area is
unlimited. So the valuation that was asked for
from the entrepreneurs was the amount that they
actually thought they could get by pledging the
property as collateral. In some cases the
property had been used for collateral guarantees
and therefore valuation was more or less known.
Of the six with assets less than Rs 1000, four
went into industry where the requirement was less
than Rs 25,000 and of the remainder, one each in
the next two categories i.e. 25,001 - 1,000,000 and
100,001 - 500,000. Similarly we find that
entrepreneurs with considerably less assets went
into industry where the requirement for industry
was even greater. There were, for instance, 91
entrepreneurs in the 100,001 - 1,000,000 asset
category of whom 25 went into industry where the
requirement was between Rs 500,0001 - 1,000,000

Table 5.1: Assets and Requirements for Industry

Assets	1	2	3	4	5	6	7	Total No.
1. Less than 1000	4	1	1	–	–	–	–	6
2. 1000 – 50,000	10	5	7	1	1	–	–	24
3. 50,000 – 100,000	1	5	9	1	–	–	–	16
4. 100,000 – 1,000,000	–	5	48	25	13	–	–	91
5. 1,000,000 – 5,000,000	–	1	2	4	21	3	3	34
6. 5,000,000+	1	–	1	2	8	2	5	19
	16	17	68	33	43	5	8	190

Key:

1 = 0-25,000, 2 = 25,001 – 100,000, 3 = 100,001 – 500,000, 4 = 500,001 –
1,000,000, 5 = 1,000,001 – 5,000,000, 6 = 5,000,001 – 10,000,000,
7 = 10,000,001+

and another 13 where the requirement was 1,000,001-
5,000,000. In the highest asset owning entrepreneur category (19 with 5,000,000± the industrial
ventures required finances on a very high scale
(see Table 5.1). The analysis of the entrepreneurs' risks will be undertaken by the value of
their personal assets and these will be compared
to the requirement for industry, the equity
participation, the debt, both from friends and
relatives as well as from investment agencies.
The difficulty of course in such comparisons is
that all these are by class intervals, whether
in absolute money terms or in percentage figures
(as debts, equity etc). In order to overcome this
difficulty the method utilised was to consider
the mid point of the class interval as representative of that class, the assumption necessarily
being that the observations in the group are
evenly scattered between the two extremes of the
class interval.

For convenience there are six such asset
groups. The first group is the less than Rs 1000/-
asset group whom we shall refer to as the first
group, the second group similarly would be the
1000 - 50,000 group and so on. We shall analyse
the manner in which the groups rationalised their
risk and possibly, covered uncertainty.

First Group
In this group there was a total of 6 entrepreneurs
(Table 5.1). The industrial classification into
which these six entrepreneurs were placed were
footwear and leather, metal machinery, electric
fans, auto equipment and ceramics. Entry into
engineering industries, which means metal machinery,
electric fans and auto equipment, can be started
with minimal capital and at a very small scale. In
fact these places can start as small service centres
and improve gradually by 'small increments' (4) by
adding machines which subsequently give it the
appearance and capability of a small manufacturing
concern.

The entrepreneurs in the footwear and leather
and ceramics industry required craft skills. The
footwear entrepreneur started as a small time shoe
maker and since the raw material (hides and skins)
was a commodity in abundance they could operate at
that level. The ceramics entrepreneur similarly
had to contend with his reputation as a craftsman.
The skills required for this sector's entrepreneurs
were therefore those which came with a long

association with the craft.

Four of these entrepreneurs viewed that the amount for entry was anything up to Rs 12,500 (mid point value of 25,000) while the other two considered that this was Rs 62,500 and Rs 300,000 which gives the ratio of assets to requirement for industry as 1:25, 1²125 and 1:600. The risk therefore is ever increasing. How did the entrepreneurs meet the balance requirements? Of these, three had 96 - 100 per cent equity, two had no equity participation and one had participation to the extent of 26 - 50%. Whatever equity participation there was emanated from the extended family system, the rules governing which are quite different. In the setting up of the firms, four of the entrepreneurs had no loan while one had a loan to the extent of 51 - 57% and another to the extent of 96 - 100%. However, when the loans obtained from investment agencies were considered the pattern of financial management become clear. Only one of the entrepreneurs had borrowed from the investment agencies and to the extent of 51 - 75% of the total financial requirement.

At this level, where the assets were less than Rs 1000/- (5) (currently $100) the entrepreneurs perceived the opportunities distinctly and differently. At least one entrepreneur made up his financial requirements from two distinct sources. Firstly a loan from friends and relatives was obtained (26 - 50%) and material purchased; secondly a loan between 51 - 75% from investment agencies and bank. A second entrepreneur borrowed from friends and relatives to the extent of 51 - 75% to augment his own resources (26 - 50%). Four entrepreneurs were in the manufacturing sector only because they were initially subcontractors to a larger manufacturing concern, the working raw material all being provided by the large sector. So far as these entrepreneurs were concerned their survival was dependent on the job orders of the larger concerns. The other two, who had borrowed extensively from the financial market and from friends, were in a different situation altogether. How could an entrepreneur seek financial resources in the ratio of 1:125 or 1:600 in an Ldc? The answer: in one case it lies in the extended family system and for the other in political patronage.

This can easily be seen by the time periods in which these units were created. Two of the enterprises were established in 1940-49, one in 1950-59, two in 1960-69, and one in 1970-79. The

distinguishing feature is that in metal machinery
manufacturing there is ease of entry and despite
the different time periods the financial requirements for industry did not undergo any substantial
change. Only skill was essential. What was
required was that entrepreneurs need to have skill.
So entry, despite a lapse of 30 years, was deter-
minable by the ability and skill of the entrepreneur. Two of the entrepreneurs, in the shoe and
electric fan industry, were established in 1960-69.
They were able to acquire credit facilities only
because the time was propitious and they perceived
their opportunities. Both these entrepreneurs
were from Gujrat where political activity has
always been intense. The period 1960-69 was the
period of intense industrial activity (6) and
economists portrayed Pakistan as a model country.
Financial intermediate institutions had been
established and activated. Their results were
judged by the number of applications granted.
One of the entrepreneurs was a major force in the
political and industrial intensity which was a
feature of this period. This combination enabled
him to operate at a status level. This combination
provided him with the necessary 'muscle' to have
easy credit lines. This was also the period when
foreign exchange limitations were covered by
commodity and project aid.

In terms of education both these entrepreneurs
who had access to financial institutions were
educated and had post graduation degrees while of
the other four, three had spent 6 - 10 years in
education, while one had between 1 and 5 years in
education. Of these, three had no experience but
had changed their occupation from private trade,
one had 6 - 10 years of experience and one had
16 - 20 years of experience, indicating that at
least three had skill and ability par excellence,
two had knowledge of marketing channels and were
aware of production requirements as they were
employed in the same trade. If we looked at the
pattern of father's occupation greater clarity was
obtainable as to the entrepreneurial disposition.
The father of one entrepreneur was an agriculturist, one was in trade and four were indigenous
industrialists with machine servicing facilities
and therefore served as an ideal training ground.

In terms of performance, and if profitability
is to be considered the yardstick for success, then
their success is indicated in Table 5.2

Table 5.2: First Group of Entrepreneurs

Industry	Year	Assets (Rs)	Require-ment	Risk Ratio	Perform-ance(Rs)	Size by Employee
Auto Equipment	1940-49	500	12,500	1:25	31,000	11-50
Ceramics	1970-79	500	12,500	1:25	31,000	11-50
Leather & Products	1960-69	500	300,000	1:600	3,000,000	5000+
Metal Machinery	1940-49) 1950-59)	500	12,500	1:25	3,000,000+ 300,000	1001 - 5000 201 - 1000
Electric Fans	1960-69	500	62,500	1:125	2,000,000	101 - 200

a. Midpoint of group intervals. For details of group intervals
   please see Table 5.1.

The success as indicated is phenomenal although the present day profit could not have been built by the mere wave of a magic wand. Where the risk was highest, profits have been greater. So where the risks are high, ultimately profit seems to be on the high side as well. At least two of the units are definitely competitive in the modern industry along with one in the progressive sector. The export orders of the leather and electric fan enterprises have been substantial for Pakistan. The leather industry is also in fact in competition internally with a multinational and subcontracts tennis and sports shoes for another multinational.

Of the six industries in this group two are in the 11 - 50 size (7) category, one is in the 101 - 200, one in 201 - 1000, one in 1001 - 5000 and one in the 5000± category, indicating that entrepreneurs were perceiving profitable opportunities and taking advantage of these opportunities.

High Risk. All the six entrepreneurs in this first group really belong to the very first group of pioneering entrepreneurs who had extremely limited resources and who literally burned their boats when they entered such a high risk venture. That their skill and ability enabled them to survive the initial years and later on rewarded them with very high profits is amply indicated by the performance ratios of 1:62, 1:4000 and 1:6000. That subsequent opportunities were not missed by them was equally apparent (Table 5.3).

Second Group

The second group comprises entrepreneurs whose personal assets were in the range Rs 1000 - 50,000, i.e. a midpoint value of Rs 25,500. This group was represented in textiles (ancillary like calendering, bleaching etc) hosiery and garments, glass and products, metal machinery, sports goods, ceramics, cutlery, agricultural implements etc. Most of these industries have interesting characteristics which negate the implementation of and escape the planners efforts at planned industrialisation. Firstly every textile industrial units needs substantial services, especially if it is a composite unit. These industrial services are sizing, bleaching, calendering, and the ginning of raw cotton. In fact all the processing in a textile unit can, when required, and in time of great demand, be contracted out to smaller units.

Table 5.3: Risk, Profit and Performance of Entrepreneurs - Group 1

Industry		Risk Ratio High	Profit	Performance
1. Auto Equipment		1:25	31,000	1:62
2. Ceramics		1:25	31,000	1:62
3. Leather and Products		1:600	30^6+	1:6000
4. Metal	(a)	1:25	30^6+	1:6000
Machinery	(b)	1:25	30^5+	1:600
5. Electric Fans		1:125	20^6	1:4000

Key 30^6 = 3,000,000
       30^5 = 300,000

As a result of this a number of indigenous units
have sprung up around large modern textile units.
To hedge against being at the disposal of the large
units, in time, came the effort to develop an
indigenous power loom industry and a third rural
semi-town sector - involving not power looms but
the very basic hand loom. Thus these service
industries had specifically three potential
customers i.e. the modern textile sector, the
power loom and the hand loom sector. Similarly the
hosiery industry, the metal engineering industries
and the agricultural implements industry all have
ease of entry. The agricultural implements
industry's potentiality for rural industry is
significant for the large rural sector. Because
of the huge market in Pakistan and because of
import of tractors and farm machinery this sector
is likely to be vigorous. Such links in the
tubewell industry led to the manufacture of engines
in far off remote villages in Punjab. So far, then,
as the characteristics of these sectors are
concerned, the majority of them escape the benevo-
lent eye of the planners and establish themselves
along small, insignificant lines. In fact there
are no water tight compartments and one sees that
besides the industries in the first group some
more are added but with one difference. The size
and the scale at which they enter is determined by
their personal assets and not by any principle of
economics i.e. economies of scale or gap in the
market, or increase in capacity utilisation.
    Table 5.4 states the assets of this group
of entrepreneurs at Rs 25,500/- while the requirement varies from Rs 12,500/- to Rs 750,000/-
indicating, as we shall see later, that entrepreneurs can enter at any scale and possibly improve
production capacity as (a) demand picks up (b) as
they become more adept and skilful in understanding possible market forces and the nature of
uncertainties and risks with which they have to
cope.

Low Risk. Some distinct patterns of risk were
noticeable. Nine of the entrepreneurs eventually
took the risk with half their assets in the ratio
1:0.5. These were in electric fan, cutlery, glass
and products, agricultural implements, hosiery
and garments, sports goods, ceramics and marble
and products. Two industries (cutlery and sports
goods) in the above category are typical of
Sialkot, a town 80 miles from Lahore. The

Table 5.4: Second Group of Entrepreneurs

S. No.	Industry	Year	Assets	Requirement	Risk Ratio	Performance	Size by Employees
1.	Electric Fan	1940-49	25,500	12,500	1:5	300,000	201-1000
		1950-59	"	300,000	1:12	2,000,000	11-50
2.	Cutlery	1940-49	"	62,500	1:2.5	Loss	11-50
		1960-69	"	12,500	1: .5	75,000	11-50
3.	Glass and Products	1950-59	"	12,500	1: .5	750,000	0-10
4.	Metal Machinery	1950-59	"	12,500	1: .5	Loss	0-10
			"	62,500	1:2.5	75,000	11-50
			"	300,000	1:12	2,000,000	51-100
5.	Auto Equipment	1950-59	"	300,000	1:12	300,000	11-50
6.	Surgical Instruments	1950-59	"	750,000	1:29	2,000,000	201-1000
7.	Agricultural Implements			62,500	1:2.5	300,000	101-200
		1950-59	"	300,000	1:12	75,000	11-50
		1960-69	"	12,500	1: .5	300,000	11-50
		1970-79	"	300,000	1:12	300,000	11-50
8.	Miscellaneous	1950-59	"	62,500	1:2.5	12,000	11-50
		1970-79	"	300,000	1:12	300,000	11-50
9.	Hosiery & Garments	1960-69	"	12,500	1: .5	750,000	101-200
			"	62,500	1:2.5	75,000	11-50
10	Sports Goods	1960-69	"	300,000	1:12	300,000	51-100
		1970-79	"	12,500	1: .5	750,000	101-200
11	Ceramics	1960-69	"	12,500	1: .5	12,000	11-50
		1970-79	"	12,500	1: .5	75,000	11-50
12	Textile	1970-79	"	300,000	1:12	300,000	11-50
13	Marble and Products	1970-79	"	12,500	1: .5	12,000	11-50

entrepreneurial ability is normally established
after formal education and an amount set aside for
the 'new' entrepreneur. Two facilities are given
and provided - (i) adequate cash to purchase raw
materials (ii) facilities in the ancestral house
to set up an office and a production managing area.
The production managing area is normally where all

the production workers bring their products for inspection. The production system is the old putting system, whereby villagers/workers take away the raw material and come back with the finished goods. Since the odds against the production worker were very high, payment being made on the basis of acceptable levels of export workmanship, the performance levels were surprisingly very high. The penalty for unacceptable workmanship was rather severe. Since the raw material was provided to the entrepreneur, the cost of this raw material was deducted from the earnings of the putting worker. Under extreme circumstances this could mean hardly any earnings if the work was rejected. In one case for instance the rejection rate was 3.2% for surgical instruments (8). As many as 13 different criteria were used for quality checks. The maximum rejections (0.9% and 0.8%) were due to finish and cleanliness, and not because of any other defect like pits, cracks, catchet, serration etc, indicating that maximum loss was due to the aesthetic aspect, dependent more and more on machine paced technology. The strength throughout in the system is one of bargaining. Despite the fact that the putting system is seen as exploitative, a good skilled worker has an immense premium attached to him. With the market for skilled workmanship, as perfect as one can expect it to be in an Ldc and in an area where entry is not limited by any government constraints, bargaining skills are required to acquire the most reliable workers. Once an entrepreneur has this on his side the rest comes to him in export earnings. Despite the very primary form of production, these manufacturers solely dependent on the putting system maintain trade offices in Western countries, from where they strike out to various industrial fairs. To get started then, only limited assets will do. With the passage of time and vigorous bargaining methods their export potential and profit would increase. This was what current profit rates indicated.

The other industries where the risk ratio was 1:0.5 was in the electric fan industry, glass and products, agricultural implements, hosiery and garments, ceramics and marble products. At least three of the industries, namely, electric fan, hosiery and garments, and ceramics are to be found primarily in the Gujrat and Gujranwala areas where the intensity of industrial activity is quite

astonishing. The two cities are about 30 miles
apart. The 1940-49 electric fan entrant is even
in the size by employees category in the large
sector. Despite the level of initial investment,
growth and development have been rapid. The 1950 -
59 entrant with a much larger ratio (1:12) is in
the small to medium size, but the pickings have
been excellent. Despite less requirement for
wages, the profits have not been quite as much as
for the earlier entrant. In the ceramics industry
the level of technology is not quite as variable as
is evident from the cost structure in the electric
fan industry. The ceramics technology is very
basic. It is obvious that in the two decades i.e.
1960-69 and 1970-79 the entry cost was the same.
The technology was entirely indigenous and in this
industry family labour was and is available. In
the original manufacturing process these potters
used red clay. They have now moved into glazed
pottery and location wise to the industrial estates.
In fact, it seemed, although confirmation of this
was not possible, that the decision to move to
industrial sites was taken by this caste collectively.

The marketing channels established by these
entrepreneurs are also a mixture of the indigenous
and the modern. Since they cater for the needs of
the lower segment of the market, travelling sales-
men carry wares to the rural areas on cycles
where payment for articles purchased was not
necessarily by cash. In fact any kind of metal
object or old iron or alloy material could be
transacted and the barter exchange would be to the
mutual benefit of both parties. Needless to say
that ability to grasp the worth of an alloy would
determine the profit margin, as these otherwise
useless articles can be used in the recycling
process. So the profit was determined by the
knowledge of prices of the alloy obtained in barter.
This was normally more beneficial. When the market
in this sector was in recession i.e. when crops
had failed or the travelling salesman was unable
to sell his wares for whatever reason, a one off
operation was launched by taking their wares to
big cities i.e. Karachi (750-1000 miles away),
Lahore (60-80 miles away) and disposing of the
goods in the cities' densely populated low income
areas. The goods were thus taken, literally, to
the doorsteps of the buyers. This sector, i.e.
the ceramics entrepreneur, thus adapted selling and
marketing strategies to suit its requirements. The

only difficult time that these entrepreneurs
complained of was in wartime. Both times they
suffered because it was not possible to market
their goods.
     Similarly ease of entry into the agricultural
implements and marble industries and the relatively
cheap requirement of tools and implements assured
the entrepreneur of remaining profitable. In both
these industries, credibility is established by the
quality produced. In both industries, in fact in
all labour intensive industries robustness and
longevity matter (as in agricultural implements)
and aesthetic value is dependent on initial
purchase 'eye' on colour, strain, grain (as in
marble industries). The industry, which was
surprising in this category, pertained to glass
and allied products. The raw material (silica sand)
was available in abundance but the cost of
machinery and the asset required were on the low
side. The entrepreneur, who has now gone into
expansion (via two independent units), is a
Chartered Accountant by profession and fiercely
independent. Although not technically qualified,
indigenous machinery was fabricated and marketing
channels carefully planned. The product, sheet
glass, necessarily delicate, is utilised in the
building industry. A total prohibition of imports
has helped the levels of profitability, which in
this particular case was in the region of
Rs 750,000/- i.e. for a risk of 1:0.5 the profitability was 1:78 (Table 5.5).

Medium Risk. The medium risk category was the 1:2.5
risk ratio category. The performance of risk to
profit to performance may be gauged from Table 5.5.
Five such entrepreneurs are in the 1:2.5 risk ratio
category in the second group of entrepreneurs who
invested Rs 25,000/- on average. These are
entrepreneurs who invested 2½ times their assets.
Barring the performance of one i.e. in agricultural implements manufacturing where returns were
of the nature of 1:12, the others have either shown
a loss or have not shown profits of the level
expected. The agricultural implements industry
at the moment has primary consideration. Policies
have been devised to remove government inconsis-
tencies in the agricultural sector. Industries
establishing links with agriculture are happily
placed. Their current demands are for import of
modern machinery, availability of raw materials,
long term and short term credit facilities and

curiously enough, research facilities and extension work on research (9). The last named demand indicated the ever increasing desire to improve the structure and quality of the product. Two of the medium risk industries showing reasonable profits are the sports goods and the metal machinery industries. The importance of these two industries has already been highlighted earlier. The most surprising performance was in the cutlery industry. Noneconomic reasons were responsible for the loss in the industry.

High Risk. In this high risk category, the maximum risk was 1:29 in the surgical instruments industry while the remaining entrepreneurs were in the 1:12 risk category. The industries which featured in this were the electric fan, metal machinery, auto equipment, agricultural implements, sports goods and textiles industries. The export oriented industries i.e. electric fan, surgical instruments, and sports goods industries can be identified by the nature of their trading pattern. Most of these industries and specifically the last two maintain informal trading offices abroad where important trading activities are covered. Since these offices operate from 'back drawing rooms' in the West and are manned by relatives of the entrepreneurs, the maintenance cost is minimal. Trade enquiries are made after their normal avocations. The important point is that collective effort in another country is constantly going on. In the process, persevering with chain sports stores etc. pays off.

The ability to see profitable propositions is evident but clearly the greater ability to organise such opportunities also stands indicated. The correlation between high risk and high profitability is strong. All these high risk areas have shown a performance ratio of 1:78, barring one which has 1:12.

In terms of occupational mobility, of the 24 entrepreneurs comprising this group 10 had changed their occupations. As many as 4 were former civil servants, 3 were from private employment and 3 were from trade. In the small asset category there were, therefore, more individuals from other avocations than from trade. So far as father's occupation was concerned, 3 came from agricultural backgrounds (explaining the preponderance in the agricultural implements sector), the fathers of four entrepreneurs were civil servants, four were from trade and 11 entrepreneurs were merely carrying on their father's industrialisation effort independently of him in a separate unit.

As a group only 5 of them utilised consultants, 3 of them local and 2 of them foreign. This does indicate the relative conservatism of this group towards acquiring capital intensive machinery. The local consultants were utilised for advice while the foreign consultants invariably were there for running the machinery on the basis of Turnkey arrangements. So far as foreign travel (10) was concerned, in respect of their quest for technology, 10 had travelled outside more than 8 times, 3 had travelled between 4-7 times and 2 had travelled between 1-3 times. So the informal learning effect from travel abroad could not be altogether ruled out. Those who had travelled abroad most frequently (i.e. 8± times) were the ones who sought advice (3) and turnkey consultancy (2).

Of the 24 firms in this group, 17 were small in size i.e. less than 50 employees, 5 were in the medium size and only 2 in the large modern sector. The proponderance of the small sector though is no bar to profitability (Table 5.5)

Third Group
The third group comprises entrepreneurs whose personal assets were in the range Rs 50,000 ÷ 100,000 i.e. a midpoint value of Rs 75,000/-. The industries in this group were textiles, footwear and leather, glass and products, metal machinery, electric fans, pharmaceutical, agricultural implements, and cycles and parts (Table 5.6). Three industries are prominent in this third group - Table 5.6. These are textiles, metal machinery and electric fans.

The textile sector illustrates the point regarding early entry advantage abundantly well. The textile entrepreneur in 1940-49 with assets of Rs 75,000/- and a risk ratio of 1:0.16, one of the lowest, was making profits in the ratio of 1:40 (Table 5.7). In fact the low risk with early entry meant monopoly profits. The entrepreneurs who came in sugsequently i.e. in 1950-59 and in 1970-79, with this kind of asset had much lower profits than the entrepreneurs who invested in 1970-79. In fact the entrepreneurs are in three categories. The entrepreneur with the maximum return and the lowest risk was a political entrepreneur, the medium risk was the progressive entrepreneur and the only high risk performer, a later entrant in 1970-79, an

Table 5.5: Risk, Profit and Performance of Entrepreneurs - Group 2

S. No.	Industry	Low Risk	Profits	Performance	Medium Risk	Profits	Performance	High Risk	Profit	Performance
1.	Electric Fans	1:0.5	300,000	1:12	-	-	-	1:12	2,000,000	1:78
2.	Cutlery	1:0.5	75,000	1:3	1:2.5	0	Negative	-	-	-
3.	Glass & Products	1:0.5	750,000	1:29	-	-	-	-	-	-
4.	Metal Machinery	1:0.5	0	Negative	1:2.5	75,000	1:3	1:12	2,000,000	1:78
5.	Auto Equipment	-	-	-	-	-	-	1:12	300,000	1:12
6.	Surgical Implements	-	-	-	-	-	-	1:29	2,000,000	1:78
7.	Agricultural Implements	1:0.5	3,000,000	1:12	1:2.5	300,000	1:12 a)	1:12	75,000	1:3
							- b)	1:12	300,000	1:12
8.	Miscellaneous	-	-	-	1:2.5	12,000	1:0.5	1:12	300,000	1:12
9.	Hosiery	1:0.5	750,000	1:29	-	-	-	-	-	-
10	Sports Goods	1:0.5	750,000	1:29	1:2.5	75,000	1:3	1:12	300,000	1:12
11	Ceramics a)	1:0.5	12,000	1:0.5	-	-	-	-	-	-
	b)	1:0.5	75,000	1:3	-	-	-	-	-	-
12	Textiles	-	-	-	-	-	-	1:12	300,000	1:12
13	Marble and Products	1:0.5	12,000	1:0.5	-	-	-	-	-	-

Table 5.6: Third Group of Entrepreneurs

S. No.	Industry		Year	Assets	Require- ments	Risk Ratio	Perform- ance	Size by Employees
1.	Textiles	a)	1940-49	75,111	12,500	1:0.16	3,000,000+	1001-5000
		b)	1950-59	75,000	300,000	1:4	750,000	101-200
		c)	1970-79	75,000	750,000	1:10	12,000	11-50
2.	Leather & Products		1950-59	75,000	300,000	1:4	300,000	11-50
3.	Glass and Products		1960-69	75,000	62,500	1:0.8	31,000	11-50
4.	Metal	a)	1940-49	75,000	300,000	1:4	750,000	11-50
	Machinery	b)	1950-59	75,000	62,500	1:0.8	750,000	51-100
		c)	1960-69	75,000	300,000	1:4	300,000	51-100
5.	Electric	a)	1950-59	75,000	62,500	1:0.8	Loss	0-10
	Fans	b)	1950-59	75,000	300,000	1:4	3,000,000+	11-50
		c)	1970-79	75,000	62,500	1:0.8	31,000	11-50
		d)	1970-79	75,000	62,500	1:0.8	3,000,000	1001-5000
		e)	1970-79	75,000	300,000	1:4	2,000,000	201-1000
6.	Pharmaceuticals		1960-69	75,000	300,000	1:4	75,000	0-10
7.	Agricultural Implements		1960-69	750,000	300,000	1:4	300,000	11-50
8.	Cycles and Parts		1950-59	750,000	300,000	1:4	2,000,000	201-1000

Table 5.7: Risk, Profit and Performance of Entrepreneur - Group 3

S. No. Industry	Low Risk	Profits	Performance	Medium Risk	Profits	Performance	High Risk	Profit	Performance
1. Textile	1:0.16	3,000,000+	1:4	1:4	750,000	1:10	1:10	12,000	0:0.16
2. Leather	-	-	-	1:4	300,000	1:4	-	-	-
3. Glass and Products	1:0.8	31,000	1:0.4	-	-	-	-	-	-
4. Metal Machinery	1:0.8	75,000	1:1	a) 1:4	750,000	1:10	-	-	-
				b) 1:4	300,000	1:4	-	-	-
5. Electric Fans a)	1:0.8	Negative	-	1:4	3,000,000+	1:40	-	-	-
b)	1:0.8	31,000	1:0.4	1:4	2,000,000	1:27	-	-	-
c)	1:0.8	3,000,000	1:40	-	-	-	-	-	-
6. Pharmaceuticals	-	-	-	1:4	75,000	1:1	-	-	-
7. Agricultural Implements	-	-	-	1:4	300,000	1:4	-	-	-
8. Cycles and Parts	-	-	-	1:4	2,000,000	1:27	-	-	-

economic entrepreneur barely subsisting and performance wise, the least significant. In the electric
fan industry, two of the enterprises were established in 1950-59 and three between 1970-79. One
of the concerns was a losing one, not for any other
reason but for the fact that after the death of the
Karta Dharta (11) family feuds had started. The
eldest son was unable to assert his ability and
this resulted in the younger sons asking for their
share and moving out of the area altogether. The
enterprise was in a run down condition despite its
earlier pristine position. The inherited entrepreneur was subsisting not on the basis of any
production but on the earnings of disposed of
machinery.

There were two entry cost requirements i.e.
Rs 62,500 and Rs 300,000 and therefore determining
two categories of risk, low and medium. In the
metal machinery the 3 entrepreneurs were in 3
different time periods i.e. 1940-49, 1950-59,
1960-69 and the entry cost requirements for the 3
enterprises were different. The 1940-49 and the
1960-69 was Rs 300,000/- whereas the 1950-59 was
in the low risk at Rs 62,500/-.

Low Risk. Of the 16 firms in this category, 6
entrepreneurs were in the low risk configuration.
These low risk configurations were in the textile,
glass and products, metal machinery and in the
electric fan industries. The lowest risk was in
the textile industry, and was for the very first
firm developed in the Textile industry in Pakistan.
This entrepreneur was from the mercantile sector
and was one of the original traders and merchants
who moved from Bombay to Pakistan. The industrial
environment was such and the needs so great that
the new government of a new independent state
would have gone to any extent for the sake of some
industrialisation. Since its early entry provided
it with profits, this was only the beginning of
establishing themselves as one of the leading
entrepreneurial families. The entrepreneurs are
definitely front runners and have maintained their
position, initially by early monopolistic entry,
and later by a curious and intelligent blend of
technological acquisitions, as well as managerial
advancements. Of the others, in the low risk
category, two of the entrepreneurs' profit was low
(ratio of 1:0.4), one had a one to one ratio and
one was in loss. One of the entrepreneurs with a
risk ratio of 1:0.8 had a profit of 1:40,

commensurate with the entrepreneur in the textile
sector. Again the real reason was early entry but
over the years, and here credit must be given to
the entrepreneurs, they have maintained their
initial advantage and remained industrial front
runners. The main difference between the two was
to the extent that the textile entrepreneur could
and probably did utilise the bureaucracy and did
manipulate government economic policies, whilst the
other manipulated the economic environment as given.
In terms of efficiency the latter (electric fan)
entrepreneur was competitive in world markets,
whereas the former (textile) political entrepreneur
performed behind high tariff walls and extensive
direct and indirect subsidies and props. In terms
of size by employees the political entrepreneur
had grown to mammoth proportions with the size of
this one enterprise being in the large sector
(1001-5000 employees) whereas the economic entrepreneur was in the 11-50 category. As to the
question of capacity creation when demand was high,
the economic entrepreneur relied on subcontracting
to other economic entrepreneurs. As to quality
maintenance, especially producing for international
markets, control was exercised by providing sub-
contraction only to those economic entrepreneurs
as had been originally in the firm and later
developed as entrepreneurs. No such benefit
accrued to the economy from the political entrepreneur, although there were industrialisation and
external economies effects (12).

Medium Risk. Nine of the firms were in the medium
risk with a risk ratio of 1:4. The textile firm
showed performance ratio of 1:10, i.e. better than
the risk ratio. Similarly one of the metal
machinery firms showed a similar performance ratio,
while the other was in a 1:4 ratio. But it was in
the electric fan industry and in the cycles and
parts industry that profits and performance by the
medium risk industry was par excellence. First of
all the electric fan industry has, as already
pointed out, certain strong points. Domestically
the urban boom has meant a rise in local demand.
This explains a considerable amount of profitability. Anything that can be produced and even if
qualitatively inferior can still sell with a not
too different price margin. The weather is of
course one major reason. With stifling heat for
9 months in a year a fan is almost the first 'ease'
requirement of any family.

For the quality producers the Iran and Middle East markets provide an easy outlet. Since the majority of the labour force in these areas is from Pakistan, the weather effects are reduced by a combination of air coolers, air conditioners and fans. Most of the electric fan producers also manufacture air coolers and in order to make it more effective have modified the design of an air expeller (exhaust), with various kinds of locally manufactured devices with raw materials which absorb water and thus bring in a cooling effect more devastatingly effective than the air conditioners. The system of air cooling breaks down during the monsoon months when the humidity is already in the region of 85-90 per cent. During this period the air coolers are utilised as dry air throwers i.e. no water for cooling is utilised. The ingenuity and adaptation of technology did lead to a product that caters for local needs. Interesting product improvements are visible in the market and even the rich realise that a combination of air conditioners and air cooling is much more effective. The product improvement though continues and the products continuously show characteristics of modern technology i.e. a better handling and movement capability (product sophistication and compactness) and a better technical aspect i.e. better air propulsion through the rooms and the house. The product is an improvement over the fan in terms of countering the weather effects (the drier and greater the heat, the more effective). Its maintenance costs are nil to negligible over the air conditioner, which is particularly vulnerable to voltage fluctuations and therefore requires an electric stabiliser, a machine to control another machine, and it would require this with every unit in the house. The other disincentive is that an air conditioner has two major components, a compressor and ammonia gas. Major expense and inconvenience is encountered to rectify either of the two faults. All these factors account for the strength of the elctric fan and the products industry. It does explain that although research and development is not as organised as elsewhere in the developed countries, the effort, more informal, less well organised, is nevertheless there.

Where and which category of entrepreneur was responsible for these technological and product improvement? Our research indicates that product improvement and marketability are more conducive and applicable where entrepreneurial ability stands

strengthened by technical ability i.e. at the level
of the economic and progressive entrepreneur.
Therefore it was not surprising to find high
variability in profitability. Out of a total of
five entrepreneurs in this asset category, three
have shown profits in the ratio of 1:40, 1:40, and
1:27. Of the remaining two, one was actually in
loss and the other had modest profits. Both these
units were in the small sector - one by choice and
the other had merely just started (a polytechnic
student turned economic entrepreneur). By size,
of the five enterprises, three were in the small
sector, two were in the large sector. The two
in the large sector were regular exporters, as
also was one of the smaller sector entrepreneurs.

The other area with high entrepreneurial
performance was the cycle industry. Cycle sale
is rationed. The demand for this mode of
travelling exists in rural areas and for the poor
condemned to the urban cities, living at distances
from their place of work. The demand is much in
excess of supply resulting in exhorbitant premium
prices. The industry is inefficient and has not
taken to technological innovation. The cycle (13)
industry has existed under tariff protection and
there is not the same vigorous and entrepreneurial
innovation approach as was noticeable in the
electric fan and products industry.

The only two industrial categories, with
modest profits, were the pharmaceutical industry
and agricultural implements. In Pakistan 80 per
cent of the pharmaceutical markets are with multinationals. The remaining 20 per cent are with the
indigenous entrepreneurs. In the early 1970s the
strength of the multinationals in the drug market
was affected by the removal of brand and company
names from the marketed product. This meant that
only generic names could be utilised. A number of
new entrepreneurs entered the market. Quality
control was not effective any more and a generic
name was utilised by both multinationals and
indigenous manufacturers. A number of abuses,
the most serious of which was spurious drugs or
simply non-potent drugs, was the outcome. The
system was changed again, in late 1970s. During
this period the multinationals' profitability was
affected. The removal of the system led to these
multinationals recovering their earlier markets,
for not only do they have strength in 'life saving'
drugs but in ordinary every day common household
medication, the indigenous entrepreneur having

124

been exposed during the 'generic system'. The
market understandably has been affected. Only
those indigenous entrepreneurs are now likely to
survive as are those producing medicines under
licence from their multinational principles and
therefore utilising their brand names.

High Risk. Only one entrepreneur (14) was in the
high risk area in this sector and that too in the
textile sector. The performance ratio was poor and
the timing of establishment of unit in 1970-79
indicates that the entrepreneur was political in
nature and did not have any of the entrepreneurial
qualities attributed to either of the categories
i.e. economic, progressive or political entrepreneurs. The result obviously was none too promising.
Dependent on other considerations, like relevant
partnerships or poaching' of critical human
elements from other concerns, might enable this
enterprise to improve its performance. The textile
industry, indeed, is bugged by such entrants. They
operate to the benefit of the existing/early
entrants in as much as they project a crisis in
industry and since these are influential entrepreneurs they do manage to have government policies
modified. Such policies are advantageous to all
yet the benefits to the earlier entrants is in
larger measure.

Fourth Group
The fourth group (Table 5.8) comprises entrepreneurs
whose personal assets were in the range Rs 100,000
to 1,000,000 with a midpoint value of Rs 550,000.
This group was represented in all the categories,
and by far the maximum number of entrepreneurs
featured in this category (i.e. 92), with the
largest number of textiles (16), metal machinery
(14) electric fans (9), agricultural implements
(7), steel rerolling (7), chemicals and products
(6), and furniture and products (6).
    The pattern and requirement for textile units
indicates how monopoly profits were permitted. Of
the 16, two units each were established between
1940-49 and two in period 1950-59, while the
remaining 12 units came up in the period between
1970-79. Of the 4 units established prior to 1960,
3 had similar financial requirements while a fourth
required 10 times the amount. In other words the
size of one composite unit (yarn and weaving) was
more than the combined size of all the three units
established in that period and in our sample. The

125

requirement for industry from 1940-49 to 1970-79 seems to have been the same fixed amount for a non composite unit i.e. Rs 300,000. Of the 16 in the textile sector, 12 were allocated this amount (15). Three of them, in the period 1970-79, had different financial requirements. Two of the entrepreneurs required Rs 750,000/- while one required Rs 3,000,000/-. The overall risk ratio was low in most cases, indicating that in the modern sector individuals with large personal assets were involved. Only two from the 16 entrepreneurs in textiles were in high risk, the remaining being in low risk. Similar indications were visible in the other sectors i.e. furniture and products, chemicals and products, steel rerolling, metal machinery, electric fans and agricultural implements etc. However, what did distinguish the textile industry from the others was the poor performance of the textile units set up between 1970 and 1979. The textile sector, a highly profitable one in 1950-59 and in 1960-69, saw an increasing number of political entrepreneurs enter this industry. With the visibility of high profits but unaware of the actual requirements most of them showed a loss, something that had never happened in the textile industry. Market conditions were also responsible for this drastic change in the 1970s. Former East Pakistan had provided a market for low quality yarn, which was utilised by the industry. In the 1970s this market was no longer available. With the loss of East Pakistan the excess capacity textile industry could not be utilised elsewhere. The high cost of production and poor quality meant it was not competitive in international markets. However, these new entrepreneurs were needed by the earlier political entrepreneurs of the 1950s and 1960s. Since they were linked to the new political system emerging in Pakistan, one based on adult franchise, they served a purpose. New recruits to the political entrepreneurial field could reflect this new power base and help remove any political and ideological uncertainty that the new democratically elected government could create. The threat of nationalisation was to be checked through these new entrants. In any case the early entrants were so far ahead that subsequent entrants could hardly break monopoly power in the markets.

A similar advantage accrued to them in the procurement of chemical and raw material inputs. Why should these be important? The chemical inputs are normally banned items as most of these

chemicals are produced in the nationalised industries. Demand for these chemicals is excessive
as compared to supply. Years of supply input
relationships between the earlier entrants and
the producers is not disrupted by the new entrants.
So reluctant as the admission to their fold was,
the textile tycoons accepted these late comers for
reasons of their own. Primarily they were willing
to share the market rather than lose the production
processes entirely through forced acquisition by
the state. The earlier entrants also knew that
the new entrepreneurs' knowledge and judgement was
questionable as most of them were still to learn
the requirements. They were neither traders not
from the industrial sector. They were speculators
looking for 'quick' profits and if these were
denied them, these very industries could be up
for sale in a couple of years' time.

Of the 92 in this category, as many as 78 were
in the low risk category i.e. less than a risk
ratio of 1:2 so far as personal assets and requirement for industry were concerned, and 14 in the
high risk area i.e. risk ratio being more than 1:4.
There were no entrepreneurs at the medium risk
level. By size, most of the textile enterprises
(Table 5.9) were in the large modern sector
barring three highly capital intensive servicing
industries, which were in 0-10 category and 4 in
the 11-50 category. The small sector in textiles
comprises of enterprises specialising in sizing,
calendering, bleaching etc. Only the machine
paced work is capital intensive; drying, building
etc. is labour intensive. Manipulation of labour
employee statistics is also helpful in increasing
projects. Temporary labour is not provided with
wage increments and the lesser number of employees
is helpful in a reduction in tax base, so that in
actual fact profitability is determined not only in
the market place but also in terms of how to evade
and avoid various kinds of expenses (16). Profits
are due not only to the demand of the product but
also due to holding back production so that
scarcity value for the product was created,
especially during the time of political uncertainty
when decisions/production in the nationalised
industry would not be to optimal capacity levels.
In all the industries barring the large corporate
textile sector, variability in size ranging from
very small to very large is noticeable. What does
this indicate? For one thing it does show that
careful and considered entrepreneurship was possible,

Table 5.8: Fourth Group of Entrepreneurs

S. No.	Industry	Year	Personal Assets	Require-ments	Risk Ratio	Performance	Size by Employment
1	2	3	4	5	6	7	8
1.	Textile	1940-49	550,000	300,000	1:0.6	30^5	11-50
		1940-49	"	3,000,000	1:5.5	30^6+	1001-5000
		1950-59	"	300,000	1:0.6	31,000	0-10
		1950-59	"	300,000	1:0.6	30^5	11-50
		1970-79	"	300,000	1:0.6	Negative	201-1000
		1970-79	"	300,000	1:0.6	Negative	101-200
		1970-79	"	300,000	1:0.6	Negative	201-1000
		1970-79	"	300,000	1:0.6	Negative	201-1000
		1970-79	"	300,000	1:0.6	Negative	201-1000
		1970-79	"	300,000	1:0.6	Negative	201-1000
		1970-79	"	300,000	1:0.6	Negative	201-1000
		1970-79	"	300,000	1:0.6	31,000	0-10
		1970-79	"	300,000	1:0.6	75,000	0-10
		1970-79	"	750,000	1:1.4	300,000	11-50
		1970-79	"	750,000	1:1.4	750^4	11-50
		1970-79	"	3,000,000	1:5.5	2,000,000	51-100

Table 5.8 (Continued)

S. No.	Industry	Year	Personal Assets	Require-ments	Risk Ratio	Performance	Size by Employment
2	Footwear & Leather	1950-59	550,000	750^4	1:1.4	30^6+	201-1000
		1960-69	"	30^5	1:0.6	31,000	51-100
		1960-69	"	30^5	1:0.6	30^5	5000^+
3	Hosiery & Garments	1950-59	"	30^6	1:5.5	750^4	11-50
		1970-79	"	30^5	1:0.6	30^5	51-100
4	Plywood and Veneer Products	1950-59	"	30^5	1:0.6	20^6	201-1000
		1950-59	"	750^4	1:1.4	30^6	201-1000
		1960-69	"	750^4	1:1.4	750^4	11-50
		1970-79	"	6250^2	1:0.1	310^3	0-10
		1980+	"	300^5	1:5.5	310^3	11-50
5	Glass and Products	1950-59	"	300^5	1:5.5	Negative	201-1000
		1960-69	"	300^5	1:0.6	310^3	0-10

Table 5.8 (Continued)

S. No.	Industry	Year	Personal Assets	Requirements	Risk Ratio	Performance	Size by Employment
6	Chemicals & Products	1930–39	550,000	300^5	1:0.6	120^3	11–50
		1950–59	=	300^5	1:0.6	300^5	51–100
		1970–79	=	300^5	1:0.6	310^3	0–10
		1970–79	=	300^5	1:0.6	750^3	11–50
		1970–79	=	750^4	1:1.4	30^5	11–50
		1970–79	=	300^6	1:5.5	30^5	51–100
7	Steel Rerolling	1940–49	=	300,000	1:0.6	3,000,000+	201–1000
		1950–59	=	300,000	1:0.6	3,000,000+	51–100
		1960–69	=	300,000	1:5.5	3,000,000+	11–50
		1970–79	=	300,000	1:0.6	12,000	11–50
		1970–79	=	300,000	1:0.6	300,000	11–50
		1970–79	=	750,000	1:1.4	300,000	11–50
		1970–79	=	300,000	1:5.5	200,000	101–200

Table 5.8 (Continued)

S. No.	Industry	Year	Personal Assets	Require- ments	Risk Ratio	Performance	Size by Employment
8	Metal Machinary	1930-39	550,000	750,000	1:1.4	300,000	11-50
		1950-59	"	62,500	1:0.1	Negative	0-10
		1950-59	"	300,000	1:0.6	3,100	11-50
		1950-59	"	750,000	1:1.4	3,000,000+	11-50
		1960-69	"	300,000	1:0.6	31,000	11-50
		1960-69	"	300,000	1:0.6	31,000	11-50
		1960-69	"	300,000	1:0.6	300,000	11-50
		1960-69	"	750,000	1:1.4	300,000	11-50
		1970-79	"	62,500	1:0.1	31,000	11-50
		1970-79	"	300,000	1:0.6	31,000	11-50
		1970-79	"	300,000	1:0.1	300,000	11-50
		1970-79	"	750,000	1:1.4	300,000	51-100
		1970-79	"	750,000	1:1.4	200,000	201-1000
		1970-79	"	300,000	1:5.5	3,000,000+	201-1000
9	Electric Fans	1950-59	"	300,000	1:0.6	300,000	11-50
		1960-69	"	62,500	1:0.6	31,000	11-50
		1960-69	"	300,000	1:0.6	75,000	11-50
		1970-79	"	300,000	1:0.6	12,000	11-50
		1970-79	"	300,000	1:0.6	31,000	11-50
		1970-79	"	300,000		300,000	11-50
		1970-79	"	750,000	1:1.4	300,000	11-50
		1970-79	"	750,000	1:1.4	300,000	11-50
		1970-79	"	300,000	1:5.5	750,000	51-100

Table 5.8 (Continued)

S. No. Industry	Year	Personal Assets	Require-ments	Risk Ratio	Performance	Size by Employment
10 Auto Equipment	1960-69	550,000	300,000	1:0.6	300,000	11-50
	1960-69	"	3,000,000	1:5.5	3,000,000+	11-50
	1970-79	"	300,000	1:0.6	31,000	11-50
11 Surgical Instruments	1950-59	"	300,000	1:0.6	2,000,000	201-1000
	1950-59	"	750,000	1:1.4	200,000	201-1000
12 Sports Goods	1950-59	"	300,000	1:0.6	750,000	11-50
13 Ceramics	1960-69	"	300,000	1:0.6	31,000	0-10
	1970-79	"	300,000	1:0.6	300,000	101-200
14 Cutlery & Products	1950-59	"	750,000	1:1.4	300,000	51-100
	1960-69	"	62,500	1:0.1	300,000	11-50
	1970-79	"	3,000,000	1:5.5	300,000	101-200
15 Pharmaceuti-cals	1940-49	"	300,000	1:0.6	3,000,000+	201-1000
	1950-69	"	750,000	1:1.4	2,000,000	101-200
16 Agricultural Implements	1950-59	"	750,000	1:1.4	300,000	101-200
	1960-69	"	300,000	1:0.6	300,000	11-50
	1960-69	"	300,000	1:0.6	750,000	11-50
	1960-69	"	750,000	1:1.4	750,000	11-50
	1970-79	"	750,000	1:1.4	750,000	11-50
	1970-79	"	750,000	1:1.4	300,000	11-50
	1970-79	"	3,000,000	1:5.5	2,000,000	51-100
17 Cycles and Parts	1950-59	"	3,000,000	1:5.5	300,000	11-50

Table 5.8 (Continued)

S. No.	Industry	Year	Personal Assets	Require-ments	Risk Ratio	Performance	Size by Employment
18	Marble and Products	1930-39	550,000	750,000	1:1.4	31,000	11-50
19	Community Processing	1960-69	"	300,000	1:0.6	300,000	11-50
20	Miscellaneous	1960-69	"	750,000	1:1.4	300,000	11-50
		1970-79	"	300,000	1:0.6	31,000	0-10
		1980-	"	300,000	1:0.6	Negative	0-10

133

Table 5.9: Risk, Profit and Performance of Entrepreneurs - Group 4

S. No.	Industry	Risk Ratio (Low	Pro-fits	Perfor-mance Ratio	Risk (Me-dium	Pro-fits	Perfor-mance Ratio	Risk (High)	Profits	Perfor-mance Ratio
1	Textiles	a) 1:0.6	30^5	1:0.5	-	-	-	1:0.5	30^6	1:5.45
		b) 1:0.6	310^3	1:0.1	-	-	-	1:5.5	20^6	1:3.6
		c) 1:0.6	30^5	1:0.5	-	-	-	-	-	-
		d) 1:0.6	Negative	-	-	-	-	-	-	-
		e) 1:0.6	"	-	-	-	-	-	-	-
		f) 1:0.6	"	-	-	-	-	-	-	-
		g) 1:0.6	"	-	-	-	-	-	-	-
		h) 1:0.6	"	-	-	-	-	-	-	-
		i) 1:0.6	"	-	-	-	-	-	-	-
		j) 1:0.6	"	-	-	-	-	-	-	-
		k) 1:0.6	310^3	1:0.1	-	-	-	-	-	-
		l) 1:0.6	750^3	1:0.25	-	-	-	-	-	-
		m) 1:1.4	30^5	1:0.4	-	-	-	-	-	-
		n) 1:1.4	750^4	1:1.4	-	-	-	-	-	-

Table 5.9 (Continued)

S. No.	Industry		Risk Ratio (Low)	Profit	Performance Ratio	Risk (Medium)	Profits	Performance Ratio	Risk (High)	Profits	Performance Ratio
2	Footwear & Leather	a)	1:1.4	300^6	1:5.45	–	–	–	–	–	–
		b)	1:0.6	310^3	1:0.6	–	–	–	–	–	–
		c)	1:0.6	30^5	1:0.55	–	–	–	–	–	–
3	Hosiery & Garments		1:0.6	30^5	1:0.55	–	–	–	a) 1:5.5	750^4	1:1.36
									b) 1:5.5	310^3	1:0.056
4	Furniture (Plywood & Veneer)	a)	1:0.6	20^6	1:3.6	–	–	–	–	–	–
		b)	1:1.4	30^6	1:5.4	–	–	–	–	–	–
		c)	1:1.4	750^3	1:0.25	–	–	–	–	–	–
		d)	1:0.1	310^3	1:0.056	–	–	–	–	–	–
		e)	1:0.4	750^3	1:0.25	–	–	–	–	–	–
5	Glass & Products		1:0.6	310^3	1:0.6	–	–	–	1:5.5	Negative	–

Table 5.9 (Continued)

S. No	Industry		Risk Ratio (Low)	Pro-fit	Perfor-mance Ratio	Risk (Me-dium)	Pro-fits	Perfor-mance Ratio	Risk (High)	Pro-fits	Perfor-mance Ratio
6	Chemicals and Products	a)	1:0.6	120^3	1:0.2	–	–	–	1:5.5	30^5	1:0.55
		b)	1:0.6	30^5	1:0.55	–	–	–	–	–	–
		c)	1:0.6	310^3	1:0.6	–	–	–	–	–	–
		d)	1:0.6	750^3	1:0.14	–	–	–	–	–	–
		e)	1:1.4	30^5	1:0.55	–	–	–	–	–	–
7	Steel Rerolling	a)	1:0.6	30^{6+}	1:5.45	–	–	–	1:5.5	30^6	1:5.45
		b)	1:0.6	30^{6+}	1:5.45	–	–	–	1:5.5	20^6	1:3.6
		c)	1:0.6	120^3	1:0.02	–	–	–	–	–	–
		d)	1:0.6	30^5	1:0.55	–	–	–	–	–	–
		e)	1:1.4	30^5	1:0.55	–	–	–	–	–	–

Table 5.9 (Continued)

S. No.	Industry	Risk Ratio (Low)	Pro-fits	Perfor-mance Ratio	Risk (Me-dium)	Pro-fits	Perfor-mance Ratio	Risk (High)	Pro-fits	Perfor-mance Ratio
8	Metal & Machinery									
	a)	1:1.4	30^5	1:0.55	–	–	–	1:5.5	30^6	1:5.45
	b)	1:0.1	Negative	–	–	–	–	–	–	–
	c)	1:0.6	310^3	1:0.06	–	–	–	–	–	–
	d)	1:1.4	30^{6+}	1:5.45	–	–	–	–	–	–
	e)	1:0.6	310^3	1:0.06	–	–	–	–	–	–
	f)	1:0.6	310^3	1:0.06	–	–	–	–	–	–
	g)	1:0.6	30^5	1:0.55	–	–	–	–	–	–
	h)	1:1.4	30^5	1:0.55	–	–	–	–	–	–
	i)	1:0.1	310^3	1:0.06	–	–	–	–	–	–
	j)	1:0.6	310^3	1:0.06	–	–	–	–	–	–
	k)	1:0.6	30^5	1:0.55	–	–	–	–	–	–
	l)	1:1.4	30^5	1:0.55	–	–	–	–	–	–
	m)	1:1.4	20^6	1:3.6	–	–	–	–	–	–

Table 5.9 (Continued)

S. No.	Industry		Risk Ratio (Low)	Pro-fits	Perfor-mance Ratio	Risk (Me-dium)	Pro-fits	Perfor-mance Ratio	Risk (High)	Pro-fits	Perfor-mance Ratio
9	Electric Fans	a)	1:0.6	30^5	1:0.55	–	–	–	1:5.5	750^4	1:1.4
		b)	1:0.1	310^3	1:0.06	–	–	–	–	–	–
		c)	1:0.6	750^3	1:0.14	–	–	–	–	–	–
		d)	1:0.6	120^3	1:0.02	–	–	–	–	–	–
		e)	1:0.6	310^3	1:0.06	–	–	–	–	–	–
		f)	1:0.6	30^5	1:0.55	–	–	–	–	–	–
		g)	1:1.4	30^5	1:0.55	–	–	–	–	–	–
		h)	1:1.4	30^5	1:0.55	–	–	–	–	–	–
10	Auto-Equipment	a)	1:0.6	30^5	1:0.55	–	–	–	1:5.5	30^6+	1:5.45
		b)	1:0.6	310^3	1:0.06	–	–	–	–	–	–
11	Surgical Instru-ments	a)	1:0.6	20^6	1:3.6	–	–	–	–	–	–
		b)	1:1.4	20^6	1:3.6	–	–	–	–	–	–
12	Sports Goods		1:0.6	750^4	1:1.4	–	–	–	–	–	–

Table 5.9 (Continued)

S. No.	Industry		Risk Ratio (Low)	Pro-fits	Perfor-mance Ratio	Risk (Me-dium)	Pro-fits	Perfor-mance Ratio	Risk (High)	Pro-fits	Perfor-mance Ratio
13	Ceramics	a)	1:0.6	310^3	1:0.06	–	–	–	–	–	–
		b)	1:0.6	30^5	1:0.55	–	–	–	–	–	–
14	Cutlery & Products	a)	1:1.4	30^5	1:0.55	–	–	–	1:5.5	30^5	1:0.55
		b)	1:0.1	30^5	1:0.55	–	–	–	–	–	–
		c)	1:0.6	750^3	1:0.25	–	–	–	–	–	–
15	Pharma-ceuticals	a)	1:1.4	20^6	1:3.6	–	–	–	–	–	–
		b)	1:0.6	30^{6+}	1:5.45	–	–	–	–	–	–
16	Agricul-tural Implements	a)	1:1.4	30^5	1:0.55	–	–	–	1:5.5	20^6	1:3.6
		b)	1:0.6	30^5	1:0.55	–	–	–	–	–	–
		c)	1:0.6	750^4	1:1.4	–	–	–	–	–	–
		d)	1:1.4	750^3	1:0.14	–	–	–	–	–	–
		e)	1:1.4	30^5	1:0.55	–	–	–	–	–	–
17	Cycles & Parts		–	–	–	–	–	–	1:5.5	30^5	1:0.55

Table 5.9 (Continued)

S. No.	Industry	Risk Ratio (Low)	Pro-fits	Perfor-mance Ratio	Risk (Medium)	Pro-fits	Perfor-mance Ratio	Risk (High)	Pro-fits	Perfor-mance Ratio
18	Marble & Products	1:1.4	310^3	1:0.06	–	–	–	–	–	–
19	Commodity Processing	1:0.6	30^5	1:0.55	–	–	–	–	–	–
20	Miscellan- a) eous	1:1.4	30^5	1:0.55	–	–	–	–	–	–
	b)	1:0.6	310^3	1:0.06	–	–	–	–	–	–
	c)	1:0.06	Nega-tive	Negative	–	–	–	–	–	–

In the sense that any entrepreneur unable to
determine the probabilities of outcome could start
at a relatively less risky level and proceed on the
basis of the outcome and divergence of the probabilities i.e. range of profits that accrue over a
period of time, probability and predictability of
outcomes improving with confidence levels. So as
confidence grows, profits are reinvested. It was
and is almost impossible to determine the level of
the profits reinvested. Thomas Timberg came across
similar patterns in India ..... this paper could
have utilised some other financial detail as an
indicator of a firm's net worth' (17), and regarding
profits, 'the under reporting of profits may be a
considerably more serious problem than that of under
reporting assets'. Many firms are milked at both
ends by privately (i.e. closely held) owned
supplying and marketing firms, who overcharge and
underpay the firm. Because these firms are private
and subject to less publicity, they can inflate
expense, or otherwise serve as devices for reducing
tax liability (18). Besides these semi legal
methods, brought about by 'human corporate ingenuity'
there was also '..... a black cash flow parallelling
that recorded in their books. Sales and purchases
have black elements that are never recorded but are
placed directly in Manager's hands' (19). The
problem stands identified by Timberg but the
awareness of this problem and its magnitude has a
restricting influence on the environment. For one
thing, wherever double standards are visible and
noticeable, trust is limited to close relatives,
friends, trusted and loyal workers. The rest stand
excluded. That also means that there is a
restriction in participation by the nation as a
whole.

Low Risk. Of the 92 in the category as many as 78
were in the low risk area i.e. with risk less than
a ratio of 1:2. In fact, 5 of the entrepreneurs
committed only 0.1 of their assets. The least
assets committed were in the metal machinery,
electric fan and cutlery and products industries
(Table 5.8). These are industries where skill and
craftsmanship can and do substitute for other
production means. Thus in the electric fan industries merely subcontracting carbon brushes for the
large sector on a very basic level could initiate
an entrepreneur, and usually does, into the
manufacturing process.
     The largest category belonged to those who

committed slightly more than half their assets i.e.
0.6, the balance being provided not by the extended
family but by the financial institutions. To
understand the nature of risk the time period in
which investments were made is necessary. Prior
to 1970 the textile industry in particular enjoyed
a boom period. The markets were not limited.
With yarn replacing homespun cotton in West Pakistan
and supplying the needs of former East Pakistan
weavers, the textile entrepreneurs enjoyed
unlimited profits. Effective protection determined
by rate of exchange, the level of tariffs, import
duty exemptions on inputs and the incompetence of
the administrative structure ensured high profits
and ironically higher inefficiency in the use of
resources. Wastage to the extent of 15-20 per cent
(20) was and is a common feature leading to the
continuous demands of this sector for subsidy.
Thus once protection (21) was established and the
East Pakistan market lost because of civil strife,
the textile industry could only become viable by
export subsidies. The net result was that entrepreneurs in this sector invariably looked towards
government to help make them profitable. The
government response, despite there being enough
firms in the sector was not to encourage competition, thus allowing the weak and the inefficient
to stay in business; but to permit protection, and
provide direct and indirect subsidies (22). For
every response the entrepreneur in this category
would look towards the government for resolving
problems: a state of continuous dependence on
government's micro policies.

The progressive entrepreneur in this low risk
category was located mainly in the footwear and
leather, furniture and products, steel rerolling,
metal machinery, electric fan, surgical instruments,
auto equipment, pharmaceuticals and agricultural
implements industries. Barring footwear and
leather, furniture and products and pharmaceuticals,
the remaining industries were ferrous/metal industries, where abilities and skill requirement were
a necessity. In fact these entrepreneurs
established themselves initially on the basis of
their ability and skills. The other progressive
entrepreneurs were those who had taken specialised
course in pharmaceuticals, leather technology and
modern furniture and woodwork requirement in the
building industry. The response from those
qualified for the woodwork industry indicated the
perceptual ability of the progressive entrepreneur.

Despite no shortage of natural forests (although the price was ever increasing), some entrepreneurs realised the aesthetic appeal and 'finish' that could be brought on veneered woodwork. Exploiting this ability and initially providing a price differential they could exploit and turn the market towards their own products despite the obvious durability and unquestioned strength of natural wood. In terms of size, the majority of these entrepreneurs remained in the 11-50 employee category.

High Risk. In the high risk category, the entrepreneurs were from textile, two from garments and hosiery, one from glass and products, one from chemical and products, two from steel rerolling, one from metal machinery, one from electric fans, one from auto equipment, and one each from cutlery and products, agricultural implements and the cycle industry. The two from textiles were political entrepreneurs and both showed extreme ability in terms of performance, while those in the garment industry were new entrants, one from an agricultural background but with experience in one of the elite services. The garment industry is export oriented. One of the units has been in operation for some time and has already a market for its goods, whilst the other showed nominal profits in its first year of production. Profits in the high risk industry (Table 5.9) were substantial and occasionally equalled the risk ratio, devised for determining financial risk. In terms of performance, even in the high risk area, it was doubtful whether the pay back period in most cases would be more than two years.

Fifth Group
The group on average had assets of Rs 3 million each. They were thus firmly in the large corporate sector. Once again the pattern was the predominance of the textile industry, and again the negligible amount of textile investment in the 1960s leading to a 'gold rush' in the 1970s. The other industries predominant in this group are steel rerolling, metal machinery, and electric fans. The entire range may be seen in Table 5.10. The requirement for industry does not vary and because of the nature of assets most of the entrepreneurs were in the low to medium risk category (Table 5.10).

Low Risk. Of the 34 entrepreneurs in this category
of personal assets, 26 were in the low category, 6
were in the medium category and data for 2 was
not available. Of the 26 in the low risk area
one had a risk ratio of 0.02, one of 0.1 and 3 of
0.25, the rest i.e. 21 had a one to one risk
ratio. (Table 5.11).

Only one of the enterprises was in the negative
and its problems were incurable. This unit was in
the chemical and products category and problems
stemmed from the nature of foreign consultancy.
Despite ever rising demand for the products
(utilised for textiles), the production had come
to an end because of corrosion of metal pipes by
the chemicals produced. Since this was part of a
foreign aided project provided through the
government, the entrepreneur was desirous of, and
had a case of seeking government aid so as to
ensure the return of the foreign consultants who
had set up the enterprise. The entrepreneur had
already tried for two years, ever since the
problem of corrosion was noticed but efforts
so far had not borne fruit. The stalemate is
likely to continue. The performance understandably was on the low side but profit in absolute
terms was substantial in the majority of the
cases and equivalent to the original assets of
the owners.

Medium Risk. In the medium risk, the performance
was much worse, despite the fact that risk was
higher. For instance, where the risk ratio was
1:2.5, in the textile sector, the performance
indicated a return equivalent to 1:0.004. Only
in one case in the textile industry was the return
or performance ratio anywhere near the levels of
the other groups. Of the six in this group, one
was indicating negative performance, one poor,
and three average, according to standards
established for the present analysis (Table 5.11).

Sixth Group
The sixth group comprises of entrepreneurs with
assets of over Rs 5 million. The industries
represented in this category are textiles, glass
and products, steel rerolling, metal machinery,
agricultural implements, cycle and parts,
commodity processing and some other miscellaneous
industries (Table 5.12). Of the 16 entrepreneurs
in this category, 8 were established in 1970-79,
3 in 1950-59, and 5 in 1960-69. Textiles was still

in favour as the most sought after industry and the units bar one were in the larger or very large category.

<u>Low Risk</u>. As many as 12 entrepreneurs were in the low risk area (Table 5.13) and indicated performance ratios comparable to the risk ratios, except in four cases. The textile sector again produced a poor performer out of a possible 7 in this category. Two other entrepreneurs were in loss and one in agricultural implements had poor performance ratios. The performance conditions for groups 4, 5 and 6 are similar and therefore only the sampling is being indicated here.

<u>Medium Risk</u>. The remaining four were in the medium risk area (Table 5.13) and the performance ratios indicated that the payback period according to the ratios would be between 1 and 2 years.

Table 5.10: Fifth Group of Entrepreneurs

S. No.	Industry	Year	Personal Assets	Requirement for Industry	Risk Ratio	Profits	Size
1	Textiles	1950-59	30^6	30^6	1:1	750^4	1001-5000
		1950-59	"	750^5	1:2.5	20^6	1000-5000
		1960-69	"	30^6	1:1	20^6	1001-5000
		1970-79	"	750^4	1:0.25	Negative	201-1000
		1970-79	"	750^4	1:2.5	120^3	11-50
		1970-79	"	10^7	1:3.3	750^4	201-1000
		1970-79	"	10^7	1:3.3	30^6+	5000+
2	Hosiery & Garments	1970-79	"	30^6	1:1	30^5	51-100
3	Furniture	1980 -	"	30^6	1:1	310^3	0-10
4	Glass and Products	1960-69	"	30^6	1:1	30^6+	101-200
5	Chemical & Products	1960-69	"	30^6	1:1	Negative	11-50
		1970-79	"	30^6	1:1	30^6	201-1000

Table 5.10 (Continued)

S. No.	Industry	Year	Personal Assets	Requirement for Industry	Risk Ratio	Profits	Size
6	Steel Rerolling	1950-59	30^6	30^6	1:1	20^6	51-100
		1960-69	"	30^6	1:1	20^6	101-200
		1970-79	"	750^5	1:2.5	30^6	101-200
		1970-79	"	30^6	1:1	30^6	51-100
		1970-79	"	30^6	1:1	30^5	11-50
7	Metal Machinery	1960-69	"	30^6	1:1	30^5	11-50
		1970-79	"	30^6	1:1	30^5	51-100
		197-79	"	30^6	1:1	30^{6+}	51-100
8	Electric Fans	1960-69	"	30^5	1:1	20^6	201-1000
		1960-69	"	30^6	1:1	20^6	291-1000
		1970-79	"	750^4	1:0.25	310^3	11-50
		1970-79	"	750^4	1:0.25	30^5	51-100
9	Auto-Equipment	1970-79	"	30^6	1:1	30^5	51-100
10	Sports Goods	1960-69	"	30^6	1:1	30^{6+}	201-1000

Table 5.10 (Continued)

S. No.	Industry	Year	Personal Assets	Requirement for Industry	Risk Ratio	Profits	Size
11	Agricultural Implements	1960-69	30^6	30^6	1:1	30^5	51-100
12	Cycles & Parts	1950-59	"	625^2	1:0.02	30^6+	1001-5000
13	Commodity Processing	1960-69	"	30^6	1:1	20^6	201-1000
14	Miscellaneous	1960-69	"	750^4	1:2.5	Negative/Loss	101-200

Key $Rs.30^6$ = Rs.3,000,000
$Rs.30^5$ = Rs. 300,000

148

Table 5.11: Risk, Profit and Performance of Entrepreneurs - Group 5

Industry		Risk Ratio Low	Profit	Performance Ratio	Risk Ratio Medium	Profit	Performance Ratio
Textiles	a)	1:1	750^4	1:0.25	1:2.5	20^6	1:0.7
	b)	1:1	20^6	1:0.7	1:2.5	120^3	1:0.004
	c)	1:0.25	Negative	-	1:3.3	750^4	1:0.25
	d)	-	-	-	1:3.3	30^7+	1:1
Hosiery & Garments		1:1	30^5+	1:0.1	-	-	-
Furniture		1:1	310^3	1:0.01	-	-	-
Glass & Products		1:1	30^6	1:1	-	-	-
Chemicals & Products	a)	1:1	Negative	-	-	-	-
	b)	1:1	20^6	1:0.7	-	-	-
Steel Re-rolling	a)	1:1	20^6	1:0.7	1:2.5	20^6	1:0.7
	b)	1:1	20^6	1:0.7	-	-	-
	c)	1:1	20^6	1:0.7	-	-	-
	d)	1:1	30^5	1:0.1	-	-	-
Metal Machinery	a)	1:1	30^5	1:0.1	-	-	-
	b)	1:1	30^5	1:0.1	-	-	-
	c)	1:1	30^6+	1:1	-	-	-
Electric Fans	a)	1:0.1	20^6	1:0.7	-	-	-
	b)	1:1	20^6	1:0.7	-	-	-
	c)	1:0.25	310^3	-	-	-	-
	d)	1:0.25	30^5	1:0.1	-	-	-
Auto Equipment		1:1	30^5	1:0.1	-	-	-
Sports Goods		1:1	30^6+	1:1	-	-	-
Agricultural Implements		1:1	30^5	1:0.1	-	-	-
Cycles and Parts		1:0.02	30^6+	1:1	-	-	-
Commodity		1:1	20^6	1:0.7	-	-	-
Miscellaneous		1:1	20^6	1:0.7	-	-	-

Table 5.12: Sixth Group of Entrepreneurs

S. No.	Industry	Year	Personal Assets	Requirements for Industry	Risk Ratio	Profits	Size
1	Textiles	1950-59	5,000,000±	30^6	1:0.6	20^6	5000+
		1950-59	"	10^7+	1:2	30^6+	5000+
		1950-59	"	10^7+	1:2	30^6+	5000+
		1960-69	"	30^6	1:0.6	20^6	201-1000
		1960-69	"	30^6	1:0.6	30^6+	1000-5000
		1960-69	"	750^5	1:1.5	30^6+	1001-5000
		1970-79	"	30^6	1:0.6	30^5	51-100
2	Glass and Products	1970-79	"	750^4	1:0.15	Negative	N.A.
3	Steel Rerolling	1970-79	"	30^6	1:0.6	750^4	201-1000
4	Metal Machinery	1960-69	"	30^6	1:0.6	20^6	51-100
5	Agricultural Implements	1950-59	"	750^4	1:0.15	30^5	11-50

Table 5.12 (Continued)

S. No.	Industry	Year	Personal Assets	Requirements for Industry	Risk Ratio	Profits	Size
6	Cycles & Parts	1970-79	5,000,000	10^7+	1:2	30^6+	11-50
7	Commodity Process	1960-69	"	10^7+	1:2	30^6+	5000+
8	Miscellan-eous	1970-79	"	750^4	1:0.15	20^6	11-50
		1970-79	"	30^6	1:0.6	Negative	51-100
		1970-79	"	750^5	1:1.5	20^6	1-50

Tab.e 5.13: Risk, Profit and Performance of Entrepreneurs - Group 6

Industry		Risk Ratio Low	Profit	Performance Ratio	Risk Ratio Medium	Profit	Performance Ratio
Textiles	a)	1:0.6	20^6	1:0.4	1:2	30^6+	1:0.6
	b)	1:0.6	20^6	1:0.4	1:2	30^6+	1:0.6
	c)	1:0.6	30^6+	1:0.6	-	-	-
	d)	1:1.5	30^6+	1:0.6	-	-	-
	e)	1:0.6	30^5	1:0.6	-	-	-
Glass Products		1:0.15	Negative	-	-	-	-
Steel Rerolling		1:0.6	750^4	1:0.15	-	-	-
Metal Machinery		1:0.6	20^6	1:0.4	-	-	-
Agricultural Implements		1:0.15	30^5	1:0.06	-	-	-
Cycles and Parts		-	-	-	1:2	30^6+	1:0.6
Commodities		-	-	-	1:2	30^6+	1:0.6
Miscellaneous	a)	1:0.15	20^6	1:0.4	-	-	-
	b)	1:0.6	Negative	-	-	-	-
	c)	1:1.5	20^6	1:0.4	-	-	-

NOTES

1. In the case of waste recycling machinery the United States quoted $500,000, Italy 450,000, Spain 400,000 and Sweden 400,000. The United States' included an inflation clause.
2. Gordon C. Winston 'Over Invoicing and Industrial Efficiency' in K. Griffin & A.R. Khan (eds) Growth and Inequality in Pakistan, London, MacMillan Press Limited, 1972.

3.   Deregulation is now taking place.   This is
the current fad.
4.   J.J. Berna - Industrial Entrepreneurship
in Madras State, Asia Pub. Ho., Bombay, 1970, p. 88.
5.   1-80 exchange rate.   The dollar rate now
is Rs 16.00.
6.   G.F. Papanek - Pakistan's Development,
Harvard University Press, Cambridge, 1967.
7.   By labour employed.
8.   A.N. Armbruster & H.J. Mallin, 'Manual on
Quality Inspection', Lahore, Punjab Small Industries Corporation, 1980. Annex 4.
9.   Ghulam Mustafa Ghazi - Problems and
Suggestions for Farm Mechanisation in Pakistan -
Memo submitted to the Government of Pakistan, G.T.
Road, Mian Channu - Pakistan.
10.   Till very recently Pakistanis could travel
outside the country once in two years.   Anybody
wanting to travel more frequently was to seek
special permission from Ministry of Finance.
11.   Head of the extended family.
12.   Z. Altaf - Pakistani Entrepreneurs, Croom
Helm,London, 1983, the case of Lawrencepur at
Attock.
13.   More units have now come into production.
The industry is now trying to emerge from technological stagnation.
14.   Interview with an entrepreneur.
15.   The government plays a large part in the
fixing of allocation.   It seems this allocation
has not been modified though different category
of permissions have enabled entrepreneurs, at least
some of them, extra finances.   These have been
entrepreneurs with some 'pull'.
16.   Dues and cesses like the social welfare
(Health), Education, old age benefit etc.
17.   Thomas A. Timberg - 'Industrial Entrepreneurship among the Trading Communities of India:
How the Pattern Differs', Economic Development
Report No.136, Harvard University, 1969. p. 112.
18.   Ibid. pp. 112-114 passim.
19.   Thomas A. Timberg, 'Industrial Entrepreneurship among the Trading Communities of India'
p. 113.
20.   Zaigham M. Rizvi - The Cotton Textile
Industry in Pakistan, Karachi, Industrial Development Bank of Pakistan, 1978. pp. 108-111.
21.   Tariff protection stands at 86% ad valorem
plus 20% sales tax.

22.   The Government of Pakistan provided direct subsidy for purchase of raw cotton despite the fact that cotton prices had been kept artificially low.

Chapter Six

ENTREPRENEURIAL PERFORMANCE

Variability in Performance

The profits and indeed the overall performance
indicates a high degree of variability between the
various categories of entrepreneurs, as well as
between entrepreneurs within the same category
whether we see it by size or by industrial classification. Explanation of this variability in
performance needs to be amplified. It is proposed
to consider this variability by analysing the
reasons for:

(1) Profitability and excellent performance
as seen by the entrepreneurs.

(2) Analysing the consequences of and results
of government incentives; and

(3) How uncertainty and risk created in the
real world either as a result of the government or
due to market conditions were met by the entrepreneurs. What entrepreneurial response redressed
any imbalance thus created in the system?

Entrepreneurs' Reasons for Success

Entrepreneurs were put an open ended question
towards the end of the interview eliciting reasons
for success. No indication was given as to the
kind of response needed. The majority of them gave
multiple responses and indicated a sharpness for
market requirements. Of those giving this response
65 entrepreneurs were in the small sector, 37 in
the medium sector and 42 in the large sector
(Table 6.1).

Since multiple responses were possible, some
of the more aware gave a number of reasons while
others gave a single response. The significant
points to be kept in mind pertain to (a) the
unawareness of reasons for success does not mean
that the response may not have been made and

(b) that the indication of the reasons for success
did not exclude the other reasons. All that could
be deduced was that certain entrepreneurs saw
certain specific reasons for their success. So
the insight that could possibly be developed needs
to be carefully balanced between absolute and
relative knowledge. The responses to that extent
would indicate merely the fact that although certain
economic concepts were utilised, the entrepreneurs
were not aware of these and did not consciously
maximise their objectives.

Table 6.1: Reasons for Success

S.No.	Reasons	Response
1	Supernatural Help	25
2	Market Demand	144
3	Hardwork and Personal Effort	130
4	Better Technology	114
5	Better Quality	124
6	Price Competitive	106
7	Human Relations	17

Market Demand. Table 6.1 gives the responses of the
entrepreneurs. Response for market demand at 144
indicates that the majority of the entrepreneurs
were aware of what goods were required in the market
place. They may not have been aware of the quantity
but the 'gap awareness' was there. Initial tenta-
tive steps led to subsequent increases in production. Although a time dimension and stage by stage
growth of the firm was not procured it was noticed
that frequently a small initial start ended up ten
years or more in the large corporate sector. A
humble beginner in group 1 (Table 5.2) for instance
starting with initial assets of Rs 500 in 1960-69,
did by 1979-80 reach the industrial zenith and did
have an enterprise which employed 5000± employees.
In fact the firm was considered important enough
to be nationalised in 1972-73, whereupon the entrepreneur moved to the Middle East where his two sons
set up a similar metal machinery firm and he himself
started from scratch about 20 miles from the former
site. In 1977-78, after the political turmoil, the
firm was one of two units to be denationalised. The
performance ratio (Table 5.3) was 1:6000. In fact
of the six entrepreneurs in this group three were in

the large corporate size, two were in the medium
and only one was still small by employee category.
Such instances are common, where an entrepreneur
initiated from very humble beginnings and moved to
the large corporate sector (Tables 5.2 to 5.13).

If the level of knowledge and the state of the
art left much to be desired how can this phenomenon
be explained? The answer lies in the complexity of
market size and structure. Firstly the conven-
tional statistical method of computing demand by the
level of imports leaves much to be desired. Kilby
appreciated this in Nigeria when he identified four
submarkets in the bread industry (1). The low level
of per capita income, the regional differences in
purchasing power, and the rural-urban gap, all
affect demand. It is virtually impossible to
assess, for instance, the intensity of desire for
modern goods in rural Punjab. Complexities of
determining aggregate demand, individual consumer
preferences and behaviour are difficult to
ascertain. In some uncanny way the entrepreneur who
develops and grows with the consumer nuances, who
understands the implications of development projects,
who can realise the geographic spread because of a
new road to a rural area, does have high profits.
The consumer on the other hand relishes personal
relationships. He is not the impersonal consumer
in a departmental store. Even in the capital goods
industry, the farmer would rely on credibility of
entrepreneur and not on the brand name of a machine.
That is why in Okara, the indigenous sewing machine
industry can drive a nail into multinational
(Singer, Toyota etc.) competition. Price plus
certain intangibles influence consumer behaviour.
In fact there are various levels of demand.

In the urban areas and for 'improved' markets,
the products of the large corporate sector assume
importance. Given the taxation policies and the ban
of import goods, this sector entrepreneur receives
rich rewards. Whereas in the sub markets, demand-
price may be subjected to severe competition, in
the modern sector this is rarely so. Cartels,
oligopolies and collusive behaviour, do exist.
Common fronts are forged to induce government policy
in directions beneficial to the entrepreneur.

So when awareness of knowledge was indicated
by the entrepreneurs it was as they understood the
market, not as import substitution or as aggregate
demand is computed.

There are virtually no marketing channels
either. The only industry where marketing channels

are in existence is the footwear industry where
competition between a multinational and two
corporate sector enterprises assumes proportions
which are extremely valuable for the consumer.
Vendors, in the consumer goods, do help to extend
the market. The non-existence of marketing
channels helps to reduce cost for the manufacturing
industries. Many of them do 'gate trading' and
occasionally push sales, utilising informal
channels.

Hardwork and Personal Effort. At 130, this response
was second to market demand. Since the majority of
the entrepreneurs were from the Punjab and the
majority of them were craftsman/economic entrepreneur and progressive entrepreneur, this attitude
towards work was not surprising. Punjabis, for
unaccounted reasons, enjoy the reputation of being
extremely hardworking. This follows, probably,
from the extremely difficult nature of agricultural
work which made the Indus Basin the grainery for
undivided India. For the economic entrepreneur hard
work and personal effort would indicate involvement
with production, a pride in one's work, more a case
of an artist, waiting once the quality and trait
stand established, to be picked up by customers.
The 70 respondents from the small sector would
pride themselves in their work. The 35 in the
progressive sector would be balancing towards
market requirements as well as their own work.
Typically these would be entrepreneurs who have
progressed out of economic entrepreneurship, someone
whose word would be law. The 25 in the large
corporate sector would have a completely different
idea of hard work. Typically this would be keeping
contacts in order, managing the marketing side,
influencing policy decisions. Their quality
products would depend on, not their own ability but
the ability of the hiring of such factors of production as they would consider critical. This is an
improvement. Previously the 'critical' factor was
not there. All the production factors were hired.
Over the years, they may not have learnt to set
the thing right, but they do have (a) an ability to
diagnose what is going wrong and (b) an ability to
determine how to correct the problem.

Production Oriented. A further distinction between
two kinds of entrepreneurs needs to be pointed out.
These two categories are the production oriented
and the market oriented entrepreneurs. The

The production oriented entrepreneurs would normally be those given to getter technology utilisation, better quality. These would be found in all categories of entrepreneurs. But the lowest level, the craftsman/entrepreneur, would seem to be prominent in this category. The responses for better technology and better quality were 124 and 114 respectively, indicating that there was a high positive correlation between them.

Table 6.2: Entrepreneurial Response for Quality and Technology

	Size of Firms by Employment		
	Small (0-50)	Medium (51-200)	Large (201+)
Better Quality	49	33	42
Better Technology	44	29	41

The production oriented entrepreneurs, conscious of both quality and quantity, were strongly placed in all three categories. To the economic, progressive and political entrepreneurs the responses meant different means to achieving firm or corporate objectives. For the craftsman entrepreneur it meant excelling in the production and skilled art. For the progressive entrepreneur it meant not only understanding the skills as a modern corporate entrepreneur but also knowing the skills. A skilled entrepreneur, who understood the implications of quality and technology and who was prepared to push technological frontiers, was an innovator in the Schumpeterian sense. The machine was not seen as a 'unitary product' creating means but as capable of doing many functions besides those listed in official brochures. Such entrepreneurs emerged from technical and industry experience oriented backgrounds. In many ways these entrepreneurs blended the modern with the traditional.
    The political entrepreneurs response to better quality and better technology was not based on intrinsic/acquired production skills but on placing the 'machine reputation' of various Western countries. This led to reputation list compilation. For instance in the bread industry, the check list

was Switzerland, the U.K. and Russia. And when the
option was Russia, the decision rested on why not
local fabrication, which was many times cheaper and
repair facilities being available. So to the
political entrepreneur it meant getting hold of the
scarcest good and the best possible technology.
This was only possible by having either a 'clout'
or an association with the bureaucracy. Normally
a bit of both helped. The clout used as a sword of
democles on the bureaucracy.

Price Competitive. As many as 106 entrepreneurs
provided this as a response. Despite the nature of
protection there was still a limit to price in the
market place. Except for the footwear industry,
price wars are unheard of in Pakistan. There are
no consumer welfare societies and no statutory
protection and no Trade Description Act for the
benefit of the consumer. How then çan the entrepreneur talk of price competition. Where a brand
name has not been established and the product was
sold under a generic product name the price was
lower. Artificial scarcities are created to push
prices, and even where the government keeps a
strict control, as in the cycle industry, it is
unable to check prices. As already pointed out
elsewhere, there were substantial price differences
between the two products manufactured on either
side of the Pakistan-India border, the significant
difference being in the investment policies which
affected the overall industrial competitive
policies.
     In the Bazaar type markets i.e. where the
economic entrepreneurs operate, prices were worked
out differently. Modern concepts were not in
operation. There was no value to self effort. The
only costs to cater for were raw materials and
power overheads. Machine time was not calculated,
human endeavour not included, premium for unsocial
working hours unheard off. Typically, for the
economic entrepreneurs work starts at first light
and ends at last light. If there was more work,
the hours were even further extended. Regular
customers' needs were to be met. Since the relationship was personal, what happened in the economy
was not reflected in the pricing or costing. The
'kills' in this sector were made not only when
innovative premium was added to a product but when
requirement by a consumer was at a premium i.e. a
diesel engine water pump for the agriculturist at
sowing time. The consumer's requirements had to be

weighed. That was why an almost 'vendor' kind of
market place was in operation (in fact still is)
where the goods have no fixed price and bargaining
matters.

For the progressive entrepreneur there is a
different yardstick. Operating for a higher share
in the world markets (cutlery, sports, leather and
products) their efficiency and pricing would be
what the international market determines. Their
real source of profits was from the various export
subsidies provided by the government. To encourage
export, capital was/is priced at discriminatory
lower levels (i.e. credit for export was at 3 per cent
while the normal interest rate was 20%). This
discrimination was also visible in project aid (2)
available in the earlier years of industrialisation.
Even now China provides machinery at one 1/4 per cent
repayment after 40 years as against some countries
who do so at 8% or more with shorter repayment
period.

Supernatural Help. Table 6.1 indicates the entrepreneurs' response. At least 25 per cent entrepreneurs
gave this response. This is consistent with the
Islamic concept - all benefits flow from the
Almighty. The entrepreneurs with this response were
mostly in the small sector. On analyses it meant
produce and leave the rest to the will and strength
of the supernatural. Thus 18 were in the small
sector, five in the medium sector and two in the
large sector (borderline with medium sector). Some
of the entrepreneurs strongly came out against
usury and held it to be against the tenets of
Islam. At least two of the small entrepreneurs were
exporters of high quality products to Europe and had
cracked the EEC market.

When questions were put to them pertaining to
special training, the answers from this category
were in the affirmative. It later turned out that
the only training they considered important was
religious education, which in Islam is compulsory.

The objectives of this category of entrepreneur were considerably different from the others.
These were (1) The fulfilment of one's own needs
in moderation (2) Meeting the needs of the family
(3) Provision for future contingencies (4) Social
service and contribution to the cause of Allah.
The Islamic orientation seemed to be extreme. But
two distinct features emerged after the interview.
One was the distinct ability of working extremely
hard and under unostentatious surroundings, and

second was the ability to keep their word which led
to establishment of credibility with all those they
came in contact. What was even more astonishing
was the fact that this kind of entrepreneur seemed
well satisfied. Industrial relations problems were
unheard of. Working together, there was no conspicuous difference, there was no way to differentiate
between the workers and the owners. It was a
shared world.

In marketing they had not lost a customer and
at least one entrepreneur was aware of the latest
technology in the industry in which he was involved.
Marketing ability was astonishingly high.

Human Relations. At least 17 of the entrepreneurs
(Table 6.1) gave credit for their success to the
labour force working in the enterprise. In Pakistan,
and possibly in other Ldcs, the labour force can and
does get violent. Despite the fact that Pakistan
has only a 2 per cent organised labour force
dealings during political turmoil become extremely
hazardous. During the 1960s, the labour force was
not given any protection which, led to general
discontent. In the early 1970s the pendulum swung
to the other extreme and it was the turn of the
entrepreneurs to grumble. In the late 1980s the
pendulum swung back in favour of the entrepreneurs.
Pakistan as such has not come to terms with the
work force. In order to maintain peace and harmony
all strikes are banned and with negotiation in the
modern sector completely absent, there is no means
of knowing grievances or even redressing imbalances.

The real wages of an already underpaid work
force were considerably lower. Every few years
survival response by this labour force leads to
violence. But entrepreneurs were now realising
the importance of coming to terms with the work
force. Most of these entrepreneurs (i.e. 9) were
in the large modern sector with the remainder in
the medium sector. In the small sector where
personal ties develop this problem of human
relations simply did not arise.

Motivation and Reasons for Success
How does an intention reflect in performance? To
check this the various motivations were tabulated
with reasons given by the entrepreneurs for their
success.

Work Independence. The responses to the reasons for
success were multiple (Table 6.3). First let us

consider the average responses which were simply
averages of total column responses. It was
apparent that market and intricacies in the market
were placed at the highest premium, collectively.
However, the highest response came from those who
wanted to work independently. These entrepreneurs
were not the ones to depend on personalised
attributes for their success. They believed in the
competence of the market place, so often held out
by the proponents of development as responsible for
misallocation and inefficiency. Papanek (3) argues
that lack of knowledge and foresight of the entrepreneurs (as decision maker) need to be augmented.
Besides the usual argument regarding inefficiency
of the market system it was felt that government
influence can determine industrial direction as
well as consumer requirement. Papanek's contentions
at a point in time may have held validity but the
main argument against government intervention and
interjection is that governments do not know when to
stop intervening. Like protection there is an ever
growing demand for limiting scarce resource and
liberalisation of economic actions becomes distinctly remote. By the creation of the 'ignorance'
image virtually anything in the Ldcs can be
justified. This indeed was and is a classical
argument. It may well be argued that it was a
case of the 'blind leading the blind'. There was
certainly no indication of shining light then or now.
    Where benefits or productive assets are
limited, the injection of government as a benefi-
cient godfather has always had catastrophic results.
Consider the textile industry where there was this
misallocation of resources by creating excess
capacity (4). Protection provided under the infant
industry pretext is even now in operation in the
textile industry. The classical situation now is
that for every problem encountered or likely to be
encountered, subsidies are provided for purpose of
raw material (5). So there are no limits to this
argument. Why should it not be argued that
entrepreneurs are capable of taking their own
decisions, within their own spheres of knowledge
and if they do not take 'correct decisions' as
determined by the market place, they suffer
consequences caused by inefficiency and ineptness?
With the government injection into decision making
there is no 'sufferance of consequences': in fact
for the same products i.e. cotton yarns of count
10 and 21, Khan found immense differences in
domestic resources costs and came to the conclusion

Table 6.3: Motivation Conversion to Success

S. No.	Motivation	Super-natural	Market	Hard work	Better Tech-nology	Better Quality	Price Compe-titive	Human Relation
1.	Inherited	8	42	45	30	37	31	7
2.	Make more money	9	81	64	64	68	64	12
3.	Security	5	32	26	26	26	24	2
4.	Born to do it	1	5	7	1	3	2	7
5.	Accidentally doing it	2	6	7	2	2	1	1
6.	Importance & status	5	35	31	33	33	29	4
7.	Happy & enjoying	7	50	47	38	46	38	6
8.	Get away from family	3	6	7	2	4	3	1
9.	Jobs for relatives and friends	11	33	33	28	29	20	1
10	Helps the country	15	95	91	76	83	67	11
11	Work independently	17	97	78	78	83	71	12
12	Experience	16	70	67	56	59	50	9
13	Any other	–	11	6	10	10	11	1
	Average response	6	43	39	35	30	32	6

that the inefficiencies were firm specific. In
examining the domestic resource cost (drc) Khan (6)
found that firms were efficient earners of foreign
exchange if the drc (7) was less than 1 and
inefficient if more than 1 (Table 6.4). Although
not conclusive as to the degree of inefficiency the
study does prove that firstly the small sector
(Sports, surgical instruments, carpets) were net
efficient earners of foreign exchange, secondly the
drc difference between the firms was not excessive,
indicating a lesser degree of inefficiency, thirdly
that the modern corporate sector was an inefficient
source of foreign exchange earning and fourthly
that the absolute inefficiencies were much greater.
The analysis does provide instances of state
intervention at the two levels. In the modern
corporate sector they have virtually controlled
every aspect from paper work to final export while
in the latter i.e. smaller sector the state has
intervened only to keep check on quality control.
The effects of state intervention has led to misallocation of resources as well as inefficiency
within the system. With the existence of barriers
to entry inefficient firms have been allowed to
remain in business.

The response from entrepreneurs indicates
awareness of situations in the market - the supply
and demand factors and the critical price signals.
There certainly is no substitute to learning from
an operative market system. To assume that after
a period of time, market knowledge will improve
suo motto in entrepreneurs not used to price
signals is difficult to accept (8).

An analysis of the entrepreneurs' responses
indicates that 22 out of the 33 in the economic
sector had provided this response, while of the
progressive, 15 out of 19, and of the political
entrepreneurs only 9 had provided this response
i.e. a declining trend from small to large sector,
the irresistible conclusion being that entrepreneur competitive strength and efficiency from the
market is reflected in price, quality and
innovative technology. To survive the entrepreneur
needs to be up and about, the information systems
utilised being more informal, more personalised.
The entrepreneurs' 'ears and eyes' provide the
information and their own personal skills and
abilities determine the response. To stay ahead
they need to achieve improvements in products.
For the progressive entrepreneurs the response has
to be more 'energetic' especially if they were

Table 6.4: Domestic Resource Cost of Selected Products

S.No.	Firm	Product	DRC	Location	Established
1.	Nagina ...	Cotton Yarn 10 Count	.39	Swat	1960-69
2.	Adamjee ...	Cotton Yarn 10 Count	-1.22	Karachi	1950-59
3.	Ayesha ...	Cotton Yarn 10 Count	7.48	Lahore	1960-69
4.	Nagina ...	Cotton Yarn 21 Count	.40	Swat	1960-69
5.	Ayesha ...	Cotton Yarn 21 Count	1.45	Lahore	-
6.	Jubilee ...	Cotton Yarn 21 Count	1.12	Karachi	1950-59
7.	Gul Ahmed ...	Cotton Yarn 21 Count	.49	Karachi	1950-59
8.	Jubilee ...	Grey Cloth	.27	Karachi	1950-59
9.	Adamjee ...	Grey Cloth	.56	Karachi	1950-59
10.	Gul Ahmed ...	Grey Cloth	1.07	Karachi	1950-59
11.	Gul Ahmed ...	Towels	.49	Karachi	1950-59
12.	Mohammadi ...	Towels	.69	Karachi	1950-59
13.	Pak Punjab ...	Carpets	.70	Lahore	1960-69
14.	Swat ...	Carpets	.76	Lahore	1960-69
15.	Khawaja ...	Tennis Racquets	.43	Sialkot	1940-49
16.	Shabbir ...	Tennis Racquets	.33	Sialkot	1940-49
17.	Hilbro ...	Surgical Instruments	.42	Sialkot	1940-49
18.	Elahi ...	Surgical Instruments	.77	Sialkot	1940-49

operating in internal and external markets. In the
case of the electric fan and metal machinery industries such competitive pressures led to product
innovation. Since entry to industry at a lower
level was not restricted, these entrepreneurs
developed on the basis of their intrinsic skill plus
the 'opportunities' provided by the environment
i.e. industrial and fiscal policies. In the case
of the political entrepreneur the dependence was
entirely on the 'opportunity' provided by the state.
Cuddled and cotton wooled against any jerks from the
market environment the state acted as a 'shock
absorber'. The manipulation followed two or three
distinct patterns, the media and the Chambers of
Commerce providing the initial articulation, and a
systematic attack on the bureaucracy so that any
likely official policy impediment was counteracted.
This was followed by a stream of personal appoint-
ments with top echelons in which the political
entrepreneur never handed anything in writing but
merely brought to the notice of the top authority
the many failings which were not allowing them to
support to the fullest extent the government in
power. By doing so the benefits were many. Firstly
it was an assertion of 'loyalty' to the one in
authority. Secondly it was an indication to the
bureaucracy to behave itself (9). Thirdly it meant
access to influencing decisions in the way desired.
The method usually was to denigrate the previous
authority and to be a sycophant to the present one.

Having seen the response that different kinds
of markets invoke in the entrepreneurs let us see
which categories were motivated to work independently in the market place. All three categories
scored high on market demand while 68% of economic,
87% of progressive believed in market determining
goods according to its traditions and rules, and
78% of the political entrepreneurs did not relish
the idea of competing with the foreign sector in
the home market. They wanted that market for
themselves and despite the number of corporate
manufacturing enterprises they managed a 'collusive'
price on their products. In fact this set up a
typical response in the power loom industry which
was developing and was a midway house between the
hand loom and the powerful modern sector. Utilising
locally manufactured power looms ....., 'the hand
loom and power loom industry now produces a fine
variety of fabrics ..... sarees, striped long cloth,
furnishing fabrics, table covers, curtain cloth,
cotton rugs and blankets .... it has been estimated

that about half of the domestic demand for cotton
cloth is now met by this sector' (10). The modern
sector has since met this threat by increasing the
price of yarn for non association buyers as well
as providing poor cotton yarn for such buyers (11).

Those entrepreneurs whose chief motivation was
the desire to work independently, to be masters of
their own destination, did score consciously and
heavily on all the reasons given by entrepreneurs
for their success i.e. hard work, better technology,
better quality, price competitiveness. Some of them
even attributed this to God fearing policies so far
as employees within the enterprise were concerned
i.e. a just policy towards them (Table 6.3).

Similarly price competition was also positively
and high correlated with independent work indicating
that these were undaunted entrepreneurs with courage
of their convictions and willing and able to stend
up to fair competition (Table 6.3).

Altruistic Motives. Two motives cover altruism i.e.
to help the country and as a particular extension
to a special case, provide jobs for friends and
relatives. There have been some objections from
economists on altruistic motives. A reference has
already been made to Pakistan (12). Since these
motives are non economic, reasons to explain must
necessarily emanate from non economic logic. To
do this one must go back to 1947 when mass migration of population, the largest ever in the history
of mankind, took place. What were the reasons for
this movement? Why should illiterate, unknowing
ignorant humans suffer hardships and move to a new
place, not knowing what was in store for them? All
personal belongings were left behind and people
literally came with what they had on their person -
clothes. It was not an orderly movement. Caravans
were looted, families lost their children,
daughters were abducted. There was no police or
military cover. Sacrifices of such magnitude can
only be made where there is extreme love for a
cause. Such indeed was the love for the cause of
Pakistan. That generation today holds the fort and
key to Pakistan's success. It is in this main
respect that the three categories of entrepreneurs
need to be considered. The strength of the motive
would obviously be different. The mercantile
traders till the mid 1950s maintained two offices,
one in Karachi and the other in Bombay and it was
only when the Indian Government enacted a law that
restricted their movement that they left India.

Some of them were apprehensive as to the viability of the new state. The progressive and economic entrepreneurs had no such choice. Their boats were burnt. So it was not surprising that there was such a response towards the country and towards one's friends and relatives. Of the two motives 'help the country' was at least three times the strength of helping friends and relatives i.e. aggregate response was roughly in the ratio of 3:1 for market, hardwork, better technology, better quality and price competitive as reason for success, indicating that entrepreneurs with this motive had a positive high correlation with economic reasoning. The preponderance of these entrepreneurs' responses would be as indicated in Table 6.5

The higher the relative value the stronger the motive strength. Thus market success for those helping the country the strongest response came in the political entrepreneurs sector. Such a high response had two reasons. Firstly the majority of these entrepreneurs were from Bombay mercantile traders and were close to the founder of the nation and initially provided the funds for the state exchequer. In fact one of these houses was the State Bank for the country. Secondly Muslim entrepreneurs all over the world were asked to come to the new land of opportunities. They did respond, though their sacrifice could hardly be compared with the sacrifices provided by the progressive and economic entrepreneurs, who also scored strongly i.e. 4 and 2.5 respectively, on helping the country. When it came to the question of providing help and jobs to relatives the response of the political entrepreneur was weakest, being strongest in the progressive and economic entrepreneur. There was consistency as the manpower requirement, at least at the management level, was provided by the extended family system. The score of 3.5, 2.5 and 1.33 reflects this consistancy in the case of progressive, economic and political entrepreneurs respectively. In other Ldcs the extended family system, on the basis of research, was clearly identified as a major obstacle (13). The evidence from Pakistan has already been identified elsewhere (14). The fact remains that the extended family system exists in Ldcs and in Pakistan and this system has provided capital and vital decisions at critical junctures in the life of the entrepreneur. To have a balanced view, not only should the expenditure items be identified but also the beneficial aspects be computed. Most of the

entrepreneurs were no longer single unit entrepreneurs but the extended family entrepreneur i.e. at
a certain stage, family members were encouraged to
strike out independently and therefore the extended
family forms a strong base for the supply of fresh/
new entrepreneurs. The nature of the help extended
varied, as human actions and concepts of 'help'
could mean a variety of possible actions. The
weakest link in the correlation was of course where
the jobs were to be provided by the political
entrepreneurs to their relatives. Modern value
systems had emerged but a significant and growing
number of family members were asked to become part
of a 'managing agency' system. They were thus set
up independently on a commission basis. The benefit
to the manufacturing entrepreneur of course was a
reliable marketing agent pushing goods into the
market.

Hard Work. Of those who provided jobs to the
families and friends hard work was scored heaviest
by the progressive entrepreneurs at value 8, and
least by the political entrepreneur at 0.75
(Table 6.5). What are the determinants of hard
work. For the progressive entrepreneur hard work
entails supervision of not only the manufacturing
process but also managing the office and taking
non-manufacturing decisions. For the economic
entrepreneur it meant being personally involved
in the manufacturing process. For the political
entrepreneur it was usually a complete isolation
from the manufacturing process, existing in the
'push button' executive offices and working on
modern managing concepts, believing in public
relations, wooing the bureaucracy and treading the
powers of corridors.
    The same sequence was noticed for those who
had stated that one of the primary forces propelling
them on was to help the country i.e. progressive,
economic and political entrepreneurs. The work
ethic pattern indicated by these values does not
indicate that those who had not replied in the
positive on any particular score were totally
devoid of that particular motive. What it did
indicate was that at that particular time that
motive was not strong enough to be consciously
related and therefore the probability of its weak
existence was likely. Such is the world of determining human motives. There cannot be guaranteed
an absolute existence: rather it must be considered
in relation to other obtaining conditions in the

Table 6.5: Motive: (1) Provide Jobs for Friends and Relatives, (2) Help the Country.

S. No	Success Reason	Economic Entrepreneurs		Progressive Entrepreneurs		Political Entrepreneurs	
		Jobs for Friends Relatives	Help Country	Jobs for Friends Relatives	Help Country	Jobs for Friends Relatives	Help Country
1.	Market	2.25	2.15	3.5	4.0	1.33	8.75
2.	Hard work	2.7	2.9	8.0	5.0	0.75	1.18
3.	Better Technology	1.27	0.96	3.5	1.72	1.0	2.88
4.	Better Quality	1.16	1.1	3.5	3.28	1.33	3.37
5.	Price Competitive	0.73	0.8	0.8	1.14	0.55	1.91

Source Construction: The Table is based on cross tabulations of reasons for success with motives. The numerator is the positive response and the denominator is the negative response. Ratios were calculated by dividing the positive with the negative responses.

environment.

Production Oriented - Better Technology. For those
who desired to help the country, the technological
aspect was highest in the minds of the political
entrepreneur, followed by the progressive and the
economic entrepreneur at 2.88, 1.72, and 0.96. For
the political entrepreneur the determinant of
technology was dependent on the various aid packages
available to a country. So technology meant
obtaining machinery from a particular country, not
the variations available within that country, it
being presumed that technology within a country was
uniform. For the progressive entrepreneur unable
to make a dent into the world of the political
entrepreneurs, it meant obtaining whatever they
could from wherever they could. Thus for a plastic
manufacturer it meant obtaining a 'robot arm' and
the electronic programmer and attaching it to a
vintage manufacturing machine, and utilising local
raw materials in conjunction with imported materials.
These were entrepreneurs with an 'eye', with a
perception. Living with technological details
themselves it was easy to identify these individuals,
living as they were within a few yards of their
factory premises, with offices within the factory.
Maintaining no regular office hours but a total
involvement they were in and out between meals and
maintained a very rigorous work schedule. The
economic entrepreneur existed on obsolete machinery
and basic tools. Machine technology was unimportant to them. Their existence was in their own
skill and craftsmanship.
    For those desirous of providing jobs to
friends and relatives the most conscious on technology were the progressive entrepreneurs, followed
by the economic entrepreneurs and the political
entrepreneurs with scores of 3.5, 1.27 and 1
respectively. These entrepreneurs were developing
an executive cadre and in doing so were moving away
from traditional organisational levels and into
capitalistic organisational structures. The
consultant shortage in managerial and executive
strengths would be satisfied in the first place by
relatives, in the second by friends and finally
from a source (15) once removed. There has never
been a case of a management job being advertised
in the job market. For the economic entrepreneur
the entire work force may consist of relatives and
friends. In some cases apprentices would also

emerge from a similar recruiting area. In the case
of the political entrepreneur, the recruiting was
normally done through informal 'milking' knowledge.
Any specific individual with a known qualification
would be picked up irrespective of job vacancy -
one was created for the extraordinary.

Production Oriented - Better Quality. Of those
entrepreneurs who wanted to help the country follow
a similar pattern as technology the political entrepreneur scored 3.37, the progressive entrepreneur
3.28 and the economic entrepreneur 1.1. The product
quality of the political entrepreneur was dependent
on machine paced technology and superior raw
materials (mostly imported) while that of the progressive entrepreneur was dependent on excellence
in product modification. Although utilising
machine paced technology, the progressive entrepreneur did utilise recircled raw materials for non
critical products. This was a natural corollary to
maintaining their production levels. Occasionally
this did lead to the loss of an export market as in
certain cases quality was not maintainable. For
the economic entrepreneur quality was dependent on
the expertise and skill of the producer in charge
(usually the entrepreneur himself).

For such entrepreneurs as wanted to help their
friends and relatives to be meaningfully and gain-
fully employed, the progressive entrepreneur with
3.5, the political entrepreneur with 1.33 and the
economic entrepreneur with 1.16, indicate that such
motives were conciously employed at recruiting time.
One would imagine that such a recruitment basis
could affect quality but this need not necessarily
be so. Such recruitment policies do reduce conflict
and industrial relations are that much easier to
supervise. It is normal practice even in the
modern corporate sector to have the entire work
force from a single tribe (16). The imposition of
tribal culture on the modern corporate sector
ensures, amongst other factors, a peaceful production basis. Not a single day, to date, has been
lost due to industrial unrest. This has prompted
three other textile mills to be constructed in this
area.

In fact even quality can be rigorously maintained. The identification by the work force goes
beyond the mill premises. There are as such no let
downs.

Merit oriented recruitment policies require
amongst other things an identification of education

and demonstrated or demonstrable ability. Neither
is there a desire to develop such management
concepts. Even the limited number of multinationals
recruit on the basis of informal orientation. For
them a raw MBA from a Western business school with
links in the country was and is far more useful then
a 'purist' with experience.

Market Oriented. Both motives, i.e. help the country
and provide jobs for friends and relatives, scored
poorly on market oriented policy i.e. competitive
pricing of their product. Given the ever scarce
supply conditions in the economy and the demand
factor which is ever increasing it was not surprising that the response was poor. The political
entrepreneurs were the pace setters so far as
prices were concerned. Multiple price structures
exist in the economy. The state subsidises flour,
sugar and essential commodities. Although essentially meant for the population living at the
subsistence level, this benefit is utilised by the
majority of the population. Of this sugar, industry
(17) sells its entire production to the government
which then distributes to the urban areas at a
fixed price. The market or the traditional supply
and demand factors do not determine price. Similarly in the durable consumer industry, the prices
of televisions and bycycles etc. were and are
determined by the government. Where prices have
not been regulated, the government has created
'Fair Price Shops'. For the elite there were
certain other 'canteens' where goods are sold at
less than market prices for certain categories of
consumers. Similarly the custom authorities sell
confiscated goods at prices ridiculously marked and
again these are meant for only those who have
access to these special markets. Once goods were
supplied by entrepreneurs to these elite markets
the pricing policies so far as those goods were
concerned could not be controlled, the usual
stance being that prices subsidised elsewhere have
to be borne by the general consumer. Suffice it to
say that with markets so unpredictable the majority
of the entrepreneurs depend on their price bargaining abilities for making exhorbitant profits. Only
in some industries, where competition, by virtue of
ease of entry, exists, was there any degree of price
competition.

Consumer demand has also been greatly influenced by the emigrant population. The earlier
values have given way and have been replaced by

modern values. The shift has meant induction into
the modern consumer goods market. The durable
consumer goods, the portable electronic gadgetry
which replaces the necessity of electricity-run
durable goods, have meant the opening up of far
flung areas. The consequences of this are very far
reaching for those who 'desire' on the basis of
the prestige of those who 'have it'. This has
pervaded all aspects of society. All this has led
to competitive purchasing and 'tasting' of modern
goods and gadgetry. In conclusion it may be said
that the imperfections in the market, plus the
capability of political entrepreneurs to further
distort the environment, provides little credance to
the price competitive actions to these entrepreneurs.

Profit Motive. Those who stated that profit was the
main motive gave the following five responses as
their reason for success:
    Market (81), Hard work (64), Price Competitive-
ness (64), Better Technology (64), and Better
Quality (68).
    The profit motive was strongest in the large
corporate sector in an overwhelming manner with
responses at a high level (Table 6.6). This
agrees with Papanek's (18) thesis where the majority
of the entrepreneurs were motivated by profits. The
political entrepreneurs scored heavily on better
technology, better quality, price competitiveness
and market demand and poorly on hard work. This
may be due to the fact that hard work in Pakistan
is associated with physical labour. White collar
workers do not qualify for hard work as such. The
progressive entrepreneurs were able to perceive
market demands almost as well as the political
entrepreneurs and scored better on hard work.
Their response to better technology and better
quality scored higher than for the economic sector,
yet it was not all that prominent. Price competitive policies indicated the lowest response, with
those who had not responded being more than those
who had given this as one of the reasons for success.
    The economic entrepreneurs scored heavily on
demand and hard work, indicating perhaps that production is increased as and when gaps are perceived.
They scored poorest on technology. This comes as
no surprise for this category of entrepreneur
initiates its enterprise from humble beginnings.
Unable to obtain credit from modern financial
institutions they make do with whatever comes to

them easiest, their forte being their skill and expertise, the ability to initiate and manufacture anything. This sector's pricing policies of necessity were based on the 'goodwill' of the large sector or what they could obtain when their services were required in emergency.

The strength of the profit motive in the political entrepreneur as compared to the progressive and economic entrepreneur also indicates that there will always be entrepreneurs believing in 'pure money' to stimulate themselves to greater success.

Table 6.6: Profit Motive Orientation and Success Reasons

| Success Reason | Entrepreneurs | | |
	Economic	Progressive	Political
1 Market Demand	2.77	5.0	6.25
2 Hard work	2.27	2.0	0.93
3 Better Technology	0.96	1.4	8.66
4 Better Quality	1.22	1.66	8.66
5 Price Competitive	1.22	0.85	8.66

Experience. Although experience may be an important factor in explaining the entry of certain entrepreneurs, by itself it does not explain the totality of the behaviour of entrepreneurs, the condition being neither necessary nor sufficient. This inner driving force may explain a vital portion of the entrepreneurial development of the economic and progressive entrepreneurs. The discussion of experience of entrepreneurs is normally within the production and technical framework: managerial and marketing experience is seldom considered. Marketing experience though could be considered as relevant to those who had entered manufacturing from trade. In a country where managerial research is more or less non existent, the trader is the only one with the pulse for demand. Since the kind of experience and the nature of experience must of necessity be dynamic and changing in its day to day context, what was the essential ingredient, the pivotal intent which enabled ordinary apprentices

to cross the Rubicon? Four such categories of
experiences were identified, i.e. apprentice,
polytechnics, self and the more prestigious technical education at well known universities. It
seems that all four had one basic desire - not to
be subservient. This needs to be differentiated
from the desire to be independent, as a stronger
pushing desire. For such entrepreneurs it was
not necessary to 'plug into the culture of capitalism' (19), the pet social psychologist's explanation being to describe a social psychological stage
responsible for this dynamism. McClelland's
achievement motivation, Hagen's inner tension of a
social group trying to regain its long lost
prestige, does not adequately explain this dynamism.
When the entrepreneurs were asked for their
reasons for success, these four categories of entrepreneurs answered thus (Table 6.7):

Table 6.7: Experience and Success Reasons

| Success Reasons | Entrepreneurs | | |
	Economic	Progressive	Political
Market Demand	2.0	4.5	10.0
Hard Work	3.8	2.67	2.6
Better Technology	0.88	1.75	10.0
Better Quality	0.92	2.67	10.0
Price Competitive	0.65	1.75	3.4

Market demand response was maximum from the political entrepreneur (10), followed by progressive (4.5)
and the economic entrepreneurs (2). The response
from the political entrepreneurs was not so much
due to superior market knowledge as it was for their
ability to manipulate tariff barriers. The economic
entrepreneur moves in a fragmented and limited
market and therefore has limited market information,
hence the relatively poor response. The progressive
entrepreneurs continue to show their strength.
        The economic entrepreneur with a response of
2.8 considered hard work as the essential ingredient
for success. Their long hours, careful working out
of the production requirements and personal
involvement stand reflected in the responses. The
progressive and the political entrepreneurs

followed each other closely, in that order, it
being certain that hard work held different connotations for the three categories. However the
longer working hours of the economic entrepreneur
and working in twilight buildings and sweat conditions are indicated.

So far as production oriented factors were
concerned the political entrepreneur was way ahead,
modern machinery and machine paced production
definitely leading to better technology employment
and output of better quality. This response was
on the low side so far as the progressive entrepreneurs were concerned and even lower for the
economic entrepreneur. A similar pattern is
noticeable for market oriented actions i.e. price
competitiveness.

Do the success reasons throw light on inner
desires? Do they explain the why and when? The
why part, in the past, has been explained by
various alternative explanations e.g., the profit
motive by Papanek for Pakistan, the socio-psychological tensions (20) by others. Other explanations provided are that this may happen by chance
or by accident (21). Both motives were specifically put to the entrepreneurs but very few agreed
with the given criteria. Such things do not happen
by chance. However the complexity could indicate
'a slight from some source', an immediate hurt to
pride etc. Although examples of this were
available, it would be too far fetched to genera-
lise on these limited responses. The five reasons
for success do indicate to a varying degree, the
skills, temperament, and capacity to work and save
required by an entrepreneur. A critical entrepreneurial mentality and all round ability seem to be
the essentials for success. The learning process,
unknowing and conditioned by the carrot and stick
from the market place, reinforces the pleasurable
and profitable process while by the same process
the painful stands discarded. The plethora of
possibilities was in the case of Pakistan quite
astonishing. For the political entrepreneur the
carrot and stick was determined by the state,
though the carrot was obviously bigger and better
and the stick came only when political factors
become involved.

Alternatives. Other motivating forces considered
were either social pattern oriented i.e. importance
and status, security etc. and non socio-economic in
nature i.e. accidental, born to do it or inheritance.

None of these motivating forces explain by themselves, even adequately, the reasons for success
but must be seen in conjunction with other motives.
Three of the motives i.e. 'born to do it',
'accidental that I'm doing it' and 'get away from
family trade', were so poor that they do indicate
alternative strength of motives. These, if anything, indicate the conscious desire to work and
struggle for existence, there being very few chance
happenings. The strength of the family system may
be observed from those who inherited the industry.
How did this come about, since there would be many
aspiring offsprings and the Mohammendan Law of
inheritance is complicated not only by itself but
the complexity is furthered by the modifications
brought in by the various sects within Islam. Thus
in Sunni law, daughters share is non-existent while
in Shia law it is very much there. If the extended
family system is not affected by modernisation, the
eldest automatically steps in and takes the place
of the father figure. To keep the family name
alive he has to ensure that it does better. The
alternative is, of course, and where modernisation
is in effect, that the shares may be equitably
determined to the satisfaction of all individuals
either by giving the cash equivalent of the
individual's share or by setting up for each of
the make children a separate enterprise. Even in
the large corporate sectors enterprises have been
apportioned (22).

The first five success responses for the
inherited entrepreneurial groups were: market (42),
hard work (45), better technology (30), better
quality (37), price competitive (31), indicating
that the inherited had similar strengths developed
by learning on the job (Table 6.2).

The last motive, 'happy and enjoying', also
had a fairly strong response indicating that once
they had taken up entrepreneurial practices there
was considerable satisfaction and enrichment in
the roles performed. Diversity and challenges
calling for extraordinary efforts even in a protected economy cannot be ruled out. The displace-
ment of market competitiveness by social status may
explain this phenomenon. Ambitions as such seem
to have undergone drastic changes. The ambition
of the first born entrepreneur is no longer to make
money but to have elevated status in society. It
is possible that in the next generation the motive,
'to help the country' may completely disappear.
Such is the effervescent nature of human motives.

What dynamic qualities can be underpinned by
the earlier discussion? There is no doubt that all
categories showed a high degree of either saving
potential or the ability to locate funds, wherever,
whether in the informal system or the modern
capitalistic system. Certain abilities and skills
varied with the level of and kind of entrepreneur.
Thus technological skills were most important where
the economic entrepreneur was concerned. Their
tenacity, their manipulative ability and their
capability at improvisation was astonishing. The
levels to which they can grow and the ability at
satisfying input requirements from entirely local
sources was an indication of their resourcefulness
and knowledge of raw material substitution. The
progressive entrepreneurs and the economic entrepreneurs had one common factor i.e. there were no
entry barriers. The two do supply a pool of entrepreneurs. The main distinguishing quality between
these entrepreneurs was their ability to move in
two different worlds - the world of the economic
entrepreneur and the world of the political entrepreneur. The progressive entrepreneur's knowledge
of technological production being no less than that
of the economic entrepreneur, and this coupled with
their knowledge of markets and social and administrative sectors, enabled them to move and benefit
from perceived advantageous positions. And finally
the political entrepreneur seeks and obtains the
benefits apparent in the management of administrative and social networks. The free market system
was completely inoperative. To maximise long term
benefits different kinds of barriers were erected.
Excess capacity was intentionally created by early
entrants so that new entrants applying to government for permission would be denied this opportunity, in short preempting competition and ensuring
that policies were such as to benefit them. The
management of import licence also ensured benefits
in the quality of the product. The political
entrepreneurs in a nutshell had to manage subsidised
credit facilities, to additional licences for the
importation of raw materials and spares, to high
depreciation allowances, to tax holidays and to
subsidised domestic inputs. This was not a simple
matter. Competition for these resources was
intense but White (23), calculating this for the
43 largest houses, found that during the second
plan period government agencies issued licences
for Rs 2968 million in imported capital goods to
non government companies. Of this Rs 1512 million

or 51 per cent of the total went to the 43 largest
houses. The aspiring entrepreneurs of Pakistan
were in competition for the remaining 49 per cent.
    Theories propounded by Hagens, Hoselitz, Weber,
and McClelland are difficult to implement in real
life. Hagen's suggestion to withdraw the social
prestige of a community in order to cause creativity
in it is difficult to conceive and implement.
Similarly the marginal segment of Hoselitz. The
inculcation of Weber's ethical values was equally
impossible to develop and convert into action plans.
To a degree McClelland's achievement motivation
(24) was the only theory which could be implemented
by indentifying certain achieving factors in every
society and teaching these to an identified group
of probable entrepreneurs.
    In conclusion, although motivational aspects
are important, definitve and determinate links
need to be established. Any training programme
devised for this purpose will be both time
consuming and extremely costly besides being
controversial until such time as causality links
are established. As a first step structural
problems may be attacked, in which an incremental
approach by the government agencies may be
developed. The incremental approach may mean
improving links between the various entrepreneurs
and the government agencies in which both are
mutually supportive, with the onus for positive
thinking ideally with the government agencies but
based on the entrepreneur's real world, the
assumption in this attitude being that realistically
speaking 'government's in Ldcs will continue to
have an egoistic attitude' of knowing more about
the assumptive world.

Government Policy - Effects on Entrepreneurs

Less developed countries have been obsessed with
the idea of industrialisation and Pakistan was no
exception to the rule. What was the effect of
such policies? Did they in fact create an environment which induced entrepreneurs to come forward?
All Ldcs when seeking entrepreneurs do so on the
basis of rhetoric and moral exhortation. There is
very little by way of analytical or empirical help.
Most governments devise policies at the macro level
hoping that that is a sufficient condition for
entrepreneurs to respond. The response invariably
has left much to be desired. Such was not the
case iñ Pakistan. There was, despite an overriding
preoccupation of government agencies with the large

corporate sector, a vigorous response at the lower
level i.e. small and medium scale enterprises.

The effects of six major incentives provided
to the entrepreneurs by the government formed a
basis for determining the effects of government
policy. These major economic policy measures have
already been indicated (25). The entrepreneurs'
opinion of government policy is based on the nature
of their experiences with the bureaucracy. The
immediate factor which strikes is that the entrepreneur expects the government official to be aware
of his immediate requirements. Given the fact that
knowledge will always be limited, more so in the
Ldcs, the knowledge level of the two sides is
extremely difficult to reconcile. This encourages
entrepreneurs to utilise other means to achieve
perfectly reasonable ends. As technology becomes
more complicated, as the input requirements become
more refined, so too will this irreconcilability
increase. This sets up different response states
in the entrepreneurs. So far as the political
entrepreneurs are concerned they have moved into
a position where they sweep whatever they can, which
led S.R. Lewis Jr. to state in respect of Pakistan
Industrial Credit & Investment Corporation that
'while it is a Government Corporation it has been
dominated by large private businesses' (26) and
this process gives them easier and subsidised (27)
access to foriegn exchange. They are now in a
position where they can influence the economy in
the manner they desire.

Political Entrepreneurs. In the sample the political entrepreneurs indicated their ability regarding
exploiting the industrial environment, tax holidays,
accelerated depreciation, reinvestment allowance,
import duty relief, tariff protection and import
licences received.

Political entrepreneurs utilised all the six
incentives provided by the government. However, it
is also equally clear that benefits even at this
stage are not evenly distributed, that besides
there being an intra sectoral rivalry, there exists
an inter sectoral rivalry for scarce goods. This
makes the job of the bureaucrat that much more
difficult. Now there has to be a value judgement
between powerful forces of the same sector. The
ultimate winner for these scarce resources, needless to say, being the one visualised as the closest
to the powers that be; so that in the ultimate,
entrepreneurial efficiency and ability takes a

further knock. So despite the fact that there may
be competent government officials around, the
decision may be based on factors other than pure
economic rationale. The net result for marginal
cases where the official is not quite sure of
the outcome, is to allow the case to float, the
entrepreneur with the maximum connective strength
eventually coming out successful.
Even amongst the limited sample of entrepreneurs' responses (Table 6.8) a definite pattern of

Table 6.8: Political Entrepreneurs and Government
Incentives

	Benefits Received	No. of Benefits Received	(Per cent) No. of Respondents
Tax Holiday	44	56	43
Accelerated Depreciation	73	27	41
Reinvestment Allowance	53	47	39
Import Duty Relief	55	45	40
Tariff Protection	57	43	40
Import Licence	80	20	40

preferences is discernible. Import licence for
obvious reasons is a first priority - both for
spares as well as for raw materials. In the case
of the modern sector incapable of perceiving
substitutes available in the local market this
becomes critical for continuous production.
Because of the nature of import substitution
policies followed, there have been balance of payments difficulties. The engineering and differences in other specifications, tool size, and spare
parts inventories pose further headaches not only
for the entrepreneur but also for the economy at
large. To be on the safe side the entrepreneur
needs to have a balanced inventory of spares and
raw materials based not on the production and demand
requirements but on the scarcity value. This
scarcity value in translation means that both the

time period involved in obtaining the spares be
calculated plus the time in obtaining the special
import licence requirement. In fact what has now
happened is that those who automatically obtain
an import licence do so and keep on clamouring
for more. The success in this depends not only
on proximity but also in continuous links with the
government official.

Inroads into official thinking can and do
create intentional errors and in conjunction with
errors of judgement can only mean distortion in
decision making and misallocation of resources.
But by far, the impact on the rest of the economy
defies calculation. It adversely affects the
development of and supply of entrepreneurs in the
short run. For the export oriented enterprises
where quality is dependent on the import of raw
material it may mean loss of an international
market. This would further reflect in the balance
of payments position.

Accelerated depreciation (Table 6.8) was
the next in order of preference. This normally
is provided where tax holiday is not in operation
and the majority of the entrepreneurs benefited
from this incentive. The 27 per cent who did not
utilise this incentive were normally operating in
the no benefit area i.e. well developed industrial
zones. Tariff protection at 57 per cent was the
next best utilised incentive. There are normally
two types of tariffs i.e. 'protective' and 'revenue
tariffs'. In theory the former are imposed to
equate the imported price of a commodity with the
fair selling price of the domestic competitor.
Normally this work was carried out by the Tariff
Commission, which is no longer functioning, the
functions having been handed to an anomalies
committee based in the Commerce Division. Despite
very high tariffs, initially based on the infant
industry argument, Pakistan has not been attractive
to foreign investment. The distortions in factors
for certain industries no longer holds water but
once tariff barriers come into existence these are
difficult to remove. There is no doubt that the
continuance of tariff barriers has encouraged 'over
invoicing' of capital goods in the textile sector
and encouraged inefficiencies in production. The
political entrepreneurs via their social networks
have managed to keep these barriers intact (28).

The other incentives are import duty relief
and reinvestment allowance at 55 and 53 per cent,
with tax holiday at 44 per cent. The political

entrepreneurs did utilise these incentives, though
even amongst them, there was discrimination.

<u>Progressive Entrepreneurs</u>. Despite their initial
drawbacks they did possess some advantages over
the political entrepreneurs. For one, these entrepreneurs could utilise consultants to supplement
their knowledge of technical matters. In fact
these entrepreneurs could determine flexible utilisation of machinery and tools, something that the
political entrepreneurs would find impossible to do.
Table 6.9 provides the responses of the progressive entrepreneurs.

Table 6.9: Progressive Entrepreneurs and
Government Incentives

Incentives	Benefits Received	Benefits (%) Not Received
Tax Holiday	18	82
Accelerated Depreciation	61	39
Reinvestment Allowance	47	53
Import Duty Relief	30	70
Tariff Protection	45	55
Import Licence	74	26

The progressive entrepreneurs showed a preference for import licence (74%) and accelerated depreciation at 61% followed by reinvestment allowances
and tariff protection at 47% and 45% respectively.
The analysis indicates:
The crucial fact of raw material. The progressive entrepreneurs were all keen to build up raw
materials inventories whenever the economy provided
them opportunities. The entrepreneurs were aware
that under conditions of scarcity they would not
receive the necessary benefits. Further the entrepreneurs did mention that import licences were
provided after: (a) considerable delay and (b) for
one shift only. The remaining requirements are
normally met from the commercial market.
Accelerated depreciation is probably the best
utilised facility and this because it falls automatically to the lot of the entrepreneurs provided
they are assessed to tax. Although this might
come as a surprise some of the enterprises were not

assessed to tax i.e. they are not on the tax rolls.
Thus, even if an enterprise is recognised by the
provincial directorate of industries, it may still
not be on the Inland Revenue rolls. This follows
from the lack of coordination between federal
and provincial agencies. It is also dependent on
the skilful manipulation of the revenue system by
the entrepreneur.

With reinvestment allowance at 47 per cent,
indications are clear that progressive entrepreneurs
do invest their earnings to a substantial degree.
The pattern of investment though is different.
Dependent on the demand of the extended family and
the degree of independence within the male siblings,
the reinvestment may take the form of new enterprises being formed. Curiously one would think
that in time, competition would reduce the profitability of one or the other but in actual fact this
does not happen. A system of informal subcontracting comes into effect between the two enterprises
with the flow of benefits following the enterprise
in difficulty.

The progressive entrepreneurs assimilated the
tariff factor as a means to quick profitability and
joined in the chorus of cries for protection from
imported competitive goods. Some of the progressive entrepreneurs complained of unfair competition
in the sense that the 'revenue tariff' on raw
material inputs placed them at cost disadvantage
with imported competitive products. The anamalies
committee also did not seem to operate in their
case. The irresistible conclusion is the inability
of the progressive entrepreneur to coordinate like
minded sufferers to the same extent as the political
entrepreneur. Though sometimes they were able to
achieve their objectives this was done at considerable cost both in terms of time and 'speed' money
paid for pushing papers forward. The remedy for
entrepreneurs in an administrative system which is
sluggish is practically non existent. Recourse is
then made either to pleadings, or to connections,
or to graft.

The least beneficial incentives were import
duty relief and tax holiday at 30 per cent and 18
per cent respectively. The entrepreneurs utilising
these incentives were those who had a string of
small enterprises and now wanted to move into
sectors where they could be assured of high profits.
As a result of this kind of thinking progressive
entrepreneurs are moving out of their traditional
areas and taking industry to underdeveloped regions

where others, especially the political entrepreneurs
are hesitant to invest. Why should progressive
entrepreneurs move to new areas? The answer lies
in a curious mix of inner desire and perception of
markets. The factor which reduces their risk is
the fact that their reputation is not tarnished.
Such is not the case of the political entrepreneur,
who in such areas would find it very difficult to
be acceptable. The progressive entrepreneur not
given to conspicuous consumption and with no 'alien
habits' is not in such a risky and uncertain
position. The progressive entrepreneur, present
as he is on the factory premises, may find a fair
degree of help from the area. In most of the areas
the fact of being rich is unforgivable and it is
even worse when that richness is exhibited. The
stigma attached to absentee ownership flows from
the historical land tenure system. Typically the
absentee feudal is personified as a tyrant - coming
to collect the benefits of a harvest twice a year,
the characteristics of the absentee entrepreneur.
The progressive entrepreneur does not suffer from
this rather unjustified name calling as the enterprise senior management stays visible and within
the proximity of the enterprise. The holding
company concept stands modified to a more personalised and informal management, the cultural and
technological uniformity being ensured through
initial training and grounding in the parent
organisation. The fact that there has been any
kind of response in this sector is itself an indication of successful inducement of entrepreneurs.

Economic Entrepreneurs. The economic entrepreneurs
also came forward to obtain benefits from the
incentives provided by the government. Sooner or
later the entrepreneurs in all categories do
benefit from the government incentive policy. The
direct beneficiaries, of course, are the one's who
can import raw materials via the licensing procedures. The others are indirect beneficiaries and
obtain benefits either when the government pursues
extraordinary liberal policies i.e. when the IMF
team is visiting, or when these entrepreneurs find
loopholes in import policy. Their's is a generally
one off operation. Table 6.10 indicates the effect
of incentives on these entrepreneurs. There is no
doubt that the government incentive policy follows
a similar pattern so far as the economic entrepreneurs are concerned. The difference lies in the

degree of benefit provided. Indications that a
large chunk of all benefits go to the political
entrepreneurs cannot be denied. The economic
entrepreneur is at the far end of the line. Two
or three things affect him all the time. The
psychological gap between these entrepreneurs
and the bureaucracy is the widest and since they
have less or hardly any 'clout', political or
otherwise, they tend to miss out on scarce resources.
What little benefits they have been getting are via
the Small Industries Corporation. The learning
effect of the Small Industries Estate cannot be
underestimated either. Entrepreneurs, because of
Industrial Estate Offices, are now more than ever
aware of the benefits which the government provides.
So even if the Estate Offices are unable to influence policy in their favour they are at least
capable of being information centres. These Estate
Offices have recently assumed some importance
because of the regular visits of the World Bank
teams. In the 1960s these estates were more or
less isolated and unimportant.

Table 6.10: Economic Entrepreneurs and Government
Incentives

Incentive	Benefits Received	No Benefits Received
1. Tax Holiday	19	81
2. Accelerated Depreciation	58	42
3. Reinvestment Allowance	32	68
4. Import Duty Relief	21	79
5. Tariff Protection	32	68
6. Import Licence	63	37

The economic entrepreneurs still operate under
conditions which can hardly be called optimal.
They are still subject to harassment by the agents
of the provincial and federal government. One
entrepreneur listed 24 agencies of one kind or
another with whom he had to deal. These were either
tax, cess or information collecting agencies.
In sum although the incentive policies were
operative to a degree, much more could be done to
improve and streamline their operation. The other
important modification required was in respect of

equality of opportunities for all categories of
entrepreneurs. It is difficult to visualise how
this could be done now that Pakistan has gone so
far down the line of import substitution, ignoring
Marshall's contention that nature does not make
jumps. These leaps or jumps could be managed, if
considered necessary and essential, the essential
management being of market enlargement, product
uniformity, specifications and regularity or
production schedules. But that would mean development from the grass roots. Incidentally it was at
this level that the most rigid religious doctrines
were noticed. Certain entrepreneurs believed in
utilising funds from their own sources and not
from the financial institutions, as that would
be usuary.

Entrepreneurs, Scale Economies and Concentration
Entrepreneurs have maintained that the variations
in costs between Pakistan and the international
market are due primarily to firstly the infant
industry argument and secondly to the existence of
economies of scale. Both the arguments however
fall short of explaining the huge variations. In
the textile sector for instance the infant industry
argument no longer holds. Evidence is also forthcoming that there are no economies of scale in the
textile (29) industry either. In fact similar
findings have been indicated for the steel industry
as well as the sugar industry.
    Most of the entrepreneurs felt that increase
in production was less riskier and safer merely by
duplicating production processes rather than
switching to a completely new set of techniques and
processes, the advantage of course being that when
market demand fell production orders were reduced
to the same extent. The risk was further reduced
by subcontracting a part of the production to other
smaller firms. It is in any case not easy to
indulge in expansionist programmes and acquisitions
of new technology.
    So far as the political entrepreneurs were
concerned creation of excess capacity was their
intention. This benefited them in many ways. The
structure of depreciation encouraged capacity
creation (30) rather than fuller use of machine
time. Since import licences were also issued on
the basis of one shift, plants which operated more
than one shift would be forced to purchase raw
materials on the black market at much higher rates.
The effect of these and other policies linked with

the subsidised foreign exchange was to create spare capacity. Besides being more rational from the entrepreneur's point of view it created more mono-poly power. This then could be used to impede entrance of new entrepreneurs.

Whereas the progressive and economic entrepre-neurs utilised their capital according to market demand, such was not the situation with the politi-cal entrepreneurs, the political entrepreneur's financial state in the enterprise being either limited or even non existent. High concentration therefore led to under utilisation. The irony is that the sector of the economy which was supposed to 'leap into advanced technology' was and is responsible for its sluggishness.

For the entrepreneur who was able to obtain a licence for import of machinery, a problem of a different nature had to be covered. This pertained to the 'geographical linkage' of imported machinery. Given the nature and kind of aid it was just possible that once the machinery was imported, spares and other requirements would be impossible to obtain.

Industrial Efficiency

The general idea about industrial efficiency is based on the working and performance of the large corporate sector. Because of the nature of aggre-gate data and the weakness in the data, the results can never be conclusive, probably one of the most important limitations being the concealment of differences that may exist at the micro level between the submarginal, marginal and more efficient units. The sweeping assumptions that are made regarding performance based on capital-output ratio, capital-labour ratio, and such other concepts on value added therefore suffer from some limitation or the other. From the entrepreneur's point of view these ratios for improving and increasing output, or increasing employment, or value added hold no meaning. To him survival is important and this simply means the ability to generate funds so that the enterprise stays on its feet. And crucial to this is the issue that production should continue, not necessarily produc-tion efficiency. The continuity of production ensures sustenance. Given the conditions, import licensing and investment licensing provide monopoly or quasi monopoly situations for the entrepreneur. Two categories which benefit from this are the poli-tical and progressive entrepreneurs. The former has this benefit regularly, the latter when the authorities and the powers that be get liberal. Entrepreneurial attention under such conditions is diverted from efficiency and production determination to other factors. These other factors could be administrative influence, political connection or the systematic development of profitable relationships. Since these other factors are in the nature of 'social relationships' these are time consuming and require different kinds of skills and abilities.

Therefore efficiency is determined neither by economic nor by engineering efficiency. Some reasons for this state of affairs are:

(i) Government regulations do not operate on an equitable basis. Some entrepreneurs are more equal than others. Therefore underlying conditions affect different enterprises in varying degrees. Surely then the most successful should be able to push out the less successful. This does not happen simply because today's successful beneficiary may not be tomorrow's. Again the economic entrepreneur and the progressive entrepreneur are very cost conscious and can 'eat into' the large concerns. Pricing policies followed are very rudimentary and made under certain assumptions. The progressive and economic entrepreneur does not price 'management services' into the product. So anything that they sell marginally above the cost of the raw material is in the nature of profits.

(ii) The expansion of a firm is tied to government policy. Entrepreneurs in Pakistan have suffered from sloganeering by politicians and economists. The stigma thus attached has worked to keep the industrial houses in check. The response from the political entrepreneurs has varied. Some of the, understandably, have entered politics, others have divided the firms within the family members and still others have gone into medium size capital intensive industry. So the economic situation that the more profitable firm would drive out the less profitable or the more efficient would throw out the less efficient does not hold water in Pakistan and one suspects this to be true for all Ldcs.

Entrepreneurial Response to Risk and Uncertainty. The two terms are viewed basically as loss oriented and not as Knight considered them i.e. 'the risk of a loss and the uncertainty of a gain' (31). The outcomes of the two need to be illuminated. In the context of Ldcs risk may flow from economic circumstances while uncertainty may flow from wholly uneconomic considerations. The power of people in authority over other people is absolute and real. There are no softening cushions, 'no institutions which can come in to safeguard one's' presumed rights. In that sense Ldcs, ab initio, have much greater risk and uncertainty in their environment than the developed countries. The mere indication by a powerful personality in the Ldcs could mean the end of economic prosperity. The power and authority structure stands undiluted and may even have been further strengthened by the continuous state of flux in which Ldcs find themselves.

To look at risk an assessment of economic factors in the environment needs to be linked with the entrepreneurial world. The manner of that coverage, as visible in the environment and from interviews with entrepreneurs, indicates:

Coverage of Economic Risk Production. The production of goods assumes primary significance. While considering production, two types of entrepreneurs figure very prominently i.e. the political and the progressive entrepreneurs, while the third is completely outside this discussion as these entrepreneurs are not dependent on either import licences, or on capital goods import. The involvement of the progressive entrepreneur is also only partial, in as much as flexibility allows him usage of local raw materials. To keep production going the first and almost absolute requirement is to obtain import licences. This is done both at the personal level, as well as at a collective level i.e. through the various associations and Chambers. Since foreign exchange is limited, each sector seeks a bigger slice of the cake. At the individual level licences of all kinds irrespective of requirements are sought so that an inventory of spares or scarce factors is built up. This understandably pushes up costs.

Profitability thus turns out to be a function not of economic factors but of obtaining licences and keeping production going. This is the criticism most often voiced by economists (32).

Markets. The rationale for import substitution has been held out to be the creation of markets by imported goods. In countries where retailing is not done by chain stores and where markets are fragmented there are reasonably good grounds for this argument. However, the entrepreneur realises that this risk can be covered either by asking governments to build tariff barriers or by seeking the complete ban of imports of the competing articles. The political entrepreneur manages to obtain such insurance and the progressive entrepreneur covers it up in two ways. Firstly they continue to demand what the political entrepreneur obtains almost by right and secondly they undercut their competition by selling through the hawker markets, where prices for consumers are attractive - a feature of all markets in Pakistan being that the hawkers with their goods are selling in front of their main business/trading competitors. Since overheads are minimal, the goods are priced much lower. These retail outlets provide an excellent insurance against failure, the selling practices of the hawkers being much more aggressive. Nowadays even durable consumer goods i.e. locally made washing machines, water pumps etc. are being sold by the roadside.

In Ldcs fragmented markets do develop in uncanny ways. The market for electronics, for instance, developed initially with free radio/wireless sets (one band to catch local radio) given by the U.S. as part of a village aid package. This led to a boost in the purchase of sophisticated electronic goods. All of a sudden the wireless provided a means of entertainment. The fact that none of the local entrepreneurs were able to take advantage of this development indicates, on occasions, the lack of perceptiveness of the entrepreneurs and the poorness of the government functionaries in identifying and stimulating the entrepreneur along these lines. A similar market in T.Vs. has developed and the government has again failed to cover the demand requirements.

The entrepreneur on the other hand, especially the economic and progressive entrepreneurs, progress in small steps. Markets are created step by step. Demand is normally met, despite production limitations, by either extension of production hours or simply by subcontracting to others. In the metal industry shaping and finishing can be done in a variety of ways. Machinery of all kinds is available in the market place and the response to any demand is normally met. For specialised work though, other limitations i.e. raw materials, may hamper production and limit markets. Normally this sector responds by substituting raw materials.

Research is thus based on trial and error and after
a period of testing the right or the nearest to the
original alloy mix is usually developed by these
entrepreneurs. So the infinite, informal knowledge
that these economic and progressive entrepreneurs
have, if collated, could be better utilised. This
knowledge, acquired over the years by back breaking
experience, works to their advantage and limits
risk.

The political entrepreneurs are opposed to
competition. Whilst a majority of the economic
and progressive entrepreneurs seek a fair deal with
imported competitors, the former seek absolute one
sided policies. The textile sector where one would
assume such comparative cost advantage, although
much flogged as an example, indicates effectively
the manner in which risk is covered. The sugar
industry is another area. Pakistan follows rationing procedures and refined sugar through government
channels (33) is only provided to the urban population. Yet the influence on the policies is such
that the government has been to date unable to
provide sugar for the entire population. On the
input front government controls the prices for raw
materials and fixes the prices of various qualities
of sugarcane. So the political entrepreneur does
not pay the price of raw materials as determined by
the market. They thus gain on the swing as well as
on the turnabout.

The interesting feature in the textile sector
is the competition that the political entrepreneur
is having from the economic entrepreneur (four loom
entrepreneurs), the yarn being obtained from the
political entrepreneurs by these four loom economic
entrepreneurs. One should have questioned the
probability of competition but the official
Industrial Development Bank of Pakistan report had
this to say:
'The weaving mills are definitely facing a
tough competition on cost front due to mushroom
growth of four loom units in Faisalabad and other
districts .... producing cloth without much
consideration to quality. They wash their cloth,
during processing, in canals, dry that in the open
and evade all government regulations and levies
like tax, excise etc. They would stamp their cloth
for any trade mark and market it'. So that while
barrier to entry permitted the political entrepreneur to reap profits, unprecedented, in the 1960s,
in the 1970s a competitive response from the

economic entrepreneurs has them worried. There
lies the strength of the market place and probably
the future of consumer welfare.

Marketing Channels. In Ldcs and in Pakistan there
are no retailing houses. Generally the goods, if
they are in demand, are sold at the manufacturing
premises. In few markets, namely, the shoe and
the tobacco industry are there any developed
channels/outlets. These channels or outlets are
normally for the urban areas, the rural areas being
supplied by the nearest urban seller. In some
trades, an agency system has developed i.e. in the
detergent industry. The agency system is also
fragmented and not developed as a chain system.
The manufacturing houses have, under the regulations, been allowed a commercial managing agency
system. Thus, all the manufacturers are also in a
sense traders. In areas where the demand is great
this makes for two levels at which the political
entrepreneur makes profits i.e. their manufacturing
profit and their commercial profit, which is
dependent on the way they can manipulate monopoly
profits and charge commission and expenses from the
manufacturers. Thus for scarce goods, the flow of
cash is from the market as well as the manufacturer (they themselves). This system is being
systematically exploited by the political
entrepreneurs.
     The progressive entrepreneur sells not to the
main centres but to the back street seller. They
do their own selling. The economic entrepreneur's
markets are limited both in the physical and the
product sense. The ambitions are limited, being
initially those of survival and subsistence, and
these entrepreneurs tend to hit the lowest end of
the market. In the ceramics industry for instance,
a member of the family would literally sell all the
goods in the rural areas. Since the rural economy
is not monetised, barter is the form of exchange.
For instance, metal would be exchanged with pottery.
For the economic entrepreneur profit would then
depend on the metal industry and the going rate
for different alloys, so that at this level the
economic entrepreneurs are in complex actions,
sellers, buyers and sellers again. Their knowledge
helps them tide over difficult selling times. On
other occasions they simply load everything and sell
on the pavements in heavily congested, urban slum
areas.

<u>Financial</u>. Entrepreneurs have always had shortages of financial resources to contend with. Barring the political entrepreneurs whose initial requirements were satisfied by the financial institutions in the early 1950s and 1960s the other categories have had problems with acquiring capital. There is no capital demand illusion in Pakistan. Given the existing formal procedures any project will be acceptable if it is viable. This in Ldcs is a grey area. Project viability and profitability, as we have seen, is not dependent on the economic reasons of a free market society. Project analyses have tended to bring in social costs and although attempts to improve this methodology are continuously made, there is as yet a lot of ground to cover to make evaluations credible. Indeed these formal procedures are operative only for those who are political entrepreneurs or who aspire to be political entrepreneurs. Their desire for money, colossal as equity and loan participation is, needs to be backed by as close an approximation of project viability on theoretical grounds as possible. Precisely every requirement is met and at subsidised levels.

The progressive and economic entrepreneurs do not go through this process. The progressive may do so at a much later date, when machine paced technology is required or when they compete for scarce resources with the political entrepreneurs. In Pakistan we have seen that the argument of shortage of viable projects is not acceptable. This argument normally stems from a bureaucracy that wants to justify its action. The argument really is who sets the priorities for industrialisation and the direction of these priorities. Should it be the state or the market? Pakistani entrepreneurs no longer subsist under ignorance. They are capable of locating what they require.

Economic entrepreneurs' risk undertakings (Table 6.11) were much greater than any of the other categories. As against 50% of the economic entrepreneurs using 96-100% of their own resources, only 33% of the progressive entrepreneurs and 43% of the political entrepreneurs used their own resources. For the economic entrepreneurs, 10% of the friends/relatives provided 26-50% of the resources and another 10% provided 51-75% of the resources, while 9% provided more than 76% of the resources. The thesis that financial institutions play the least important role in this category

Table 6.11: Economic Entrepreneurs - Financial Arrangements

	Percentage Resources					
	0	1-25	26-50	51-75	76-95	96-100
1. Own Resources	3	30	13	3	–	50
2. Friendly Relatives, Resources	70	–	10	10	6	3
3. Financial Institutions, Resources	77	–	6	6	10	–
4. Equity	4	24	13	3	–	54
5. Debt	57	–	14	6	17	6

was amply borne out when 77% of the economic entrepreneurs had no loan or financial commitments with
the formal financial sector.

For the economic entrepreneur it was evident
that equity and debt interact quite differently.
The extended family can provide various kinds of
financial arrangements, from outright grant to
interest free loan, to working capital. Normally
and under optimal conditions no formal contractual
agreement is drawn up. That is not to say that the
funds would be in any kind of danger of embezzle-
ment. Friends and relatives provided funds ranging
from 26-50% to even 96-100%. It is quite common,
where ability is not in doubt, and where friendship
and affection are based on a deeper human relationship, to set up arrangements to help someone in
distress. Thirty per cent of the economic entrepreneurs received such benefits. Forty-three per
cent of these entrepreneurs were in debt, 14% to
the extent of 26-50%, 6% to the extent of 51-75%,
17% to the extent of 76-95%, and 6% to the extent
of 96-100%. These were mostly short term loans
from scheduled banks or money lenders normally
carrying high interest rates. Where the capital
structure was such that the entrepreneurs worked
with limited working capital all kinds of market
arrangements were utilised to cover this
shortage. Raw material is obtained on credit
or raw material is provided and the entrepreneur
only charges 'labour cost'. But basically for
this category, no challenge is too big and no
work too demeaning. They accept everything that
comes their way.

The progressive entrepreneur's financial
pattern was different in as much as it indicated
lesser utilisation of own resources at 33%, greater
dependence on friends and relatives at 51%, greater
reliance on financial institutions at 34% and
greater debt at 63%. Twenty-two per cent of the
entrepreneurs had obtained debt to the extent of
26-50%, 18% to the extent of 51-75% and 15% to the
extent of 76-95%. Thus some of the enterprises
were highly geared. As against this 37% had no
debt (Table 6.12).

The progressive entrepreneurs' strength was
their ability in two areas: firstly at the production stage and secondly at the managerial level.
They themselves were capable of managing both
aspects themselves. These entrepreneurs operated
at two levels and were cautious starters, some of

them actually starting from no resources whatsoever. This is also the area where maximum innovative practices and intermediate technology develop, these entrepreneurs having adapted developed world technology to their own requirements. As an illustration, not only have the Japanese/German power looms been modified to meet their own requirements but in certain cases the capital goods themselves are manufactured and brought on to the market in competition with imported capital goods.

The political entrepreneurs are further down the scale. So far as own resources in this category were concerned 25% had 1-25% own resources, 27% had 26-50%, 15% had 51-75%, 8% had 76-95% and 25% had 96-100% utilising their own resources. Those utilising less than 50% of their own resources can be identified as the early entrepreneurs. As many as 52% utilised own resources. A large segment, 81%, did not utilise any resources from friends and relatives and 63% had loans from financial institutions. The debt pattern indicates that 76% have some kind of loan arrangement, of which 29% have more than 50% as loan (Table 6.13).

How then do these categories cover up their risk? Understandably the rational course is to benefit from the incentives already provided and secondly to devise means to push government policies along more beneficial lines. Since consumer welfare is totally unknown in Pakistan, whatever price is put on the goods will of necessity be accepted, for the simple reason that there is no competing product or competing substitute. For instance, despite a history of over 40 years in the cycle industry, the purchase of cycles is rationed. The price is almost double the price in India. Although the extent of distortion in policies in the two countries is not known, surely Indian efficiency, if reflected in price, could not be twice that of a Pakistani enterprise. It is here that competitive policies could do much to reduce inefficiency.

The area which has the least amount of government guarantee and cover is the economic entrepreneurs. How they subsist is astonishing. Their strength lies in their own abilities and skills. With loans from financial institutions at a minimum (22%) and that too only for critical machinery, the recurring capital cost is negligible. Similarly, of the progressive entrepreneurs only 34% have the requirement for regular outgoings to scheduled banks/financial institutions, as against 64% who

Table 6.12: Progressive Entrepreneurs – Financial Arrangements

	Percentage Resources					
	0	1–25	26–50	51–75	76–95	96–100
1. Own Resources	1	24	29	6	8	33
2. Friends/ Relatives	49	10	20	12	8	–
3. Financial Institutions' Resources	65	8	14	8	4	–
4. Equity	–	22	28	6	7	37
5. Debt	37	9	22	18	15	–

Table 6.13: Political Entrepreneurs - Financial Arrangements

	Percentage Resources					
	0	1-25	26-50	51-75	76-95	96-100
1. Own Resources	-	25	27	15	8	25
2. Friends/ Relatives' Resources	81	6	12	-	2	-
3. Financial Institutions' Resources	37	8	29	12	16	-
4. Equity	-	18	24	23	10	25
5. Debt	25	13	34	10	17	2

who are in debt, indicating that roughly 30% have
used informal sources for capital at subsidised
cost or no cost.

Uncertainty. To assess uncertainty a look at the
various non economic factors may be necessary.

(i)Political Uncertainty. The emerging nations have
this chronic problem and there is no way that
political stability can come overnight. Because
development creates different kinds of pressures
the entrepreneurs need to devise ways and means of
safeguarding their interests and assets. Therefore it is with the consequences of political
instability and the response of the entrepreneurs
that we are concerned.

Entrepreneurs most affected are the political
entrepreneurs. The lives of progressive and
economic entrepreneurs are not touched by this kind
of uncertainty except in an indirect manner. The
first tendency of any entrepreneur is to have an
effective relationship with those in power in the
here and now. They cannot afford to have relationships with those who have lost power. So with each
successive change in government, entrepreneurs
pledge loyalty to the existing authority. The
institutions most active are the Chambers of
Commerce and Industry where either the virtues of
the new policies are highlighted or the past is
criticised for some policy or the other. In Third
World countries merely the praise of the existing
authority is not enough. Politics demands the
renunciation of the immediately preceding government for ineffectiveness, corruption and all ills.
This suits both parties, the entrepreneurs as well
as the new political boss, the reason being that
no political boss or political party has managed
to return to power. This reinforces the political
entrepreneur's will and desire to be loyal to the
existing authority.

(ii)Economic and Administrative. In order to cover
economic uncertainties encouraged by administrative
policies reflected in raw material shortages,
inadequacy of licensing facilities, each entrepreneur tried to get, when the going was good and he
was in with the authorities, an exaggerated number
of licences. This enabled him to keep some
production material for difficult times. Although
this meant building an inventory at some cost, it

paid off in the long run.

To cover administrative uncertainty the entrepreneurs went into permanent or semi permanent
relationships with the bureaucracy. Even if the
entrepreneur went above the heads of the bureaucracy to the political authority great care was
normally taken to see that the bureaucracy was not
annoyed. The reality of the permanent face of
bureaucracy was and is an acceptable fact. At the
implementation and field level, the local bureaucracy is also to be carefully handled. Consider
the police officer who could delay safety if a Law
and Order situation developed, or the local tax
collector who could fill excessive production
statements. All of these are real world problems
and to cater for such eventualities entrepreneurs
generally recruit influential bureaucrats.

<u>Nationalisation Threat</u>. When fashionable politics
and fashionable economics have an interface, a
number of pseudo policies, justified by the rhetoric
of the politician, come into existence. Pakistan
had such a phase from 1972-77. While the politically created enterprises suffered state acquisition the economy accepted the challenge.
Responses in such cases were quite astonishing.
The growth of small enterprises kept the economy
in a buoyant state.

As a first response, economic concentration
was made less visible by reducing size. A number
of political entrepreneurs, but notably Adamjees and
Habibs, did this. The financial statements were
less ostentatiously announced and irregularly
published.

Secondly the more adventurous went into joint
ventures with foreigners, not necessarily multinationals. Thus joint private ventures between
citizens of Pakistan and Canada became noticeable,
with normally the technical know how being provided
by the foreigner and the finances by the Pakistani.
The existing laws and statutes provide security
to the Pakistani if he is in joint operation with
a foreigner.

Thirdly in certain situations if the entrepreneurs were threatened in physical terms there was a
case of flight of capital as well as flight of
entrepreneurs. One effect of this has been that
Pakistani entrepreneurs entered other Third World
countries, notably Tanzania and the Middle East, and
such First World countries as Canada and Ireland.

And finally the threat of nationalisation from

1972-77 led to the resurgence of the small industries sector. Entrepreneurs, of different categories, started thinking in terms other than size.
There was a more conscious approach. Yes, capital
intensive projects seemed to come into fashion.
But for once the feeling was that more thought and
effort was being put into the projects. At the
progressive and economic entrepreneurial level the
response was quite remarkable as they saw a remote
chance of the economy responding to their needs.

NOTES

1. P. Kilby, African Enterprise: The Nigeriaor
Bred Industry, Stanford, Hoover Institution, 1965,
pp. 42-43.
2. The nature of aid has changed from grant
to soft loans, to hard loans.
3. G.F. Papanek, Pakistan's Development -
Social Goals and Private Incentives, Harvard U.P.,
Cambridge, 1967, pp. 221-232.
4. A.K. Tareen Pakistan Textile Industry.
5. For no apparent economic reason a subsidy
of Rs.45/- per 40 Kilograms was provided to large
textile mills to make them more viable. This was
the result of the Production and Industries Minister
himself being a cotton and industrial magnet.
6. M.Z. Khan, The System of Export Incentives
in the Manufacturing Sector Pakistan, unpublished
Ph.D. Thesis, John Hopkins University, 1979, p. 252.
7. Ibid. pp. 245-252 passim.
8. In a competitive structure survival and
profitability would have high correlation with
knowledge but in an insolated industrial structure
energies would be diverted towards such policies
as would increase profitability without the balancing danger.
9. The proof usually comes in the form of
Presidential Directives, telling the concerned
ministry what to do. These directives are routed
through the Cabinet Division and regular meeting
between the Presidential Secretariat and the
Cabinet Division ensures implementation.
10. A.K. Tareen, The Directory of Pakistan
Cotton Textile Industry - 1970, p. 22.
11. Transpired during interview with an
entrepreneur. Yarn manufacturing by modern methods
is by complicated precision machinery and therefore
not possible for small entrepreneurs to enter this
industry.

12. G.F. Papanek, Pakistan's Development: Social Goals and Private Incentives, Harvard U.P., Cambridge, 1967.

13. P. Garlick, African Traders and Economic Development in China, Oxford Clarendon Press, 1971.

14. Z. Altaf, Pakistani Entrepreneurs.

15. A source once removed would need to be a person with whom the entrepreneur would need to have frequent contact and would be 'useful' in some conspicuous way. As soon as the usefulness of the source was removed the appointee would be terminated unless otherwise proving his strength.

16. The Khattak tribe was employed by the Janana De Malucho Textile Mills Ltd., at Kohat. The mill is in the high performance sector and is exporting its entire production of yarn, grey cloth, and printed cloth.

17. This has since changed and sugar industry is now operating in a free market.

18. G.F. Papanek, Pakistan's Development: Social Goals and Private Incentives, Harvard U.P., Cambridge, 1967, pp. 27-50 passim.

19. P.T. Kennedy, Ghanain Businessmen, Munchen, Weltforum - Verlag, 1980, p. 154.

20. Z. Altaf, Pakistani Entrepreneurs, Croom Helm, London, (reference to Hagen, MeClelland etc.).

21. P.T. Kennedy, Ghanian Businessmen, Munchen, Weltforum - Verlag, 1980, p. 154.

22. The Saigol family enterprises. The Saigols were amongst the second richest family by industrial and manufacturing assets. L.J. White places these assets at Rs.529.8 million in 1970.

23. L.J. White, Industrial Concentration and Economic Power in Pakistan, op.cit. p. 122.

24.

25. Z. Altaf, Pakistani Entrepreneurs, Croom Helm, London.

26. S.R. Lewis Jr., Pakistan Industrialisation and Trade Policies, London, Oxford University Press, 1970.

27. S.R. Lewis Jr., Ibid.

28. Their latest move in the textile sector is to state that in the textile industry economies of scale are only possible at 50,000 spindles and one loom per 400 spindles. The government has accepted this according to the latest reports. The manner of exercising custom duties will vary and will be to the benefit of the earlier entrepreneurs. New entrants will have to pay 40% custom's tax while all the earlier entrepreneurs will pay

15-20% as they will fall in the balancing, modernising category.

29.   P. Uri, Development without Dependence,
op. cit.

30.   The depreciation allowed for the second
and third shifts was half the depreciation allowed
for the first shift.

31.   F.H. Knight, Risk, Uncertainty and
Profit, op. cit., p. 233.

32.   H.G. Johnson, Pakistan's Development
A Case of Frustrated Take Off, op. cit. H.J. Bruton
and J. Sheahen are some of the other economists.
More recently A.L. Krueger, The Benefits and Costs
of Import Substitution in India, op. cit.

33.   Sugar is now available in the free market.
Controls have since been removed.

Chapter Seven

CONCLUSIONS

Pakistan like other developing countries sought the way out of its economic malaise through industrialisation. It is very difficult to give an absolute judgement on whether the effort has been successful or otherwise. Barring the first few years of the process, the effort has been very regressively implemented. Bureaucratic procedures have made this process extremely complicated. It is difficult to analyse objectively a counterfactual situation. What would have been the effect if a free market system had been allowed to operate? If barriers to industry had not been as regressively observed the industrialisation process would have been distinctly different. A different set of entrepreneurs would have emerged based on local or easily available raw materials. Competitive policies would have ensured consumer welfare. All in all a more socially just, not to speak of a structurally sound industrial sector, may have emerged.

Investment allocative decisions taken by a strongly entrenched bureaucracy have been proved to have distinct disadvantages. The inability to (i) gauge market demand, (ii) to determine inter and intra industry priorities, (iii) to opt for inappropriate and/or obsolete technology, (iv) to operate behind high tariffs, (v) heavily to over invoice credit requirements, (vi) wilfully to obtain obsolete and redundant machinery in lieu of what has been approved, are some of the economic weaknesses that have been witnessed.

On the non-economic side, the creation of a powerful bureaucracy, the wilful misallocation of scarce resources, the creation of adverse human values and the intentional criminal manipulation of the market system are some of the societal

problems that will be difficult to change in the
years to come. The creation of a negative list
may well be to allow trading profits to certain
categories of individuals.

The cumulative result of all these policies
has been hazardous for the balance of payments
as well as for the consumer. Unwarranted benefits
have accrued to those members of the society as
have no claims to hard work, efficiency, honesty
and tenacity. Social justice has taken a back seat.

Implications for Entrepreneurial Theory

Early entrepreneurial theories have no relevance
to the current economic environments of less
developed countries. This economic environment
could vary from country to country and when the
personalities of the entrepreneurs is super-
imposed on this, the difficulty in analyses becomes
obvious. How can the two be made to harmonise?
So far the emphasis has been on the environment.
Virtually no effort has been made to assess and
value the entrepreneur and to tailor the economic
scene to his requirements. A synchronisation can
only occur in a liberal system. When the system
is 'ordered' by a bureaucracy it becomes restrictive. So to the economic conditions must be added
the socio-psychological world of the entrepreneur.
This again would vary from country to country, and
within a country it would be dependent on regional
cultures. In other words a distinct effort is
required to obtain an environment conducive to
entrepreneurial development.

The internal world of the entrepreneur is
dependent on a number of values and attitudes.
Motivational analysis indicates the complexity of
the process. In other words the entrepreneur has
distinctly (i) economic views and attitudes, (ii)
social obligations and (iii) psychological motivations. Any one of these may energise an individual towards taking on an entrepreneurial challenge.
Theories to that extent have explained only
partially this phenomenon. Of the typologies
listed an effort was made to indicate the different
worlds of the political, progressive and economic
entrepreneurs. The distinct existence of each one
is fascinating. What is most appropriate to the
Pakistani scene? Is there a requirement for the
political entrepreneur and if so how should he be
regulated so that he is allowed to play a positive
and constructive role in society? Is there a basis
for the existence of the economic entrepreneurs?

Conclusions

Are they to be cultivated?

Risk and Uncertainty

Of the three typologies given, what is the attitude
to risk and uncertainty? In fact is there risk
involved? An effort was made to compute risk for
the various categories. Asset formation has
distinct advantages for certain categories of
entrepreneurs. In certain industries this risk is
virtually non-existent. The operation of risk can
be virtually eliminated. Uncertainty has other
connotations. When uncertainty is all prevasive
and enters the national life, the results can
be catastrophic. Everything can come to a stand-
still. The difficulties are normally temporary in
time. Should there be a more permanent form then
a situation of total loss can occur (like in East
Pakistan when entrepreneurs lost all their assets).
        The reduction of conflict and tension in a
society is reflected in the uncertainty and risk
prevalent in that society. Sometimes this conflict
is turned to entrepreneurial advantage i.e. gun
manufacturing entrepreneurs of North West Frontier
Province. The nature of feuds led only to manufacture of sophisticated gadgetry by the small
scale (i.e. economic) entrepreneur. One would
imagine that because of 'metallurgical' and high
velocity precision requirements this response
would normally have been in areas where education
etc. would be at high levels. The consequence of
such an environment is a flourishing gun making
industry and little else. The priorities are
attached to physical survival.

Economic Entrepreneurs' Risk

The entrepreneur's risk is highest at the economic
entrepreneur's level. The reason lies not only in
the complete and total involvement of his financial
assets but also in the lack of props that are
available to him. The management of social networks at this level is very basic. The entrepreneur does not have the ability to interact with an
alien milieu. Even if he does have this ability
the entrepreneurs have to travel some distance.
Financial institutions or other economic factor
requirements are not easily available to them. To
raise the technological as well as the general
level, extension policies need to be devised.
Once the level is raised, efforts of the entrepreneurs will depend on inner propulsions.

Conclusions

Progressive Entrepreneurs' Risk

The progressive entrepreneurs have over a period of time, broken away from their earlier category i.e. economic. Their's is a case of self-reliant industrial effort. Markets have been located by them. Much would depend on the value added to exports if the shift from traditional to non-traditional is to be made. A continuous awareness of the requirements of demands in the West has therefore to be monitored. For these industries to remain viable a research oriented programme for product improvement and innovation needs to be carried out. This is only possible at either a collective level, where all the exporters develop an institute of research and standards or if the government moves in. To take an example in the sports industry, product innovation has practically revolutionalised concepts. Some of these developments have been based on shortage of natural raw materials i.e. tennis rackets, some of improvement for particular kind of play. The users (players) actually serve the manufacturers by advising on improvements, which are then carried out, and tested by the players again. All this requires a different kind of handling and effort. This certainly is the weakest link. For instance, Pakistan has done exceedingly well in certain sports i.e. squash cricket, hockey. It manufactures playing equipment but they hit the lower end of the market. So player involvement and experience in the manufacturing process means involvement of user expertise. The writer is of the opinion that product innovation in sports could lead to Pakistan taking a sizeable chunk of the higher end of the market. At the moment, it is very risky for the entrepreneurs to rake on risky research activities, the commercial gains from which are not quite obvious.

Political Entrepreneurs' Risk

For the political entrepreneurs, the game is different. Brought in as an artificial appendage into the industrial zone, these entrepreneurs are heavily dependent on acquired production processes, managerial and coordinative requirements. It is like throwing in a swimmer at the deep end of the pool and asking him to learn to swim. Learn he will but occasionally some may be lost. Similarly some of the entrepreneurs have not only learnt to swim but do so very well. It is pointless providing them with 'swimming aids' when they are so well ahead.

210

Conclusions

Some of them have risked their assets, have
come through all kinds of uncertainty, and now
require a period of consolidation. A systematic
development of these large houses (entrepreneurs)
augurs well for the country provided there is a
shift towards self reliant industrialisation i.e.
the props given in the system need not be provided
now. In other words they have reached a turning
point in the process. The more confident, and the
more skilful and able this sector is, the more
energetic the entrepreneurial response. The pitfall
and danger, of course, is that being that powerful,
they can influence policies to the exclusion of all
others.

Political and Social Instability

A passing reference in the case of Pakistan regarding
reduction of tension and conflict needs to be made.
Pakistan is a special case. The country has to
contend with all kinds of secessionist and non-
integrative trends. Pakistan has managed its
political and social conflicts in a not very
desirable manner. Many revolutions in Ldcs have
to take place simultaneously. Political and social
conflict does dampen economic activity and therefore has implications for risk and uncertainty.

The political and social uncertainty flow
from policies which are not well thought out.
Wherever economic growth and development has
occurred, political and social lags have at some
occasion or another reduced the impact of such
growth and development. Involvement and awareness
of conflicts do act as partial cures for conflicts,
creating risk and uncertainty. Pakistan has
particularly suffered. A thrust on income distribution and egalitarianism may lessen the social
cleavages and to that extent economics must give
way to basic human need determinism.

Evidence, though, from the Pakistan scene
indicates that entrepreneurs are not risk averse.
They are willing and able to take up any challenge.
Their reasons for success confirm their ability
to respond to their requirements. They are in
short able to locate their requirements. It is
for the government and other agencies to see that
this is done in the shortest possible time or
at least to create conditions which are conducive
to the development of entrepreneurs.

The motives for the majority of the entrepreneurs were not necessarily economic i.e. profit
oriented. The motive to work independently scored

heavily. McClelland's High Need achievement methodology was not utilised for testing entrepreneurial motives. It is obvious that entrepreneurs who wanted to be their 'own men' could be identified in society and encouraged to progress to other entrepreneurial levels. It may not be possible to inculcate this motive but it may be possible to identify possible sources of supply and to try to establish causality responsible for the creation of this motive.

Basically less developed countries' economic risk is minimised by various government policies. Sometimes contradictory policies are propounded. Indication of these contradictory policies has already been provided. What is required is a method and bases for limiting uncertainty. Political uncertainty as well as administrative difficulties need to be minimised.

Government Intervention

A theme which is continually prevalent in the present work is the importance attached to intervention in the industrialisation process by the government.

Governments of the day consider that they have a duty of care towards their countrymen and the nation. And although most of them advocate a number of laudable objectives the actual action seems to fall far short. We have seen the result of volatile policies which have retarded industrial progress and increased uncertainty and risk. Some times policies have been such that governments have been unable to see them through, resulting in considerable time, effort and financial loss. Sometimes policies have been based on rhetoric and moral injunctions and clearly the advocacy of such policies could mean insurmountable hurdles in actual implementation.

Pakistani entrepreneurs have now entered a phase where they could probably look after their technological and other industrial requirements. Their crying need is for some kind of security from political and other kinds of uncertainties which are thrown up with periodic regularity. However much the effort may be it is difficult to envisage reduction in these kinds of uncertainties. Pakistan has seen twenty years of military rule out of the last twenty-nine and therefore those in authority could be motivated by forces in conflict with what is being argued. Therefore an analysis of power and authority along with the recent religious resurgence seems to be equally important.

The effort has been to study human nature in an economic environment and to see whether appropriate policies can be devised. The task of generalising on human nature is difficult. It is also necessary. Simply ignoring difficult options will not allow development problems to go away. The need may be for trying to work dynamic human systems rather than static environments. It is possible to work into the economy a socially just and stable system, a system devoid of greed, dishonesty and mistrust. To do so would require policy framers to be aware of (i) societal requirements, (ii) attitudes, (iii) values, (iv) linkages with the entrepreneurial personality. The list is far longer. But what is certain is that the current institutions cannot and will not deliver the requirements of a just stable order. In fact this has been a major failing in all developing countries. Unjust policies surface in society and do create instability and uncertainty. The human factor is the critical and underlying basis for all actions in a society. To ignore this, as in the past, would mean greater turmoils in the years to come. Economic policies need to be sharpened, keeping in view societal requirements. The time has come to develop a highly sensitive corps of social philosophers and social engineers to deal with this sector.

BIBLIOGRAPHY

Ahmed, A.K.   Export Bonus Schemes,
           Pakistan Development Review,
           Spring 1966

Ahmed, N.   Peasant Struggle in a Feudal
           Setting, Geneva, Interna-
           tional Labour Office, 1980

Akeredolu - Ale, E.O. Nigerian Entrepreneurs in
           the Lagos State. Unpub-
           lished Ph.D. Thesis,
           University of London, 1974

Alexander, A.P.   Greek Industrialists,
           Athens, Center of Planning
           & Economic Research, 1964

Ali, M.N.   Mobilisation of Resources
           in Pakistan, Pakistan
           Economist, April 1980

Amjad, R.   Private Industrial Invest-
           ment in Pakistan. Unpub-
           lished Ph.D. Thesis,
           Cambridge University, 1976

Azhar, B.A. &   The Effect of Tax Holiday
Sharif, S.M.   on Investment Decisions.
           An Empirical Analysis,
           Pakistan Development
           Review, Winter 1974

Bardhan, P.   External Economies,
           Economic Development and
           the Theory of Protection,
           Oxford Economic Papers, 1964

Bibliography

Baumol, W.J.	Entrepreneurship in Economic Theory, <u>American Economic Review</u>, May 1968
Beech, R.P. & Beech, M.J.	<u>Bengal Change and Continuity</u>, East Lansing, Michigan State University, 1969
Berna, J.J.	<u>Industrial Entrepreneurship in Madras State</u>, Bombay, Asia Publishing House, 1970
Bhagwati, J.N. & Krueger, A.O.	Exchange Control, Liberalisation and Economic Development, <u>World Development</u>, 1973
Brimmer, D.	The Setting of Entrepreneurship in India, <u>Quarterly Journal of Economics</u>, 1955
Bruton, H.	Import Substitution Strategy, <u>Pakistan Development Review</u>, Summer 1970
Calkins, R.A.	Technology, Innovations and Economic Development. Unpublished Ph.D. dissertation, Duke University, Durham N.C., 1970
Cauthorn, R.C.	Contributions to a Theory of Entrepreneurship. Unpublished Ph.D. dissertation, Tulane University, 1963
Carroll, J.J.	<u>The Filipino Manufacturing Entrepreneur. Agent and Product of Change</u>, Ithaca, Cornell University Press, 1965
Chamber of Commerce and Industries (Karachi)	Annual Reports (1970-1978)
(Lahore)	Annual Reports (1972-1977)

Bibliography

Chambers of Commerce and Industries	Industrial Development and Productivity. Proceedings of Conference, August 11-13, 1977
Cody, J. Hughes, H. and Wall, D. eds	Policies for Industrial Progress in Developing Countries, London, Oxford University Press, 1980
Fritschler, A.L.	Industrialists in the Government Process in Pakistan. Unpublished Ph.D. Thesis, Syracuse University, 1965
Garlick, P.C.	The Ghanian Entrepreneur. Unpublished Ph.D. Thesis, London University. The African Traders and Economic Development in Ghana, Oxford, Clarendon Press, 1971
Geiger, T. & Armstrong, W.	The Development of African Private Enterprise. Washington D.C., National Planning Association, 1964
Ghouse, A.M. ed.	Studies in Economic Development with Respect to Pakistan, Lahore, Pakistan, Ferozesons Limited, 1962
Gledhill, A.	Pakistan, London, Stevens and Sons Limited, 1957
Grechkel, F.E.	Import Substitution in Under-developed Nations and Regions. The Mexican Experience. Unpublished Ph.D. Thesis, Indiana University, 1969
Griffin, K. & Khan A.R. eds	Growth and Inequality in Pakistan, London, Macmillan Press Ltd., 1972
Harris, J.R.	Industrial Entrepreneurship in Nigeria. Unpublished Ph.D. Thesis, North Western University, 1967

216

Bibliography

Hart, K.	Entrepreneurs and Migrants Unpublished Ph.D. Thesis, Cambridge University, 1969
Hazelhurst, L.W.	Entrepreneurship and the Merchant Castes in a Punjabi City. Unpublished Ph.D. Thesis, University of California, 1966
Hernandex, N.	The Entrepreneurial Role of the Government in Economic Development in Puerto Rico. Unpublished Ph.D. Thesis, Rutgers University, 1965
Hoselitz, B.F.	Sociological Aspects of Economic Growth, Glencoe, The Free Press, 1960
Institute of Economic Affairs, London	The Prime Mover of Progress, London Institute of Economic Affairs, 1980
Kahf, M.	The Islamic Economy, Plainfields, Muslim Students Association, 1980
Kennedy, P.T.	The Ghanain Businessmen, Munchen, Weltforum - Verlag, 1980
Khan, M.Z.	The System of Export Incentives in the Manufacturing Sector of Pakistan. Unpublished Ph.D. dissertation, Johns Hopkins University, 1979
Kilby, P.	African Enterprise. The Nigerian Bread Industry, Stanford, Hoover Institution Press, 1965
King, B.B.	Obstacles to Entrepreneurship in India. The case of Bengal. Paper presented to the Congress of Orientalists, University of Michigan, 1967
Knight, F.	Risk, Uncertainty and Profit.

217

	Boston, Houghton Mifflin & Co., Reprinted, Harper Torch book edition, 1965
Krueger, A.D.	The Benefits and Costs of Import Substitution in India. A Micro-economic Study, Minneapolis, University of Minnesota Press, 1975
Lamb, H.B.	The Rise of Indian Business Communities, June 1955
Landsberg, M.	Export Led Industrialisation in the Third World, Review of Radical Political Economics, Winter, 1979
Lee, H.S.	The Entrepreneurial activities of the Government in the Economic Development of Puerto Rico. Unpublished Ph.D. dissertation, University of Wisconsin, 1965
Lee, K.J.	Technology Transfer and Development Strategies. The Role of Large Firms in Korea. Unpublished Ph.D. dissertation, University of Hawaii, 1977
Leibenstein, H.	Entrepreneurship and Economic Development, American Economic Review, May 1968
Lewis, S.R. Jr.	Economic Policy and Industrial Growth in Pakistan, London, Allen & Unwin, 1969
Lewis, S.R. Jr. & Guisinger, S.	Measuring Protection in a Developing Economy. The case of Pakistan, Journal of Political Economy, 1968
Lorett, A.E.	Concepts of Entrepreneurship in Recent Economic Thought. Unpublished Ph.D. dissertation, University of Southern California, 1965

Nafziger, E.W.   Nigerian Entrepreneurship.
                     A Study of Indigenous
                     Businessmen in the Footwear
                     Industry. Unpublished Ph.D.
                     Thesis, University of
                     Illinois, 1967

                     Effect of Extended Family on
                     Entrepreneurial Activity,
                     Economic Development and
                     Cultural Change, October
                     1969

                     Indian Industrialist - An
                     Examination of Horatio
                     Alger Model, Journal of
                     Development Science,
                     1974-5

                     Education and Entrepreneur-
                     ship, Journal of Development
                     Administration, April 1970

                     African Capitalism. A Case
                     Study in Nigerian Entrepre-
                     neurship, Stanford, Hoover
                     Institution Press, 1977

Naqvi, S.N.H.   Protection and Economic
                     Development, Karachi,
                     Pakistan Institute of
                     Development Economics, 1967

Nulty, T.E.   Income Distribution and
                     Savings in Pakistan. An
                     Appraisal of Development
                     Strategy. Unpublished
                     Ph.D. Thesis, Cambridge
                     University, 1974

Owens, R.   Industrialisation and the
                     Indian Joint Family,
                     Ethnology, April, 1971

Owens, R.L. &   The New Vaisyas, Entrepre-
Nandy, A.   neurial Opportunity and
                     Response in an Engineering
                     Industry in an Indian City,
                     Durham, N.C., Carolina
                     Academic Press, 1978

Bibliography

Papanek, G.F.	Pakistan's Development. Social Goals and Private Incentives, Cambridge Mass, Harvard University Press, 1967
Papanek, G.F.	Pakistan's Big Businessmen, Muslim Separatism, Entrepreneurship and Partial Modernisation, Economic Development & Cultural Change, October 1972
Papanek, G.F. Falcon, W.P., eds	Development Policy II. The Pakistan Experience, Cambridge, Mass., Harvard University Press, 1971
Power, J.H.	Small Industrialist in Bombay, Delhi and Karachi, Pakistan Development Review, Autumn 1962
	Industrialisation in Pakistan. A case of frustrated take off? Pakistan Development Review, 1963
Punjab	Small Industries Survey Reports
Rowe, M.P.	Indigenous Industrial Entrepreneurship in Lagos, Nigeria. Unpublished Ph.D. Thesis, Michigan State University, 1972
Sayigh, Y.A.	Entrepreneurs of Lebanon, Cambridge, Mass., Harvard University Press, 1962
Sen, A.	Employment, Technology and Development, Oxford, Clarendon Press, 1975
Sharma & Singh	Entrepreneurial Growth and Development Programmes in North India, New Delhi, Abinar Publications, 1980

Bibliography

Singer, M. ed.	<u>Entrepreneurship and Modernisation of Occupational Cultures in South Asia</u>, Durham, N.C., Duke University Press, 1973
Singh, P.	Essays concerning some types of Indian Entrepreneurship. Unpublished Ph.D. Thesis, Michigan State University, 1966
Smith, N.R.	The Entrepreneur and His Firm. Unpublished Ph.D. Thesis, Michigan State University, 1965
Soligo, R. & Stern, J.J.	Export Promotion and Investment Criteria, <u>Pakistan Development Review</u>, Spring 1966
Spaddek, H.	Manchesterisation of Ahmedabad, <u>Economic Weekly</u>, March 13, 1965
Stewart, F.	Technology and Employment in Ldcs, <u>World Development</u>, March, 1974
Strachan, H.W.	<u>The Role of Business Groups in Economic Development. The Case of Nicaragua</u>, Cambridge, Mass., Harvard University Press, 1972
Streeten, P.	Self Reliant Industrialisation. Paper presented at International Seminar, Lahore, Pakistan, 1979
Tareen, A.K. ed.	<u>Directory of Pakistan Cotton Textile Mills</u>, 1970
Teribe, O. & Kayode, M.O.	<u>Industrial Development in Nigeria</u>, Ibadan, Ibadan University Press, 1977
Timberg, T.A.	<u>Industrial Entrepreneurship among Trading Communities of India</u>, Cambridge, Mass.,

Bibliography

Economic Report No.136,
Harvard University Press,
1969

White, L.J.   <u>Industrial Concentration and</u>
                       <u>Economic Power in Pakistan</u>,
                       Princeton, Princeton
                       University Press, 1974

INDEX